**ACPL ITEM
DISCARDED**

S0-BWX-575

STO

5-3-76

**International Trade Policy
in Transition**

# International Trade Policy in Transition

Wilbur F. Monroe

**Lexington Books**
D.C. Heath and Company
Lexington, Massachusetts
Toronto          London

**Library of Congress Cataloging in Publication Data**

Monroe, Wilbur F.
    International trade policy in transition.

    Includes indexes.
    1. Commercial policy. 2. Commerce. I. Title.
HF1411.M616        382'.3        74-34279
ISBN 0-669-98152-4

*Copyright © 1975 by D.C. Heath and Company.*

All rights reserved. No part of this publication may be reproduced or transmitted in any form or by any means, electronic or mechanical, including photocopy, recording, or any information storage or retrieval system, without permission in writing from the publisher.

Published simultaneously in Canada.

Printed in the United States of America.

International Standard Book Number: 0-669-98152-4

Library of Congress Catalog Card Number: 74-34279

To my parents,
Marjorie E. and Robert T. Monroe

1905974

# Contents

# Foreword

International trade policy, always important and enlivened by an unusual dynamism, has long attracted some of the best minds in government. However, extraordinary, sometime unforeseen trends and events of recent years have now combined to place a greater burden on the shoulders of responsible officials. Dramatic changes have brought the world economic community to a crossroads—with the United States inextricably involved in a manner both central and pivotal.

The major global changes comprising the background of present-day policy considerations can readily be recalled. Widespread production growth during the post World War II era underwrote vastly expanded world trade, but also altered the relative positions of particular country participants. Thus, absolute gain for the United States economy paralleled a weakening relative to Western Europe and Japan. Monetary repercussions of international scope were implicit in the dualist trend of rising volume alongside changing pattern, culminating in massive currency revaluations and calls for international monetary reconstruction. Concurrent with ongoing shifts of status among major developed countries, less developed countries, increasingly desirous of accelerated economic development, began to evidence a new cohesiveness. All the while, multinational enterprise, had taken root and was growing apace—a new international ingredient viewed with enthusiasm by some and with a certain skepticism by others.

With surprising swiftness and severity, additional crises forged to the forefront during the early 1970s—superimposed upon all the preceding trends and events. The concerns at issue pertained to global inflation (high and at disparate rates), access to energy (petroleum), and commodity scarcities (foodstuffs and raw materials generally). The complex formed by the trio posed a further complicating element for national entities and the international economy that, it was widely conjectured, could only inhibit constructive effort in other contexts.

One can ask a number of questions: What is the desirable international trade policy for the United States? Are present and planned policies appropriate? How do present and future needs differ from past practice? Are future issues adequately recognized now? These questions, and others, are implicit in Dr. Monroe's timely book *International Trade Policy in Transition*. Bringing to his task the impressive combination of solid scholarly training, extensive career experience, and seasoned perspective, Dr. Monroe proceeds skillfully at both the philosophical and applied levels.

Viewing the essential nature of the present-day environment and the constraints or demands it poses for successful formulation of United States trade policy, Dr. Monroe's analysis points particularly to two governing sets of circumstances. First, the American economy has become "internationalized"; the distinction between domestic and international has become far less clear. International forces play increasingly upon the domestic scene, while, conversely, domestic factors increasingly convey international implications. It follows that international trade policy is not something largely unto itself but, rather, can best be approached as a closely integrated component of the country's over-all economic policy.

Second, foreign trade today stands less apart from foreign investment or prevailing currency alignments than heretofore. With the state of the country's balance of payments reflective of all economic transactions at point of convergence between it and others, interrelationships and possible tradeoffs between trade, investment, and exchange ratios for currencies assume special prominence. Again the conclusion follows that international trade policy neither operates, nor should be formulated, in isolation but, rather, can best be approached as a closely integrated component of the country's total external economic posture.

Dr. Monroe's earlier (1974) book, *International Monetary Reconstruction*, focused on monetary matters, but viewed in the over-all context of trade, investment, etc. Now, with his *International Trade Policy in Transition*, Dr. Monroe continues the approach, sharing some of the same situational material as background, only this time focusing on trade within the over-all context of monetary considerations, investment, etc. Indeed, the work of Dr. Monroe appears particularly noteworthy for his early and clear perception of the importance of understanding and invoking interrelationships and interchangeabilities in the course of formulating international economic policy.

Bringing this view of policy formulation to bear, Dr. Monroe directs his attention to a wide range of topical material, with specific focus on three main points. First, he surveys the circumstances that led from past to present. Basics of the reciprocal trade approach, adhered to by this country in trade negotiations for over thirty years, are examined—with stress on evolutionary elements that, in due course, prompted thoughts of possible successor approaches. Thereafter, he identifies and weighs the current issues. These are considered with mature understanding, in terms of today's scene and its needs, and in terms of how they relate to particular country or bloc interests (including Russia and the People's Republic of China). To complete the sequence, he offers insights into some problems of trade policy likely to beset the future. Just as the Kennedy Round of trade negotiations (1963-67) is now displaced by the newly launched Tokyo Round, different in character because of differences in nature of issues and attitude of participating parties, so upcoming years promise a further setting with other challenges. The element of scarcity and general concern about access to foreign supplies, coupled with a growing role and voice for less developed countries, appears to assure it.

Offering a broad spectrum of relevant material competently handled, Dr. Monroe with this book makes a valuable contribution to the better understanding of problems and issues of international trade policy during the current critical years.

**Walter Krause**
John F. Murray Professor of Economics
The University of Iowa

# Preface

In recent years, the close interrelationships between trade policy, exchange-rate policy, economic assistance, and investment policy have been widely recognized. Changes in one area mesh with and affect other areas. Nowhere has all of this been appreciated more than in the context of balance of payments disequilibria and in the attempts by national authorities to come to grips with the challenging problems at hand.

August 1971 marked the collapse of the international monetary system, better known as the Bretton Woods System. The event followed a decade of upheaval in foreign-exchange markets, recurrent pressures on the dollar, chronic US balance of payments deficits, and failure of participating countries to collectively adopt measures dealing with the root causes of those ills, as opposed to their symptoms. Convinced of the need for wholesale reconstruction of the world's monetary system, nations belonging to the International Monetary Fund established the Committee on Reform of the International Monetary System and Related Issues, or the Committee of Twenty, and assigned it the task of making proposals for a new system. The major problems and issues confronting architects of reform were the subject of my earlier book, *International Monetary Reconstruction*.

Together with the pressing need for monetary reform, it was recognized that the international trading system also required major overhaul. International trade policy had been characterized by a particular approach, known as the Reciprocal Trade Approach, for some thirty-five years. It had provided a framework for reducing tariff barriers imposed chiefly on manufactured products; it had, therefore, contributed directly to the sustained and rapid expansion of international trade and to a marked improvement in economic well-being in the world, especially among the rich industrial countries. Partly because those countries seemed to reap continually and increasingly the lion's share of the benefits of trade, partly because of structural changes that had been ongoing in the world economy (including the decline in relative economic strength of the United States), and partly because detente with Russia and Mainland China signalled new and brightening prospects for economic exchange, international trade policy and the principles underlying the world trade system had entered an era of transition.

The United States, Japan, and members of the European Economic Community agreed in early 1972 that a new round of multilateral trade negotiations should take place under the auspices of the General Agreement on Tariffs and Trade. The idea won quick endorsement of many other countries. It was hoped initially that the negotiations on monetary reform and the negotiations on trade could go forward in tandem. The ultimate and larger purpose was to establish a new international economic order that would generally fulfill present and future economic and financial needs, that would provide a framework within which trade, monetary, and investment policies would work systematically and harmoniously to deal with balance of payments disequilibria as they arose, and that would facilitate the attainment of various widely agreed objectives, including a larger transfer of real resources to less developed countries, promotion of their economic development, expansion of East-West trade, and a resumption of growth, price stability, and enhanced economic well-being for the world in general. For various political and bureaucratic reasons, however, it soon became clear that negotiations to restructure the trade and monetary systems could not proceed together but instead would take place separately or sequentially, with monetary reform going first.

As the work of the Committee of Twenty was in its second and last year, and with the groundwork for a new round of comprehensive trade nogotiations already well advanced, uncertainties affecting the world economic outlook (related especially to the energy crisis and the quadrupling of oil prices, virulent worldwide inflation, and other unsettled conditions) became so overwhelming that the committee was obliged to switch its attentions from comprehensive reform to consideration of those aspects that might help alleviate immediate financial problems. Thus, monetary reconstruction was recognized to have become an evolutionary process that might take some years to ultimately bring to fruition. The change in course of monetary reform will also have an impact on trade negotiations, for the latter, too, must now be regarded as an evolutionary step rather than a single effort to construct a new international trade system and to define the appropriate role of trade policy in the new world economic order.

The agenda for the multilateral trade negotiations in this era of transition is both lengthy and complex; and it has been made more so as a consequence of the world's current economic difficulties. This volume is about the major problems and issues arising in the context of the Tokyo Round of trade negotiations; and it is, accordingly, a companion to my earlier book, *International Monetary Reconstruction*. It treats the current issues against the backdrop of the reciprocal trade approach that characterized and dominated trade policy over the last three decades, and it evaluates the issues both from the standpoint of less developed and developed countries. Finally, some of the major issues of trade policy likely to dominate the scene beyond the current juncture are identified and analyzed.

In preparing this book, I have benefited from contacts with a variety of experts in Washington, from work experiences associated with the United States Treasury Department, the Brookings Institution and the International Monetary Fund, and from my travels abroad, including my assignment to the American Embassy in Tokyo during 1970-72. My special appreciation is due to Walter Krause, John F. Murray Professor of Economics at the University of Iowa, who has provided much inspiration and wise counsel. I should also like to thank Dr. Lawrence B. Krause, Senior Fellow at the Brookings Institution, Dr. Gottfried

Haberler, Resident Scholar of the American Enterprise Institute, and Phillip H. Trezise, Senior Fellow at the Brookings Institution and formerly Assistant Secretary of State for Economic Affairs. I express my appreciation to certain colleagues in the US government and to officials of foreign governments here in Washington who will, I trust, forgive me for not mentioning their names, but who will recognize my acknowledgement of personal indebtedness to them.

The views and opinions expressed in this book are mine alone and should in no way be taken as representing the views of the United States Treasury Department, the International Monetary Fund, the Brookings Institution, or any of their officials.

**Wilbur F. Monroe**
October 1974

# 1 Introduction

A new round of multilateral trade negotiations was formally opened by ministers of more than one hundred sovereign nations convening in Tokyo in September 1973. With actual bargaining sessions now anticipated to start in early 1975, the seventh series of such negotiations to be held under the auspices of the General Agreement on Tariffs and Trade since 1947 will have begun. The issues to be addressed are numerous and complex, and the outcome of these negotiations, like the outcomes of preceding rounds, will have a major impact on the course of international trade and on the well-being of the international economy for years to come.

A number of characteristics set the current series of negotiations apart from those that have gone before. Those characteristics, which on the one hand have to do with the major problems and issues that now confront negotiators of the various trading nations and on the other with the more generalized economic problems—inflation, scarcity, stagnation—facing all nations of the world, signify that international trade policy is in transition.

For over thirty years, US trade policy was embued with a particular philosophy and bent. The reciprocal trade program, whose legal foundation was the Reciprocal Trade Agreements Act of 1934 and its numerous extensions, was based upon the propositions of classical economics. Free international trade would allow countries to obtain indirectly goods and services that could not be produced directly or that could be produced directly but at higher costs. Each country should specialize in the production and export of those goods and services that could be produced most efficiently. The more international trade could be allowed to operate unhindered, the more costs of a given level of production would be minimized or the output from a given amount of resources would be maximized. For each country and for the world as a whole, economic benefits would be maximized if free trade were to prevail.

The way to achieve freer trade in the 1930s and for years thereafter was for nations to reduce tariff barriers. After the United States Congress passed the famous Smoot-Hawley Tariff Act of 1930, and with the adoption of similarly protectionist trade legislation abroad, tariffs were considered to be by far the major inhibiting device to freer trade. The reciprocal trade approach began in 1934 with the decision to adopt a liberal trade program as one means to overcome the Great Depression. The central objective was to lower tariff duties in order to permit an increase in exports. All of this was accomplished by means of bilateral trade agreements between the United States and other trading

1

countries. Both parties made concessions by lowering tariff barriers to imports; as a result, each country achieved easier entry to the other's domestic markets for the sale of its exports.

A key principle of the reciprocal trade program was unconditional most-favored-nation treatment. According to that principle, trade concessions granted in an agreement between the United States and one of its trading partners were automatically extended to all other nations, regardless of whether equivalent concessions were made in return. The inclusion of the MFN clause in trade agreements had the effect of multilateralizing concessions.

After World War II some twenty-three nations, led by the United States and Britain, joined together to become contracting parties of the General Agreement on Tariffs and Trade. This development had the effect of institutionalizing the spirit and philosophy of the reciprocal trade approach. In the years that ensued, international trade policy continued its liberal trend; more countries joined the GATT and agreed to abide by the stipulations of the Agreement, and more and more negotiations were successfully completed, and the resulting benefits were extended to all GATT members.

When the Reciprocal Trade Agreements Act finally came to an end and was not renewed, the US Congress passed a new trade bill, called the Trade Expansion Act of 1962, that in all important respects carried forward the same basic principles. The act once again empowered the president to negotiate lower tariffs; but in recognition of changing economic circumstances in the world, and in particular the advent of the European Common Market, some new features were added to the legislation to help assure successful negotiations and thus a further expansion of US exports.

The Kennedy Round of international trade negotiations, held in Geneva under the auspices of GATT, was more grand and more complex than any that had been held previously. But the central purpose and the featured achievements of the negotiations were the same as before. In all cases, a more liberal trade policy was sold on the grounds that it would lead to export expansion. The primary technique used was reciprocal tariff reduction applied on an MFN basis. With the end of the Kennedy Round, a long and unique era in international trade policy drew to a close.

By the late 1960s a growing discontent had arisen in various quarters concerning the particular patterns of international trade that resulted from long and increasingly widespread application of the reciprocal trade approach. In the thirty or more years that the reciprocal trade program was alive, international trade prospered and increased tremendously. But at the same time, the proportion of trade in foodstuffs, raw materials, and fuels declined from about two-thirds of total trade just before 1930 to around one-third in 1970. Trade in manufactured products accounted for the lion's share of growth. Such changes in the commodity composition of trade were echoed by similar changes in the nations accounting for that trade. The great bulk of trade came to be concentrated increasingly among the rich industrial countries of the Northern Hemisphere, and the trade shares of less developed countries in Africa, Asia, and Latin America declined. The largest share of trade conducted by less developed countries was not among themselves but was with the developed countries. In the case of Communist countries, whose nonmarket economies placed a much lower priority on trade compared to market-oriented economies, only very limited exchanges of goods occurred with either the developed or less developed countries in the quarter century after World War II; but such a phenomenon was more than anything else a result of the political and economic isolation that arose during the Cold War.

For less developed countries, many of which at one time had been colonies of European nations and Great Britain but had more recently gained political independence, the disproportionate benefits of trade accruing to them appeared to be a result of the trading system itself. Without substantial changes in the system, their plight would worsen, and one critical means by which they hoped to realize objectives of economic development would be foreclosed. Spokesmen for the developing countries accordingly began to articulate an approach to international trade policy that cut across the ideals and thinking of the past: preferential treatment and nonreciprocity in future trade negotiations between themselves and developed countries.

International trade relations among developed countries came under increasing strain during the latter half of the 1960s. In part, this resulted from perfectly natural shifts in economic strength that followed in the years of initial reconstruction and ensuing prosperity of the postwar era. The relative economic power of the United States declined, while that of the European nations, especially the Common Market countries, and Japan increased. Once almighty US industries were subjected to stronger and stronger competition from abroad. At the same time, the extent to which the United States could assert its formerly pre-eminent position of world leader and effect international agreements had diminished.

In conjunction with shifts in relative economic power, mounting international financial problems created difficulties for trade relations among developed countries. US balance of payments deficits were recognized to be chronic, and this intensified strains on the US dollar, the world's most important currency and international reserve asset. The dollar had become overvalued, thereby causing the US competitive position in world trade to be substantially eroded; but neither the existing international monetary system nor the nations belonging to it seemed capable of correcting these problems in a systematic or orderly fashion. Instead, protectionist forces within the United States and elsewhere gained new footholds and acquired new reasons for being. Much of the liberal trade order that had been painstakingly built up over the course of some thirty-five years seemed in jeopardy of being torn down.

While discontent over the status quo was gathering momentum, an easing of political and military tensions between East and West was taking place. In particular, European countries and England were eager to reestablish formerly important trade relations with Eastern Europe, with the Peoples' Republic of China, and with Russia. Those trade ties had been suspended for all practical purposes as a result of political-military tensions prevailing between Communist countries and the free world throughout the 1950s and most of the 1960s.

Structural economic changes, manifested in ever larger balance of payments disequilibria, caused increasingly severe and more frequent problems for both the international trade and international monetary systems. Both had worked well in an earlier period when the economic strength of the United States and the soundness of the dollar provided a firm foundation for world economic order. The rules and regulations of the trade and monetary systems had been framed on the premise that strong leadership of the United States, based upon that country's economic and financial strength, would continue indefinitely. But as time passed and the distribution of economic power among the European Community, the United States, and Japan became more even, and as the US balance of trade and payments performance weakened still further the ability of the US to continue fulfilling that leadership role was inevitably undermined. With no country or group of countries able to step into the void, it was only a matter of time before the rules of the game would have to be redrawn. Since the United States was encountering financial difficulty in carrying its former burden, it became apparent that there would have to be a more equitable sharing of responsibilities among the leading industrial countries. The rules governing the international trade and monetary systems would need revision in order to assure greater symmetry of rights and obligations for all members, and in order to provide for improved management of problems arising in the international trade, investment, and monetary areas. Whereas in earlier times international trade, monetary, and investment (including economic assistance) matters were treated separately and as functionally distinct elements of international economic policy, developments around the turn of the decade helped to demonstrate the very close interrelationships between all three.

In August of 1971, in the face of an especially severe exchange market crisis that centered on speculation against the dollar, and in the knowledge that the international competitive position of the United States had been eroded to the point where a trade deficit was forecast for the first time in the twentieth century, the United States undertook a series of bold new economic policies. On the one hand, some of the policies were designed to arrest in the short term the deteriorating situations in both the trade and monetary areas. A 10 percent surcharge on all dutiable US imports was imposed by the president and an investment tax credit was announced which, if enacted by the Congress, would have discriminated in favor of US manufactured capital equipment over that produced abroad and imported into this country: These measures were chosen to shore up the US trade position. As a supplement, bilateral negotiations with

Japan, Canada, and Western Europe were conducted in late 1971 and early 1972 for the purpose of winning specific trade concessions that would permit an improvement in the US trade position with each of the countries involved.

On the monetary side, the president suspended convertibility of the dollar into gold, one of the main pillars of the Bretton Woods monetary system that had prevailed for a quarter of a century. The purpose was to allow the dollar to float in foreign-exchange markets and thereby to relieve US authorities of having to support a clearly unrealistic exchange rate.

In the investment area, restrictions imposed earlier on US direct investment abroad were retained, as were the Federal Reserve guidelines, which limited short-term capital movements abroad, and the interest equalization tax, which neutralized incentives for foreigners to borrow from US capital markets. Although the United States made known its intention to remove these controls, such a step could not be taken until a semblance of equilibrium had been restored to the US balance of payments.

The second major purpose of US policy initiatives was to stimulate major reforms of the international trade and monetary systems themselves. The United States had hoped that negotiations in both areas could proceed simultaneously, and that out of such parallel reform efforts a new international economic system would emerge wherein future balance of payments maladjustments, surpluses as well as deficits, would be treated in an orderly, equitable, and systematic fashion with a blend of trade, exchange rate, and investment policies. Politically and bureaucratically, however, that approach did not prove to be practicable.

Multilateral trade negotiations have proved to be slow in starting; at the time of this writing they appear likely to begin in earnest early in 1975. Monetary reform negotiations were first launched in mid-1972 within a newly established Committee of Twenty under the auspices of the International Monetary Fund. These negotiations appeared to be headed toward the commonly agreed objective of a new comprehensive monetary system designed to last for at least another quarter century. But then the international oil crisis, in the form of a quadrupling of crude-oil prices, descended upon a world already gripped by severe inflationary pressures. The uncertainties for all leading countries with respect to balance of payments and domestic economic performances were so great that participants in the monetary negotiations agreed in January 1974 to switch to an evolutionary approach to monetary reform and to concentrate their efforts on implementing interim measures specifically designed to alleviate the unprecedented financial problems that had arisen.

It is important to realize that as a consequence of the indefinite delay in implementing a new international monetary system, the current round of international trade negotiations will not be able to complete, as had been hoped, the construction of a new international economic system. The assignment of roles to trade policy, monetary policy, and international investment policy, and how all three are to work conjointly in the future for the betterment of world economic order, are major issues that lie beyond the present round of multilateral trade negotiations.

International trade negotiations were slow in getting underway for two main reasons. On the one hand, there were important foreign countries whose leaders argued they could not negotiate on trade matters until they knew what the exchange rates of their currencies were going to be. That argument had some appeal around the time of the seemingly large exchange-rate adjustments of late 1971 that culminated in the Smithsonian Agreement of December 19 of that year. But those changes were only the beginning; further exchange-rate changes began to occur just six months after that agreement, and then in February 1973 the dollar was devalued for the second time in just over one year. In the months intervening, exchange rates have been allowed to float more or less freely, and the leading currencies have experienced wide swings to and fro in relation to one another. All of this has occurred, however, in an atmosphere of relative calm compared to the foreign-exchange market crises that gripped the world in recent years as the authorities attempted vainly to defend the par values of their currencies, according to the rules of the outmoded Bretton Woods monetary system.

A second major constraint on the start of trade negotiations concerned the highly protectionist mood of the United States Congress. That mood, and a variety of proposed trade legislation and amendments to legislation, recalled to the minds of many observers an earlier period when a successful logrolling effort took over in Congress and resulted in passage of the Smoot-Hawley Tariff Act of 1931. That act, which introduced record-high barriers to trade, was a disaster not only for the United States but for its trading partners as well, all of which were then in the initial throes of a worldwide depression.

The reasons for the protectionist sentiment in the United States during 1971-72 included the already abysmal and still worsening trade position of the country, which reflected stiff competition from foreign producers, and rising domestic unemployment. Since it has been traditional for the US executive to propose trade legislation to the Congress which would authorize him to negotiate trade agreements with other countries, the administration was more or less obliged to fight defensive battles with the Congress in hopes that protectionist legislation under consideration would simply be allowed to wither and die harmlessly without being enacted. That indeed was what happened, and by early 1973 the domestic economic picture and the US trade position had both improved substantially and the mood of the Congress was more receptive to the kind of forward-looking trade legislation that the administration had in mind as an essential ingredient to building a new international economic system.

On the presumption that the Trade Reform Act proposed by President Nixon in spring of 1973 would receive prompt approval by the Congress, and that trade negotiations would open by the end of the year, the preliminary groundwork was laid in Europe and elsewhere. In September of 1973, a formal meeting of ministers from over one hundred countries was convened in Tokyo to set out the broad purposes of the negotiations and to declare them officially open. But shortly thereafter, the unforeseen oil crisis occurred, and along with that, scarcities in a number of basic materials and foodstuffs sent world prices skyrocketing. On the eve of a new round of international trade negotiations that boasted an already overloaded agenda of pressing issues, entirely new questions were being raised about security of foreign supplies and rules governing the use of export controls.

The trade bill that Congress passed just prior to its adjournment at the end of 1974 authorizes the president to negotiate not only on those trade policy matters that were deemed to be of great importance in 1973, but also on matters directly related to the recent and continuing problems of short supply. As already indicated, the United States and its trading partners will not be able to resolve at the current juncture the role that trade policy is to play in the future international economic system. Until the leading countries are prepared to implement a new international monetary system, such as the one proposed in the Committee of Twenty,[1] the desired relationships and relative responsibilities of trade, monetary, and investment policy cannot be settled.

The present study is concerned with the major problems and issues of international trade policy. Those problems and issues, whether examined from the viewpoint of less developed or developed countries, indicate trade policy is in transition. The focus of attention has been shifting away from tariff barriers, since over the course of previous negotiations they have been substantially reduce. There will, it is hoped, be declines in tariff duties as a consequence of the current round of negotiations, but progress in resolving a whole complex of other barriers to trade, known as nontariff barriers, stands to offer a greater impact on future international trade flows.

Whereas past trade negotiations have promoted trade liberalization and freer trade as the means of increasing each country's exports, and thereby giving impetus to domestic objectives of high employment levels, stable prices and rapid growth, the present negotiations will give major attention to establishing a framework of international safeguards. On the one hand, safeguards would offer a measure of protection to domestic industries injured by volatile and disruptive imports, and at the same time would spell out more carefully the circumstances or conditions under which countries could impose or maintain protective trade barriers. There is still a great deal of interest in promoting liberalization, but there has also been growing conviction that in our increasingly interdependent world, international trade, and the increasing level of government intervention therein, must be subject to ground rules that will prevent one country's salvation from becoming other countries' burdens.

The interest in safeguards indicates a further movement away from the laissez-faire attitude of the past. Indeed, many of the current problems and issues foreshadow a move toward a more active management of international trade problems through various understandings, agreements, and new rules and regulations. The idea is to ensure greater orderliness of international trade so that the economic benefits enjoyed so much in the past may continue to be savored in the future. All of this indicates a need for reform of the international trade system at various stages of operation and, in particular, a need for modifications or additions to the Articles of the General Agreement on Tariffs and Trade, the one international body responsible thus far for preserving and maintaining order in international trade.

More than on any previous occasion, these multilateral trade negotiations will be very much concerned with the problems of less developed countries. To a certain extent, there is a willingness to bend previous and still current principles of nondiscrimination and reciprocity in order to give LDCs increased opportunities to improve their share of the benefits deriving from international trade. Although such concessions may prove to be of some help to those countries just entering the "takeoff" stage of their development, they will not be of great significance to a number of LDCs whose economies continue to be impoverished and stagnant. For such countries, other economic assistance measures lying beyond the scope of international trade policy will have to be coordinated.

Another important feature of trade policy in transition has to do with the interest in access to foreign supplies which has arisen out of the international oil crisis and the world scarcity of a number of basic materials, all occurring in the 1973-74 period. The present concern with access to foreign supplies contrasts with the overwhelming attention accorded access to markets in all previous trade negotiations. Today, trading nations are not only interested in increasing exports; they are also trying to find ways to ensure a continued flow of much needed imports. These issues of short supply lend a particular balance to the current round that has not existed before. Although the long-term implications of recent and current scarcity problems are unclear, the multilateral trade negotiations may very well seek to develop some ground rules governing the imposition of export controls, a matter to which international trade policy has heretofore accorded scant attention. Another probable result of recent scarcity problems will be to redouble previously unsuccessful efforts to improve conditions of agricultural trade. Various foodstuffs have ranked high on a long list of scarce commodities, and a breakthrough in reconciling what has become over the years one of the most restricted areas of international trade would be of major importance to a great many food-consuming and food-producing nations.

In all of these respects, international trade policy has come to a juncture of especially great significance for the world economy. The resolutions to current problems and issues will in all likelihood light the path ahead for many years to come. In the balance of what is already, for better or for worse, an interdependent trading order lies the future growth and well-being of all nations comprising that order.

# 2 The Reciprocal Trade
Approach: 1934-67

For thirty-three years, 1934 to 1967, the United States pursued consistently a particular approach to international trade policy, known as the reciprocal trade approach. The extraordinarily high tariffs prevailing in the early 1930s were substantially reduced through repeated negotiations between the United States and its trading partners. Despite differences in viewpoint and emphasis, the Congress and the executive branch were able to reach mutual agreement in the basic tenets of enabling trade legislation—eleven times in the case of the Trade Agreements Act and once in the case of the Trade Expansion Act. All of those acts authorized the president to pursue and execute a liberal trade program of a particular sort.

This chapter describes the features of the reciprocal trade approach, traces in broad outline its development up to the late 1960s, and sketches in general fashion the great impact the reciprocal approach had on shaping international trade institutions and commercial practice in the post World War II era.

## The Trade Agreements Act, 1934

Domestic sentiment in favor of high tariffs reached its high point during the Great Depression. The agriculture sector in the United States, which had not fared as well as other sectors during the generally prosperous 1920s, teamed up with other sectors to favor protection from foreign competition as the effects of the depression began to be felt toward the end of 1929. In the context of those mounting pressures from various quarters, the Congress brought into being the highest import duty rates in US history when it passed the Smoot-Hawley Tariff Act of 1930. The rationale at the time was that through greater protection from foreign imports, the domestic economic depression could be overcome.

But the prescribed cure did not serve to soften the depression. Instead, the protraction of US economic ills set the stage for a victory by the Democratic party in the 1932 national election. With the inauguration of Franklin D. Roosevelt, a new approach to economic policy was initiated. Included was a completely different view toward international trade and tariff policy from that embodied in the Smoot-Hawley legislation.

The theme of the New Deal was to bring about economic recovery. While the policies designed to achieve this goal domestically were the precursors of those embraced by Keynesian economics, the flavor of President Roosevelt's policies formulated to handle trade and the external sector was pure classical economics.[1] More trade was preferable to less trade; freer trade or free trade would promote trade more than less free trade; all countries should be treated on an equal basis. These simple concepts provided the foundation for the reciprocal trade approach to US commercial policy. The success of that approach may be attested to by its great durability, for it has been the beacon light for each piece of legislation dealing with international trade since its inception in the early 1930s down to the present day.

General tariff reform was not long in coming after Roosevelt had been inaugurated. The first enabling legislation, the Trade Agreements Act, was passed in 1934. This was the centerpiece of the Reciprocal Trade Agreements Program.[2] The avowed purpose of the program generally, and of the legislation in particular, was to liberalize the US tariff structure so as to facilitate an expansion of foreign trade. Proponents of the new legislation looked upon increased trade as an integral part of the larger program to extricate the United States from its economic depression.

There were four principal features of the initial Trade Agreements Act and of its successors. First, for a stipulated period of time, the president was given by the Congress broad authority to enter negotiations and reach agreements with foreign governments in order to reduce tariffs at home and abroad. Second, any tariff reductions conceded by the United States were to be implemented simultaneously with *equivalent* concessions by other nations. This was what was meant by *reciprocal* tariff concessions. Third, tariff concessions between the United States and any other country were to be formally espoused in a trade agreement. And finally, each agreement was to bear the principle of "unconditional most favored nation."

The first feature simplified the entire procedure of reducing tariffs by Congress giving the president a legislative mandate that clearly set forth the broad limits within which he could conclude reciprocal trade agreements. Agreements so concluded were made effective by presidential proclamation and did not require congressional review. The key limitations imposed on the president included: the power to lower or raise tariffs by no more than 50 percent of the rates in effect as of June 1934; the stipulation that items on the dutiable list could not be transferred to the duty-free list, or vice versa; and the requirement that public notice had to be given prior to the conclusion of an agreement in order that interested persons could express themselves if they so wished. It was believed and intended that as a general procedure, the president would confer regularly with concerned government agencies in order to avoid conflicts between governmental policies.

Incorporation of the principle "unconditional most favored nation" in negotiated trade agreements meant that any concession granted by the United States to another country was extended automatically to all other countries, regardless of whether or not those other countries were willing to offer the

United States equivalent concessions in return. (There were a few countries excepted, including Cuba and the Philippines. Under certain conditions, the president was authorized to withhold trade concessions if it were established that other countries discriminated against the United States.) Moreover, in most cases where concessions were granted to a third country by another country with which the United States had negotiated a trade agreement, it was understood that the same concessions were to apply automatically and unconditionally to the United States. In effect, therefore, the unconditional MFN clause in the trade agreements made trade concessions multilateral, even though the agreements themselves were bilateral.

The US approach in negotiating trade agreements was to deal with countries that were the principal source of supply for a particular commodity. Then, as a result of the unconditional MFN clause, lesser suppliers benefited from the trade concessions negotiated. The object of the "chief supplier" principle, as it was known, was to win equivalent concessions where they would count most for US exports—the home markets of the most formidable competitors of the United States.

## Continuation and Elaboration of the
## Reciprocal Trade Agreements Program

The Trade Agreements Act of 1934 lasted for only three years before its renewal was required. It was extended several times (eleven in all) but, in each case, for short periods of from one to four years. During its first ten years of operation, the reciprocal trade program made considerable progress in liberalizing international trade barriers. Numerous tariff reductions were achieved by means of negotiated trade agreements. As much responsible for this success as any one person was the secretary of state, Cordell Hull, who strongly supported the reciprocal trade agreements program.

Periodic renewals of the Trade Agreements Act continued through the Second World War. Little domestic political resistance was encountered, because full employment and wartime prosperity worked to the advantage of those domestic elements—labor, management, and agriculture—that supported the program. By 1945, the scope for reducing tariffs on many items had been exhausted; and so, in the renewal of the act in that same year, a provision was included that authorized the president to negotiate further reductions in tariffs of up to 50 percent of the rates obtaining at the beginning of 1945.

The trend of trade liberalization first came under question as the US economy paused to shift gears from a wartime orientation to a peaceful one. Political pressures arose in favor of trade policies that would better relieve domestic firms suffering from competition with imported goods. In response, the president issued an executive order that required future trade agreements to incorporate an "escape clause." Such a clause gave the United States the right to alter a tariff concession if competitive domestic producers suffered or were threatened with serious injury. In 1948, protectionist forces gained further support nationally as a consequence of increased competition by foreign producers and a domestic economic recession which led to increased unemployment. As a result, the Trade Agreements Act was extended for only one year in 1948, and a special "peril-point" provision was added to it which went beyond the earlier escape-clause provision. Under the new provision, the United States Tariff Commission was instructed to determine in advance the minimum tariff rate that might be adopted by the United States "without causing or threatening serious injury to the domestic industry producing like or similar articles."

The Trade Agreements Act of 1949 renewed the authority of the president to negotiate trade agreements. With protectionist sentiment somewhat abated, the peril-point provision was dropped, but the escape-clause provision was retained. In the 1951 extension, both provisions in question were included; moreover, there was a new provision which stipulated that benefits from negotiated tariff concessions could not be extended to Communist countries. Further resistance to the reciprocal trade agreements program was incurred in 1953 when the Eisenhower administration took office. The act was renewed for only one year after a stiff battle in the Congress. In the 1953 legislation, a Commission on Foreign Economic Policy (better known as the Randall Commission) was named to study American foreign policy and to make its recommendations known to the Congress as to the appropriate course for future policy. The commission's report, symbolized by the slogan "Trade, not Aid," recommended further efforts to reduce tariffs and suggested that through increased trade the costly requirements of US foreign aid could be reduced. But in 1954, recessionary economic conditions and sharply higher unemployment levels touched off another resurgence of protectionist sentiment and sidetracked implementation of the commission's recommendations. Accordingly, the Trade Agreements Extension Act of 1954 was passed for only one year.

In 1955, the basic legislation was extended for three years. The escape-clause, peril-point, and Communist country provisions were all included. In addition, a new protectionist feature appeared which precluded the decrease in duty of any item whenever it would threaten domestic production necessary to meet projected national defense needs. Judgment as to the use of this provision was left up to the president. As an offset to these protectionist features, the president was once more given greater scope in negotiating tariff reductions. He was empowered to reduce tariffs up to 15 percent of their previous levels over a three-year period and up to 50 percent for all tariff rates above 50 percent.

The Trade Agreements Extension Act of 1958 was approved for four years. It included a more broad escape provision and a national security provision. And as had been the case in the previous renewal of the basic legislation, the authority of the president to negotiate tariff reductions was broadened to include a choice of three alternative schedules to guide duty cuts.

In 1962, the Trade Agreements Act expired for good; but during its twenty-eight years of existence, very substantial tariff reductions were achieved as the scope for reductions was widened. At the same time, resistance to freer trade became evident and had a significant impact in particular areas, as indicated by the protectionist provisions that became permanent features of the basic legislation during its later years of existence.

## World Impact of the Reciprocal
## Trade Approach After World War II:
## The General Agreement on Tariffs
## and Trade

Before World War II had ended, US leaders had already begun to think about what kind of world economic order was desired.[3] The reciprocal trade approach was still central to American thinking, but there was a desire to institutionalize it and give it greater operational relevance for the free world as a whole. Planning and discussions took place not only within the US government but also between the United States and its allies. The main, but conflicting considerations were these: first, there was a general desire for freer, nondiscriminatory trade relations as a consequence of still vivid memories of chaos during the 1930s, and because of a still abiding belief in the policy prescriptions of classical trade theory. Second, the lessons of the 1930s also indicated that countries in severe balance of payments difficulty should have freedom to impose restrictions other than tariffs, and that discriminatory trade practices might be appropriate in certain circumstances. Third, in respect of the great changes in the approach and scope of domestic economic policy, all of which had been prompted by the Keynesian revolution, the range of institutions with which planners and policy-makers were concerned had grown tremendously. The era of laissez faire had given way to a new period in which government control over, and management of, international trade would increase greatly.

It was in this period that US commercial policy was further shaped and clarified in concert with the policies of American allies in order to facilitate attainment of two broad objectives, both entirely consistent with the reciprocal trade approach. One objective was to obtain international agreement on the code and conduct of commercial matters that embraced the basic principle of nondiscrimination. The other was to reach an accord on the gradual reduction of trade barriers. In 1947, at the urging of the United States, an international conference was convened in Geneva. At that conference a draft charter was drawn up for an International Trade Organization, and a General Agreement on Tariffs and Trade was adopted.

The charter of the International Trade Organization provided a code of conduct for commercial policy and a structure to ensure its enforcement. The code of conduct included not only commercial policy per se, such as tariffs, quotas, subsidies, internal controls and the like, but also the related concerns of domestic employment, foreign investment, and economic development. In 1948, at the Havana Conference, there was general agreement on the policies contained in the ITO charter by the representatives of the fifty-four participating countries. But that was as far as the ITO ever went. The United States never ratified the ITO charter, ostensibly because of concern within the Congress that national sovereignty might be compromised by such an organization. Without US participation, other countries were unwilling to give their endorsement.[4]

The General Agreement on Tariffs and Trade (GATT), of course, was more successful—not only in the sense that it survived the test of time, but also because it went on to be one of the international organizations that contributed most to growth and prosperity of international trade in the postwar era.[5] The United States was one of the twenty-three initial signatories.[6] The first section of the Agreement included rules governing trade between contracting parties. Those rules dealt with tariffs, quotas, subsidies, and internal controls and were similar to those contained in a section of the ITO charter. Therefore, when it became apparent that ITO was not going to come into being, the GATT was able to take over and carry out that portion of the ITO charter. The second section of the GATT had to do with a schedule of concessions which resulted from various trade negotiations; and that schedule has been modified from time to time over the years as a consequence of subsequent negotiations.

The main objective of GATT, which indeed bore all the important earmarks of the reciprocal trade approach, was to diminish trade restrictions, and particularly tariffs, which were then still looked upon as the main barrier to freer trade. The way the GATT worked was that country representatives would meet periodically in conference to exchange tariff and other trade concessions. The negotiations were bilateral in each instance, but concessions were granted to third countries because of unconditional most-favored-nation treatment. Given the presence of representatives of many countries at each session, the operation had the appearance of being multilateral in nature. By this multilateral process, US negotiations under its own reciprocal trade agreements program were facilitated.

Quite akin to the early experience of International Monetary Fund, which bore responsibilities in the realm of world monetary developments, the GATT got off to a slow start for a period right after World War II. That period, popularly referred to as the period of "dollar shortage," gave rise to numerous quantitative and exchange controls in Europe and in Britain; and it also witnessed the European Recovery Program and US Marshall Plan, which combined to help restore economic order in that part of the world.

The development of the Cold War, in conjunction with the dollar shortage, led the United States for military and economic reasons to give strong support to a concept then in its infancy: European economic integration. At the time, such a concept implied first priority should be given to liberalization of restrictions on intra-European trade over liberalization of restrictions on trade between all members of GATT. This was more a matter of degree than anything else, however, and significant progress in trade liberalization did go forth in those early years under GATT.

Since its beginning, GATT has grown from a representation of twenty-three nations to one hundred countries, eighty-three full members and seventeen provisional member countries, all of which apply the rules of GATT to their commercial activities. Six negotiating sessions conducted under the auspices of the GATT have resulted in tariff concessions on items that together account for more than half of total world trade.[7] The importance of the General Agreement has been widely recognized both for its role in helping to bring about lower tariff levels for a major portion of items traded throughout the world, and for its having provided a forum for the discussion of members' commercial policies and the resolution of disputes.[8]

## Assessment of the Reciprocal
## Trade Agreements Program

During the twenty-eight year life of the Reciprocal Trade Agreements Program, the United States entered into a large number of trade agreements. By 1963, those agreements encompassed fifty-eight non-Communist countries all over the world. As a result of the trade program and the agreements born out of it, progressively lower tariff rates were enforced. The average duty in 1934 under the Smoot-Hawley legislation was 53 percent (measured in terms of duties collected as a percent of the value of dutiable imports). When the GATT came into being in 1947, the average rates of duty under US tariff laws had been reduced to 20 percent,[9] and at the end of 1962 the average was 12.3 percent. The major reduction in the average duty since 1947 had occurred by the end of 1952 when it was 12.8 percent. Growing protectionist sentiment in the 1950s slowed greatly any further lowering in rates.[10]

The impact of the reciprocal trade agreements program was most evident in the sharp reversal of a protectionist trend in US commercial policy that had emerged at the start of the 1930s. By the early 1950s trade had become substantially freer than it had been at the height of the Great Depression. During the mid- and late-1950s and up until the Trade Agreements Act finally expired in 1962, progress in reducing import duties slowed markedly. This was owing in part to growing success of protectionist elements in the United States as indicated by the increasing number of loopholes in the trade legislation that undercut concessions the United States could or had already offered. The other factor contributing to the diminished rate of duty reduction was the fact that the largest and most easily achieved concessions had been made for the most part in the early years of the reciprocal trade agreements program. That which remained to be negotiated was both narrower in scope and also less tractable, in the sense that some concessions would always evoke concerted resistance among certain quarters of US trade and industry and among their counterparts abroad.

Despite the progress made in moving toward freer trade, US duties on a number of items remained high (50 percent or more ad valorem). But in comparison with other nations, the US average duty rate was ranked approximately in the middle of the more developed countries. In 1961, countries granting less liberal treatment of industrial imports included Japan, Austria, the United Kingdom, Italy, Canada, and France. Countries offering relatively more liberal duty treatment were Germany, Sweden, Switzerland, and Denmark.[11]

Despite the longevity of the reciprocal trade agreements program, and the durability of the basic legislation, which was extended or renewed so many times, criticisms of the program and the supporting legislation arose, particularly during the 1950s. As mentioned earlier, the protectionists argued, but with only limited success, that duty reductions were injurious to the economy and to employment and that there should be a halt in the trade agreements exercises. But those who fully supported the classical economic concepts that were the foundation of the program, the so-called free traders, also had complaints.[12]

One objection was that the reciprocal trade agreements legislation was never in effect for very long before it had to be renewed. As occurred more than once when the time for extension of the law came due, domestic economic circumstances of the United States militated against a full political endorsement of the bill by those who were preoccupied with problems of the moment. If the basic legislation had been enacted for a longer period of time, some argued, then the coincidence of temporarily adverse domestic economic conditions would have been less likely to interfere with legislators' judgment as to the long-run interests of US commercial policy.

It was also suggested that concern as to the ability of the Congress to continually renew the Reciprocal Trade Agreements Act as it came up for consideration served to deter producers and investors from committing themselves fully to long-range projects. While this criticism might have had some validity when it came to anticipating future trade agreements, it should have been realized that already existing trade agreements were immune from any change or lapse in the trade agreements law.

One potent criticism by those who supported more liberal trade policies had to do with the fact that the Trade Agreements Act was being undermined through the addition of various escape provisions which either qualified the permanency of concessions being negotiated or narrowed to begin with the scope of concessions open to negotiation with foreign governments. First of all, there were the escape clauses that retained the right of the United States to withdraw any concession that might be granted if certain conditions obtained. This, it was argued, undermined the reciprocal trade agreements program by introducing a note of uncertainty. Production or investment decisions might be effected if it were believed that a relevant concession in a given trade agreement might be revoked at a later date. While the actual impact of the escape-clause provisions was relatively minor—that is, there were only a small number of cases whose claims were investigated and supported by the Tariff Commission and then upheld by the president, and they concerned items of small significance to over-all trade—the psychological impact abroad on business decisions and on assessments by foreign diplomats as to the strength of US conviction behind trade liberalization may have been more significant.

The peril-point provisions were a worse threat to tariff reform, since they prevented ex ante offering concessions that might have resulted in import competition either causing or threatening to cause serious injury.

The national security safeguard was a product of the Cold War. It was broadened in 1958 to permit restrictions for nondefense industries where import competition might weaken the domestic economy, since by the same token national security would also be adversely affected. This provision was a greater threat to the success of the reciprocal trade agreements program than either of the above two provisions.

While many industries sought to have the national security safeguard invoked for their benefit, few succeeded. Interestingly enough, one of the successful claims was that put forth by the petroleum industry. In 1959, quotas were first imposed on the importation of crude oil and petroleum products.

As with the first two provisions mentioned, it is impossible to say what the economic impact was of the national security provision. The presence of this additional safeguard, however, could not have helped but raise still more doubts in the United States and abroad as to the extent and sincerity of US intentions with respect to tariff reform.

## The Trade Expansion Act, 1962

The Reciprocal Trade Agreements Act was due to expire in mid-1962. It had been renewed a total of eleven times since it was first passed in 1934. On two previous occasions when the legislation had been up for renewal and little latitude remained for the president to undertake further action, the Congress had broadened his powers or redefined particular provisions within the legislation to inject new life into the program. The major question in 1962 was, therefore, should this approach be tried once more, in which case the administration would seek congressional concurrence to continue the long established program. Or, alternatively, should the administration present a new trade program to the Congress?[13]

The new Democratic administration under President Kennedy decided to push for much the same type of program as before, but with certain changes in implementation and a new title, to try and distinguish its own approach to economic policy from that pursued before under the previous Republican administration.

There were, however, plenty of good reasons for seeking a new trade bill with a truly fresh approach rather than simply asking Congress for an extension of the Trade Agreements Act. First, the scope for further progress under the reciprocal trade agreements program had just about run out; indeed, during the 1950s, tariff reductions under the program had bogged down in large part for this very reason. Furthermore, escape clauses and other protectionist provisions that had become attached to the trade agreements program over the years threatened further substantive progress. A third consideration was the arrival of the European Common Market on the scene. European economic integration had been a major objective of postwar US foreign economic policy in Europe. The course that integration took entailed changes in the structure of the world economy and the balance of power that prevailed shortly after World War II.[14] But for strong US support for the Common Market, integration might have taken a different approach, one in which there would have been economic cooperation and policy coordination among a larger number of European countries on the basis of their common problems and interests. This approach was favored by Britain and other countries on the European periphery; it was an approach that would have been more consistent perhaps with preserving and fostering a liberal international economic system in the classical sense, and it was an approach that would not in all likelihood have led toward the semblance of a third political power comparable to the United States or Russia.

Development of the Common Market in the late 1950s and early 1960s took place simultaneously with the emergence of chronic US balance of payments problems. Those problems were exacerbated by the Common Market through tariff discrimination against US exports and through the attraction to US direct and portfolio investment caused by that tariff wall and by rapidly expanding markets within. A major source of concern on the part of US exporters was the European Community's Common Agricultural Policy (CAP). This policy was the agricultural counterpart of internal free trade of industrial commodities in the Common Market; it was reinforced by a system of variable tariff levies on imports from nonmember countries in order to protect the generally less efficient agricultural producers within the Common Market. In broadest terms, the Common Agricultural Policy bore similarities to US agricultural policy, for which the United States had obtained a GATT waiver in 1951.

By the early 1960s, the Common Market comprised a large and prosperous group of industrial nations which collectively posed a distinct economic challenge to industrial US supremacy. Clearly, if further expansion of US trade was to be realized, the United States would have to work constructively and harmoniously with this new economic bloc that was protected by a common external tariff applicable to imports of commodities from nonmembers. Thus, the Kennedy administration sought to develop a trade program that would offer broad authority to reduce tariffs and that would directly promote meaningful negotiations with the European Common Market.

Other considerations favored a fresh approach to US trade policy in the early 1960s. US involvements with less developed countries (LDCs) were increasing, especially with Latin American countries, where the Alliance for Progress was a source of great interest and rising hope. It was recognized that interests of LDCs were not being well served in the face of numerous protective features of the Common Market that discriminated against those LDCs that were not former colonies or dependencies of EC members. New trade policies would be needed to reverse these trends and to improve the international position of the developing countries. But overriding these and other considerations was the US interest in preserving the Atlantic Alliance and in seeing to it that the advent of the Common Market entailed development of a cooperative force militarily and economically in world affairs, not a rival force.

The product of all these factors was the Trade Expansion Act, passed by the Congress in 1962. It was an act whose vital earmarks bore striking similarity to the Trade Agreements Acts of the preceding twenty-eight years. The major provisions of that legislation included authority both to reduce and to increase US tariffs, authority to extend escape-clause relief or to provide adjustment assistance to workers or firms injured by liberal trade practices, and procedures for conducting trade negotiations with US trade partners.

Under the Trade Expansion Act, the president was empowered to reduce US tariffs up to 50 percent of the rates prevailing on July 1, 1962. (Compared to what had existed under the Trade Agreements Act in late years, this authorization greatly broadened the scope of the president in negotiating tariff reductions with other countries.) In certain specific areas, the president was given authority to remove tariffs entirely.

In respect of less developed countries, the president could eliminate tariffs on "tropical agricultural and forestry products" as long as such products were not grown in substantial volume in the United States and as long as the members of the European Common Market were willing to grant similar concessions. With regard to the Common Market, the president could negotiate full elimination of tariffs on items for which the United States and the EC together accounted for 80 percent or more of world trade. Authorization to negotiate the complete removal of US tariffs on trade with the EC was extended to include agricultural goods, regardless of their weight in total world trade, as long as it was assured that US exports of those goods would be maintained or increased. The third area in which tariffs could be removed entirely concerned nuisance duties, which were defined to be 5 percent or less as of July 1, 1962.

The Trade Expansion Act also embraced the authority for the president to pursue more restrictive trade policy. In fact, he was authorized to raise tariffs as much as 50 percent above rates prevailing July 1, 1934. As a general proposition, it was understood and expected that the entire thrust of the program would be to reduce trade barriers rather than to raise them. But in certain instances, about which the legislation was quite specific, tariff rates were permitted to rise. These included injury to domestic producers, threat to national security, retaliation against foreign barriers to US exports and quotas on various agricultural imports.

With respect to the first area, the objective was to protect domestic producers from injury arising from competitive imports. Upon determination by the Tariff Commission that serious injury was caused or threatened by rising imports that resulted from concessions contained in trade agreements, the president could impose such restrictions as necessary in order to prevent or remedy the injury. This was a rejuvenation of the escape-clause provision of the Trade Agreements Act. However, the concept "serious injury" was written so as to make a finding in favor of domestic producers more difficult than before. The guidelines in determining injury were explicit and included production level, profit rate, and extent of unemployment. Eligibility requirements of the firms seeking escape-clause action were more limited than before. Only firms whose competition from imports could be shown to be the "major factor" in alleged injury to domestic production could apply for relief. Thus, resort to escape-clause action was much more circumscribed than it had become under the Reciprocal Trade Agreements Program.

It may also be noted that whereas the peril-point provision appeared in most versions of the Trade Agreements Act beginning in 1948, no such provision or anything resembling it appeared in the Trade Reform Act. But a new alternative form of relief, called adjustment assistance, which had not appeared earlier, was offered in the 1962 legislation. (This relief device is discussed below at greater length.)

According to the Trade Expansion Act, preservation of national security was the second rationale for increasing trade restrictions. The provision in the new legislation was very similar to that found in the Reciprocal Trade Agreements Acts. The president could not reduce trade barriers on any item if he believed the action would "threaten to impair national security"; and he had the authority to impose restrictive measures in order to eliminate any threat to national security arising from importation of a particular commodity. Wide discretionary power existed as to the application of this provision, since the criteria for determining whether national security was indeed threatened were very general.

The third major consideration for which the Trade Expansion Act authorized reinforcement of trade barriers had to do with US retaliation against foreign countries that continued to apply restrictions against their imports of US products. This provision was an exception to most-favored-nation treatment, which was once again the guiding principle of US trade legislation, and it was aimed at countries that benefited from trade agreement concessions granted by the United States but simultaneously enforced nontariff trade restrictions harmful to US trade. Thus, the president was given new leverage with which to coax other nations into more cooperative negotiating positions or to convince them that restrictive actions against US exports would not be to their advantage. According to the legislation, the president was to work for removal of foreign import restrictions that "impair the value of tariff commitments made to the United States, oppose the commerce of the United States or prevent the expansion of trade on a mutually advantageous basis." In respect of agricultural goods, the president could impose higher import duties and other barriers against foreign exports in the event restrictive actions were initiated abroad.

The fourth area in which the Trade Expansion Act permitted increased trade barriers concerned agricultural goods. Similar to the provisions in previous trade legislation, authority was given the president to impose trade restrictions on agricultural commodities that were included in the domestic price-support programs.

Adjustment assistance was a new feature of the Trade Expansion Act; but because of various operational limitations, its practical significance was almost nonexistent. As an alternative to increasing tariffs under the escape-clause provision, adjustment assistance offered, at least conceptually, constructive solutions to domestic pressures for relief from import competition without entailing the withdrawal of negotiated tariff concessions. In order for producers or workers to seek adjustment assistance, conditions had to exist similar to those for producers who sought relief through escape-clause action. A firm was deemed eligible for adjustment assistance if, as a direct consequence of trade agreement concessions, competitive imports reached such a point as to cause or threaten serious injury. Levels of production, profit, and unemployment were all taken into account. Similarly, workers were eligible for adjustment assistance whenever, as a direct result of trade concessions, a substantial part of the labor force in an injured firm was afflicted with unemployment. Both workers and firms had to prove that increased imports were the major factor causing injury.

"Adjustment assistance" was to be made available in different forms. Technical assistance helped firms improve their productivity or efficiency or helped them move into alternative lines of activity or production. Financial assistance involved direct loans by government or government guarantee of private loans to assist firms in modernizing or diversifying their plants. Tax assistance offered afflicted firms greater freedom to write off losses over several years and thereby to reduce their tax liability. Adjustment assistance for workers included retraining, unemployment compensation, and relocation allowances. The emphasis was placed on retraining workers who had lost their jobs and were unable to find alternative employment on their own.

Negotiation procedures under the Trade Expansion Act were similar to those practiced under the Reciprocal Trade Agreements Program. One important change, however, was that the president was authorized to negotiate tariff reductions by whole categories, rather than item by item. This was to be of significance, particularly in bargaining with the European Common Market.

There were some limitations, however. For instance, the Tariff Commission had to give its appraisal of a proposed tariff action before the president could commence negotiations; and no items subject to previous escape-clause action could be the focus of trade agreement negotiations for five years after passage of the legislation. Further, the president's authority to enter negotiations was for five years in duration, or until July 1, 1967. And finally, the amount of scheduled tariff reduction taking place in any given year could not exceed 20 percent.

### Results of the Kennedy Round

Crucial to the Trade Expansion Act was the "dominant supplier authority," which was intended to permit the largest tariff reductions to be concentrated on commodities of bilateral interest to the United States and the Common Market. (From the US point of view that prevailed, a US technological edge over Europe and the presence of greater spare productive capacity would ensure a relatively greater expansion of US exports than US imports.) But in order to make full use of the dominant supplier authority provision, it was necessary for Britain to join the Common Market by the time trade negotiations were in full swing. France vetoed Britain's application for membership in January 1963, however, which meant that the scope for tariff reduction under this provision was cut from about twenty-five to two commodity groups: vegetable oils and aircraft.[15] Thus, the initial objective of free trade for a wide range of industrial and agricultural products traded between the United States and the EC had to be abandoned, and along with that went high hopes for substantial progress in the area of agricultural trade.

Still of relevance in the Trade Expansion Act was the general authority to negotiate reduction in tariffs by up to 50 percent. The United States hoped that this would be sufficient inducement to EC countries to exchange concessions on their agricultural support prices and tariffs for reductions in US tariffs on industrial products, but that hope was not fulfilled. Instead, the EC held firm to its position of freedom to pursue its own agricultural policies, which stressed self-sufficiency. What scope remained for the Kennedy Round negotiations, therefore, was essentially reduction of tariffs of up to 50 percent on trade in industrial products.

At the conclusion of negotiations the average tariff reduction by all major industrial countries was 36 to 39 percent.[16] The great preponderance of tariff reductions achieved were the partial type, similar to but on a bigger scale than those that had occurred through previous rounds of trade negotiations under the auspices of the GATT. The largest tariff reductions occurred in industries characterized by advanced technology, a high degree of product innovation, or dominated by multinational firms. Substantially smaller tariff concessions were granted for products of interest to less developed countries; in particular, concessions on textiles and processed agricultural products were very modest.[17]

The Kennedy Round of negotiations ended in June 1967. The negotiated concessions were to be phased in over the ensuing five-year period. While the over-all exercise fell far short of initial ambitions, which were indeed more sweeping than any embodied before in the several Trade Agreements Acts, the Kennedy Round was labeled a success by those participants who favored the reciprocal approach on the grounds that it achieved a large step forward down the path of tariff reduction begun in 1934.

A weighted average of post Kennedy Round tariff rates on dutiable items for the United States was 9 percent compared to 12.3 percent in 1962. The following table compares U.S. average rates to those of other countries. Viewed broadly, and particular items notwithstanding, tariffs were no longer considered to be the major problem in world trade as they had been until perhaps the early 1960s. Indeed, other issues were moving into the forefront, and they will be the subject of attention in succeeding chapters.

## Continuity Between the Trade Expansion Act and the Preceding Trade Agreements Acts

In spite of being heralded as a new departure for US commercial policy, the Trade Expansion Act should be regarded more than anything else as a

**Table 2-1**
**Weighted Average, Post Kennedy Round**

|  | Tariff Rates, Dutiable Items Only |
|---|---|
| United States | 9.0 |
| EC[a] | 18.9 |
| Japan | 12.5 |
| United Kingdom | 12.0 |
| Sweden | 8.0 |
| Switzerland | 5.9 |
| Denmark | 9.4 |
| Austria | 16.4 |
| Norway | 10.0 |
| Finland | 14.2 |

[a]If tariffs on grains and variable levels are excluded, the average EC tariff rate is 10.1.
Source: Based on Thomas B. Curtis and John Robert Vastine, Jr. *The Kennedy Round and the Future of American Trade*, (Praeger Publishers: New York, 1971), Table 42, p. 228.

continuation of the spirit and approach to policy that had been propounded in the Trade Agreements Acts of earlier years. The purpose was to promote freer international trade in order to permit increased efficiency in the allocation of resources and to improve the process of economic growth in the world economy; but underneath all the trappings, the emphasis was on expansion of US exports in order to help alleviate this country's balance of payments deficits. The Reciprocal Trade Agreements Program was also dedicated to reducing trade barriers in order to expand international commerce generally, to increase overseas markets for US exports in particular, and therefore to help offset the domestic economic consequences of the Great Depression.

The Trade Expansion Act did include some new bargaining methods that acknowledged key changes in the world environment that had taken place over the course of more than a quarter century. Rather than dealing item by item and country by country, the president was empowered to negotiate by entire categories of trade and with blocs of countries. These new features were incorporated in the 1962 legislation to facilitate effective negotiations between the United States and the European Common Market. The assumptions of classical economics, namely, many sovereign countries dealing with each other on an equal basis, were no longer appropriate. But these changes were more a matter of form than changes in the substance of the reciprocal trade approach itself.

In one particular sense the Trade Expansion Act differed from preceding trade agreements legislation. The former provided for adjustment assistance as an alternative to reliance upon escape-clause action when injury was realized or threatened by tariff concessions embodied in trade agreements. Strictly interpreted, and indeed according to the record of slowed progress in reducing tariffs during the 1950s, injury as spelled out under the law was sufficient basis for negating the tariff action. But for meaningful tariff reductions to take place, it followed that dislocations within the domestic economy would arise. The Trade Expansion Act exhibited greater awareness of this basic fact than did the Reciprocal Trade Agreements Program and showed that legislators had sought to provide a mechanism for mitigating or amicably resolving the internal dislocations which would still permit the wider advantages of tariff reduction to be realized. As a practical matter, however, adjustment assistance was hardly ever utilized, because only a small amount of funds was appropriated to make it work and because the criteria for firms or workers to become eligible were very strict. Thus, while the idea of adjustment assistance was new, its impact was so small that in a pragmatic sense there was very little break with the past.[18]

Above all else, US trade policies emphasized tariff cuts, the tradition of tariff reductions through reciprocal concessions, and the concept of nondiscrimination in trade relations as embodied in the most-favored-nation principle. These elements, together with the goals of freer trade, more rapid growth in the world economy, and a net expansionary effect for the US economy, joined the trade agreements legislation of the past with the Trade Expansion Act of 1962.

**A Note on Other Features of**
**US Commercial Policies**

While the tariff was the central issue in US commercial policy during the long period of time that the Reciprocal Trade Agreements Program was in vogue, there were other important aspects of US policy, some of which may be noted briefly.[19]

Two types of import quotas have been used: tariff quotas and quantitative quotas. Quotas have been permitted under the Agricultural Adjustment Act as amended in 1939.[a] They were used on occasion when imports threatened to interfere with domestic agricultural programs, namely, the price-support programs. The president has been authorized to restrict imports by imposing fees over and above any existing tariffs, or by imposing quantitative quotas. A variety of agricultural products have been restricted by quotas over the years: cotton, wheat, wheat flour, oats, rye, barley, certain dairy products, and peanuts.

Besides being used on agricultural goods, import quotas have been used in conjunction with the national security provision of the Trade Agreements Acts. The knowledge that quotas could be employed has in some instances led to voluntary sales limitations by foreigners exporting to the United States. For example, in 1956, Japan curtailed the amount of cotton textiles exported to the United States, presumably out of concern that unilateral action by the United States might impose still more severe limitations.

Quotas have been a matter of continuing controversy for the United States in the GATT. Since the General Agreement prohibits the use of import quotas in the context applied by the United States, a waiver of that commitment was applied for and granted in 1951. But under the terms of the waiver, the United States had to grant extensive consultations and was obliged to report periodically to the GATT on its actions. That action has had much to do with indefinite postponement of any coming to grips with the global problem of agricultural trade barriers.

"Buy American" legislation has been another feature of restrictionist US policies. It has given domestic producers preferential treatment in contracting for the sale of merchandise to the US government. Impetus for such legislation derived from considerations of employment and national security.

An adjunct of the Buy American idea was a law enacted in 1934 that required that for goods traded internationally and obtained using any funds of a federal agency, US commercial vessels had to be used for transport, if available. In practice, this has been taken to mean that a minimum of 50 percent of the cargo in question must travel in American carriers. Indeed, provisions to this affect were included in the legislation authorizing aid to Europe after World War II

---

[a]The Reciprocal Trade Agreements Program was in fundamental conflict with the Agricultural Adjustment Act provisions for domestic price supports, import quotas, and export subsidies. This conflict erupted in 1955, when the United States requested a waiver of GATT obligations on certain actions it was required to pursue under the agricultural act.

under the Marshall Plan, and in military and economic assistance to developing countries in subsequent years under the Mutual Security Program. The rationale for this preferential treatment of US carriers has been to maintain a substantial and active US shipping fleet so as to safeguard national security.

# 3

# The International Trade Structure: Growing Discontent

The long and successful life of the US trade agreements program, and of the reciprocal approach to freer trade embodied in it, was to a large extent responsible for the particular pattern of international trade that arose. Tariff policies based on the most-favored-nation principle meant that all countries were to be treated alike and that in principle no quarter was to be given to preferential trade agreements.

Following World War II, it was the policy of the United States and other nations to work for acceptance of the principles of nondiscrimination and free trade on a multilateral scale but within a more structured institutional framework. The General Agreement on Tariffs and Trade reflected those principles, and that organization in turn helped to influence the pattern or complexion of international trade that has evolved during the past quarter century.

Indeed, it has been the growing dissatisfaction in many quarters with trade patterns that flowed from the long application of those principles that has brought about the present reconsideration as to what modifications in basic trade policy are most appropriate and necessary at this juncture in light of changes in political realities and shifts in economic strength that have taken place between nations. This chapter concerns the particular pattern of trade that arose in the course of the last thirty-five years, and developments in different quarters that revealed the general principles after which the international trade system had been patterned were due for substantial modification and overhaul.

## General Characteristics of International Trade Patterns

With respect to the commodity composition of world trade, manufactured goods accounted for about one-third of total goods traded in the five-year period 1925-29, just prior to passage of the Reciprocal Trade Agreements Act. By 1960, manufactured goods accounted for about 48 percent of all world trade, and by 1970 the proportion had risen to 58 percent.[1] The fact is that growth of trade in manufactured goods has accounted for the record rate of growth in world trade in the post World War II period. Trade in food, raw materials, and fuels has grown more slowly, and their share of total world trade has declined from about 66 percent in 1925-29 to about 34 percent in 1970.

Several reasons may be cited as to why the composition of internationally

27

traded goods changed in this fashion over time. In the rapidly growing industrial economies the manufacturing sectors were enjoying the fastest rates of growth. Discovery of new products increased, and the scale of their production soared. Such activity generated higher incomes and higher living standards, which in turn stimulated more production. Interest in and demand for manufactured goods spilled over national boundaries at such a rate that the portion of industrial production entering into foreign trade rose very substantially over time. Moreover, the fact that the greatest reduction in barriers to trade took place in the areas of manufactured and semimanufactured goods during the last three decades was of great importance in reinforcing the emerging pattern of trade.

International trade in foodstuffs did not increase as fast as total world trade, partly because many countries purposefully chose to maintain some levels of domestic food production in a desire to maintain national independence and security, or to appease strong farm lobbies. It has also been argued that international trade in foodstuffs rose less rapidly than total trade for reasons related to Engel's Law: out of a rising aggregate world income, a decreasing proportion of it was spent on acquiring food. In any event, protective barriers against imports of a variety of agricultural products comprised a fundamental part of many industrial countries' commercial policies.

Trade in raw materials and fuels historically did not rise very rapidly either. Again several reasons may be cited. Technological innovation and development of synthetics afforded substantial economies of scale in the use of raw materials and fuel in a wide variety of production processes. Moreover, there was generally little product differentiation among given types of raw materials and fuels, and except in extreme circumstances of war, there were almost always alternative sources of supply. Accordingly, prices of many raw materials and fuels tended to rise less rapidly over time than did prices of manufactured products. That meant that by value the share of raw materials and fuels entering international trade declined more rapidly than did the share of those same items in terms of volume.

During the past forty years, foreign trade activity has taken place to an ever more concentrated extent among a relatively small number of developed countries. This trend, which has been most pronounced in the quarter century since World War II, has witnessed the virtual elimination of nonindustrial countries from leading positions in international trade. Such gradual but persistent increases in concentration of international trade among a group of rich, industrialized and, for the most part, rapidly developing countries are in contrast to steady declines in total world trade shares for a much larger group of less developed countries with stagnant or slow growth economies.

In 1960, 70 percent of developed countries' international trade took place among each other, while another 26 percent occurred with less developed nations. The balance, or about 4 percent, was trade with Communist countries. By 1965, trade between developed countries had increased to nearly 74 percent. Only 22 percent of their trade was with less developed countries, while the share of trade with Communist countries remained at just under 4 percent. By 1972, about 77 percent of all trade of developed countries was trade with each other. Just under 20 percent of their trade involved less developed countries, and again the share of trade with the Communist bloc of nations remained constant.

Foreign trade of less developed countries has taken place by and large with industrial nations and not between each other. In 1960, 73 percent of all LDC trade involved developed countries, whereas only 21 percent was accounted for by trade within the LDC bloc. LDC trade with Communist countries accounted for about 5 percent of total trade. During the 1960s and early 1970s, this pattern of trade was further reinforced. By 1965, just over 75 percent of all LDC trade was with developed countries, and 19 percent was trade with each other. By 1972, 76 percent of all LDC trade involved industrial countries, and less than 20 percent of the total was trade with each other. The share of LDC trade with Communist countries has remained steady within a range of 4 to 5 percent.

For Communist nations, and especially since World War II, the great bulk of their international trade, or about 70 percent, has been directed to one another. In the 1930s, the United States and West European countries traded with East European nations to a significant degree, but that trade dwindled in the face of World War II and the ensuing Cold War. Another significant characteristic of Communist bloc trade is that it has accounted for a substantially smaller proportion of the total economic activity of its member countries than has trade for Western nations. When Communist countries have traded outside their own bloc, trade has been directed toward developed countries much more than toward less developed countries. In most recent years, trade between the Communist countries and Western industrialized countries has been increasing more rapidly than at any time since World War II.

To sum up, the composition and pattern of world trade outlined above was to a very considerable extent the product of the reciprocal approach to the reduction of existing international trade barriers, and the most-favored-nation treatment that viewed countries as equals in the foreign trade arena. The philosophy and principles underlying the rules that governed international trade during the past four decades, the tremendous expansion of manufactured products entering the trade network, and the economic isolation of Communist countries for politicomilitary reasons, all of these factors are of major importance in explaining how existing trade patterns, which were concentrated initially among a handful of rich industrial nations, were materially strengthened over the course of the past thirty-five years.

**Unrest Within Developing Countries**

Interest in, and concern about, economic development began to stir in nonindustrial lands around the period of World War II. The beginning in Latin America was marked somewhat earlier than in Asia and Africa, in part because of its proximity to the industrialized United States, and in part because for a period during World War II Latin America had enjoyed an early taste of favored export status and the sizable foreign exchange earnings that accompanied that position. By the war's end, there was widespread desire in Latin America for economic development, especially in the form of industrial development; at the time, however, the one foreign government that had ample resources, the United States, was interested primarily in helping a war-torn Europe regain its economic independence. Accordingly, foreign assistance for the purpose of helping to realize some of the dreams of economic development had to be sought in alternative ways.

Coupled with the idealism that led to the establishment of the United Nations and the International Monetary Fund-World Bank Group, various regional arrangements were introduced as affiliates of the United Nations. These included the Economic Commission for Latin America (ECLA), the Economic Commission for Asia and the Far East (ECAFE), and the Economic Commission for Africa (ECA). The head of the Secretariat of ECLA, Raul Prebisch, became a strong force, a leading thinker and spokesman, for the cause of economic development generally and for Latin American advancement in particular. Indeed, the early work of Prebisch and others sowed the seeds that led to questioning and, ultimately, to rejection of many basic tenets of classical economics and its approach to international trade.[2]

During the early 1950s, one of the themes in the literature of economic development was that the established pattern of trade between industrial countries and less developed countries was not beneficial to the former—that, indeed, it was detrimental. Such argument conflicted directly with traditional economic doctrine. LDCs traded some of their raw materials production for some of the manufactured production of developed countries. According to classical international trade theory, this pattern of production and trade, wherein each country specialized in those modes of production for which it had a comparative advantage over others, and then traded the surplus production for other goods for which the foreign countries enjoyed a comparative advantage, should yield maximum possible advantage to all concerned. Trade contributed to enrichment of nations, and more trade meant greater enrichment.

It had been recognized for some time that the production of raw materials was characterized by diminishing returns on the supply side and inelastic demand with respect to price. Prebisch expanded the argument, first showing how raw materials commodities traded internationally had been subject to great price instability and, second, demonstrating that over the long run the terms of trade of raw materials exporting countries had worsened. LDCs could not count on a given sum of foreign exchange earnings from the sale of their raw materials; moreover, an increasing amount of raw materials exports was required over time to obtain the same volume of manufactured goods imports. In both senses, international trade benefited the developed countries more than, and at the expense of, less developed countries.

The policy recommendation Prebisch offered in 1950 was industrialization.[3] He did not suggest abandonment of raw materials production; instead, new industry should be constructed by using some of the foreign exchange proceeds of raw materials exports. By altering the pattern of production, countries could achieve a more advantageous role in the world trade network. But industrialization would be a difficult proposition at best, it was thought, because new industries would have to compete against already established producers in advanced countries. In order to facilitate the process, there were several alternative approaches.

One of the first steps was to form a customs union. Countries wishing to establish their own industrial base should agree to lower and ultimately to reduce trade barriers as a means of creating a larger, more unified market. Second, countries belonging to the customs union should introduce tariff barriers on external trade. This could preempt, in effect, the customs union market for producers within. This two-stage approach placed heavy reliance on the technique of import substitution. An enlarged market area protected from competition of producers in nonmember countries should offer incentives for the development of new industry, especially firms capable of producing goods previously imported. The infant industry argument of classical economics that provided a rationale for tariff protection was thus adapted to fit the requirements of less developed countries. Advocates of the approach saw the infant industry, whatever it might be, as providing a first step in a cumulative process of industrial growth.

In Latin America, the Prebisch proposal had great impact. Indeed, it led ultimately to the development of two common markets in the region: the Central American Common Market (CACM), established in 1958, and the Latin American Free Trade Association (LAFTA), begun in 1960.

Even though the regional integration approach was pursued vigorously in Latin America, substantial problems were encountered. The scope for import substitution was circumscribed owing to the fact that imports had always been quite restricted. With no great latitude for import displacement by domestic production, there was a question of whether industrialization could indeed become cumulative, as Prebisch had suggested, or whether it would advance to a certain level and then taper off. It became apparent, therefore, that the industrialization approach would also have to give attention to production for export.

Beyond that realization, there was growing awareness that a broader forum and an approach offering more general appeal were needed in order to embrace developing countries through the entire world and in order to mobilize more widespread cooperation and interest for the purpose of achieving global trade policies that could better help to promote economic development of the nonindustrial countries. In other less developed areas, namely Asia and Africa, there was little feeling of identification or of common interests, which might have been combined with sentiments in Latin America so as to comprise a more forceful bargaining device in negotiations with developed countries. Such lack of cohesion among countries in the less developed world manifested itself economically as well as politically. Often, countries would be producers of the same kinds of raw materials, and they would compete with each other for markets in developed countries, the result being that a smaller amount of revenues was forthcoming to help finance desired industrial development.

A more global focus did begin to develop in the early 1960s. In 1963, Prebisch published a book that contained policy recommendations more amenable to, and in keeping with, the needs of the underdeveloped world as a whole.[4] The major recommendations are worth a brief review here.

An income retransfer from developed to less developed countries was one important proposal. Without fundamental changes in production patterns or trading relationships, the observed worsening trend in terms of trade was bound to continue, in which case LDCs would have to give up ever increasing amounts of raw materials just to maintain past levels of manufactured goods imports. Owing to aspirations for economic development, however, import requirements of LDCs were growing over time. Given this two-way squeeze on the outlook for LDCs, Prebisch argued that some means had to be found to allocate more foreign exchange to them. An international income retransfer could be achieved either through measures aimed at restructuring production and trade so as to halt or reverse the secular adverse movement in their terms of trade, or through acceptance by industrial countries to transfer back to LDCs a portion of the income accruing from their long-run terms of trade improvement. Prebisch favored the former approach on the grounds that it would give LDCs a better chance to pay their own way internationally in the future.

A second feature of Prebisch's recommendations was a set of policies designed to stimulate exports. The years preceding had shown that the scope for import substitution as a means to industrialization with regionally integrated LDCs was limited. He therefore advocated development of industries whose output would have a good chance of being sold in markets of developed countries. Indeed, he suggested that LDCs should not be prevented from developing export-oriented manufacturing industries because of previous inability to gain access to markets of industrial countries. As a practical matter, however, this would involve a restructuring of world tariffs, which in fact was the next major recommendation Prebisch put forth.

During the early 1960s the developed countries continued to impose import duties of varying levels on industrial imports, but raw-materials imports remained practically duty free unless there was a substantial base of domestic production that needed protection from world competition. Less developed countries imposed relatively higher duties on imports of industrial commodities in order to raise revenue or to protect domestic industries, but they too allowed raw-materials imports to enter largely duty free. The global tariff structure, therefore, was very favorable to the existing raw-materials orientation of LDCs, but it discouraged their entering into new industrial production for export.

As has been discussed before, such a tariff structure was based on a philosophy of trade long held by the United States and many other developed countries and one on which the General Agreement on Tariffs and Trade had been founded after World War II. Essential to that philosophy were the assumptions that freer trade was desirable since a greater value of trade would result, and that reduction of tariffs was good for all trading countries and therefore should be pursued on reciprocal, most-favored-nation basis.

From the viewpoint of LDCs, this approach to trade lent a bias in favor of a particular pattern of production and trade; as tariff cuts took place, there was a stimulation of trade in manufactured goods between advanced countries that already possessed a broad industrial base, but there was no parallel impetus to LDC production of, or trade in, raw-materials products. Moreover, reciprocal tariff reductions on industrial goods conceded on an MFN basis by developed and less developed countries gave the latter no help in building their own industries—indeed, quite the contrary, since tariff reductions stimulated even greater production of competitive goods abroad, which could then be placed more easily either in LDC markets or in markets of other developed countries. Prebisch concluded that the global tariff structure and the philosophy on which it was founded served to strengthen the status quo. And it was a status quo from which LDCs should be trying to extricate themselves, inimical as it was to their long-run interests.

With increasing emphasis on export promotion, Prebisch's third principal recommendation called for a new global tariff structure which would break with past precedent. He advocated, on the one hand, opening the markets of developed countries (abolishing tariffs) to products of new export-oriented manufacturing industries in LDCs, and, on the other hand, retention of LDC tariff duties on imports in order to protect home markets for LDC producers.

Prebisch's recommendations on tariff reform were radical in that they ignored the reciprocity and most-favored-nation principles so strongly endorsed before. What he maintained was that the global tariff structure should be modified, even manipulated, in ways that would help directly to reshape the global pattern of production; world tariffs should not continue to accommodate the existing pattern of production and trade as it had for years past.

While the need for new industry was stressed greatly by Prebisch, his fourth main recommendation concerned measures to strengthen raw-materials exports, since, in his view, that sector would clearly be the one to generate the bulk of foreign-exchange earnings necessary to finance new industry. With that in mind, LDC participation in international commodity agreements and compensatory finance schemes was looked upon as the way to help alleviate the problem of price instability of primary products traded internationally and, hence, to help reduce the problem of wide variations in foreign-exchange earnings of LDCs that made long-range economic planning extremely difficult.

By the mid-1960s, the basic emphasis of Prebisch and other economic development economists had turned toward promotion of export-oriented industry in LDCs. The global relationships and common interests among LDCs were taking root. There was growing dissatisfaction with the basic raw-materials orientation associated with poorer, underdeveloped countries, for that was viewed increasingly as a dead end which offered no promise of a better future. The time was ripe, therefore, for an amalgamation of strength among the LDCs of Asia, Africa, and Latin America under the auspices of the United Nations.

The first United Nations Conference on Trade and Development, a new organization known as UNCTAD, began in April 1964 in Geneva, Switzerland.[5] The agenda was concerned with matters of trade and development. All members of the United Nations, developed and less developed, were represented; in all, 120 countries attended, including eighty-eight less developed and thirty-two developed. It was the first assembly ever that brought together so many countries to discuss problems of trade and development. Discussion during the conference illustrated the wide gulf between rich and poor countries, and only in a few areas was there general agreement as to how to proceed. Recommendations emanating from the conference took the form of requests that industrial nations undertake policies domestically and internationally in order to help promote economic development of the third world. Socialist countries attending the conference supported LDCs on a number of points.

One of the issues highlighted most during the UNCTAD I conference concerned "tariff preferences." Embodied in the Final Act and Report of the Proceedings was a clear beginning of an alternative approach to the multilaterialist, reciprocal trade approach that had been in vogue for so long.[6] Recognized was the fact that international trade was one of the most important factors in economic development, that all countries should cooperate in establishing conditions conducive to attainment of a rapid increase in export earnings of LDCs and to the expansion and diversification of trade between countries, irrespective of differences in their levels of economic development or their social systems. It was further recognized that trade expansion and diversification depended upon increasing access to overseas markets and on fair prices for exports of raw materials. Developed countries should reduce and eliminate trade barriers and other restrictions that hampered trade and consumption of products from LDCs and should take steps to increase markets for LDCs. There should be cooperation among all countries through appropriate international arrangements to increase and stabilize primary product export receipts and to maintain a mutually satisfactory relationship between prices of industrial commodities and raw materials goods.

While it was stipulated in the Final Act of UNCTAD I that international trade should be carried out to mutual advantage on an MFN basis and should not involve measures detrimental to other countries' interests, an important caveat, offered by the United States, was that advanced nations should grant concessions to all LDCs, including all concessions they grant to one another, but should not require reciprocal treatment in return from LDCs. Such preferential tariff and nontariff concessions should be extended to LDCs as a whole but should not be made applicable to developed countries. Related to this was the caveat that LDCs need not extend preferential treatment in trade among themselves to industrial countries. Finally, there was a statement to the effect that special tariff preferences then in existence (namely, the preferences accorded by certain European Common Market countries to their former colonies and by Great Britain to members of the British Commonwealth under British Imperial Preference) should be progressively reduced and eliminated as soon as appropriate measures could be introduced to guarantee equivalent advantages to the countries concerned. 1905974

Following the end of UNCTAD I in June 1964, the permanent working groups of UNCTAD that included the Trade and Development Board and its sundry committees went to work on the difficult tasks of attempting to reconcile the divergent interests of less developed and developed countries. After approximately two years, enough progress had been made so that a second conference, UNCTAD II, was scheduled to be convened in New Delhi in February 1968.

Any substantive success for that conference was, however, foredoomed. At that time, many developed countries were beset with domestic budgetary problems, or balance of payments difficulties, or both, thus constraining the concessions they might otherwise have been willing to offer; others came seemingly still not prepared to accept the kinds of changes LDCs maintained were necessary in order to help pave the way for meaningful contributions to their economic development. On the other hand, LDCs opposed social and economic reforms suggested by developed countries, and resisted some of the disciplines of traditional economic planning.

Tariff preferences were again high on the agenda. Developed countries had moved significantly away from their previous position, which strongly endorsed the most-favored-nation approach. Yet, there was inability to proceed and to negotiate the principles of a general system of preferences embracing discrimination and nonreciprocity. For one thing, the two groups could not agree on the products to receive preferential treatment. Developed countries preferred a limited list of manufacturers and semimanufacturers, while less developed countries pushed for inclusion of processed agricultural products. The scope of the list of products was important, since the narrower lists would have allowed only a small number of well-to-do LDCs to benefit from tariff preferences.

Another stumbling block was the problem of how to deal with existing discriminatory trade preferences, or reverse preferences, if a generalized preference scheme were implemented.

The problem of the so-called reverse preferences granted by certain groups of LDCs to particular developed countries was of especially great concern to the United States, which believed that any further development of such discriminatory schemes would help prompt evolution of world trade into trading blocs that would be detrimental to US interests. Thus, for the United States, dismantling existing preference schemes was essential. While the United States supported a generalized preference scheme in principle, it was unwilling in the face of its own domestic and external economic problems to go further than that at New Delhi.

On the matter of access to developed countries' markets, no progress was made at the conference. The LDCs had requested that a share of incremental demand for primary commodities in developed countries be reserved for production in developing countries, but no agreement was reached.

Some positive results were secured in the areas of trade expansion and economic integration among less developed countries. There was general support for regional ties among LDCs. A resolution of the conference established a framework for action by all countries to help promote successful efforts toward such regional cooperation. As envisaged, assistance from developed countries could take the form of commercial policy concessions, such as a waiving of MFN treatment, or it might be financial and technical assistance to help support the regional arrangements.

The marked lack of progress on the major issues before the conference caused several matters to be referred to the Trade and Development Board. A mood of pessimism and the inevitability of further delay hung over the conference as it adjourned in March 1968.

By 1970, events indicated greater promise of change. A series of meetings took place in Geneva, hosted by UNCTAD and attended by major developed countries. The meetings were held in order to develop guidelines for generalized preference schemes, on the basis of which countries might then proceed to introduce their own particular versions of preferential tariff treatment toward LDC exports. Indeed, shortly thereafter, the European Common Market and Japan in 1971 and Britain and several other European countries in 1972 introduced generalized tariff preference programs. The United States did not act on the matter because of severe balance of payments problems and because of growing protectionist sentiment domestically that seemed sure to foredoom any enabling legislation that might be introduced before Congress.

For less developed countries, the reciprocal approach to international trade, based as it was on the principles of nondiscrimination and free trade, proved to be more of a hindrance than a help in their efforts to promote change and development within their economies. The prevailing international trade system seemed to work well for the developed countries but not for less developed nations, and accordingly, the gulf in economic well-being between the two worlds widened over time. Gradually during the early 1950s and then more rapidly as time went on, a new body of economic thought with policy recommendations quite contrary to classical economic doctrine began to build up. The principles of this new approach to trade were nonreciprocity, discrimination, and preferential treatment. Spokesmen became more numerous and increasingly articulate in a number of multilateral forums. In the latter 1960s, doubts began to surface in some developed countries concerning the wisdom of further application of traditional trade policies to less developed countries. By the end of the decade, a breach had been opened, and acceptability of special treatment for the third world began to be recognized as desirable and necessary.

## East-West Trade and the Policy
## of Containment

In the wake of World War II, the comprehensive system of export controls (applied in conjunction with the military effort of the United States and its allies) began to be dismantled. Certain controls on US exports were continued for a time on items in especially great demand by allied countries in order to prevent severe shortages and to moderate inflationary pressures within the United States. Those controls were applied on a nondiscriminatory basis and in accordance with US Marshall Plan commitments.

With respect to trade with the Soviet Union, with its satellite countries, and with the Communist forces on Mainland China, a more forceful body of US export controls emerged in the late 1940s and early 1950s. A policy of containment of the Communist bloc was prompted by evidence of Soviet expansionism in Europe and of Russia's unwillingness to cooperate in postwar efforts, such as the Marshall Plan and the various new international organizations then being born. In effect, it was the "economic equivalent of political containment,"[7] prompted further in 1948-49 by the Communist takeover in Czechoslovakia, the Berlin Blockade, and the defeat of Chiang Kai-Shek and his forces at the hands of the Communist Chinese. It was believed that by depriving the Communist bloc of superior Western technology, embodied particularly in military and strategic goods, Russia and her partners could be more easily held to a position of relative military and economic inferiority.

The key piece of legislation enacted by Congress to carry out this policy was the Export Control Act of 1949. It required the use of export controls in order "to exercise the necessary vigilance over exports from the standpoint of their significance to the national security."[8] The president was thus given broad discretionary authority with respect to enforcing the policy of containment.

At the same time, the United States entered into negotiations with other industrial countries for the purpose of establishing a collective embargo of strategic exports to Communist countries. In November 1949, a Consultative Group-Coordinating Committee (COCOM) was formed. Its membership included

Japan and all fifteen nations belonging to the North Atlantic Treaty Organization (NATO), with the exception of Iceland. COCOM drew up a list of goods whose export to Communist countries was to be completely embargoed; any exceptions to the embargo required the unanimous consent of COCOM members.

Even at COCOM's inception, there was opposition from various quarters in Western Europe to a bloc-wide embargo policy. West European nations were more accustomed historically to trade with Eastern Europe; accordingly, those countries anticipated greater economic losses from such an embargo than was expected by the United States, which in the past had traded with East European countries to a far less extent.

COCOM's embargo efforts were directed for the most part at military goods and nonmilitary products of strategic importance. The range of goods that the United States embargoed unilaterally was always more comprehensive, however. This came to be known as the "COCOM differential." The Battle Act of 1951, which provided for US participation in COCOM, directed that a wide range of military and strategic goods be embargoed from shipment to any nation threatening the security of the United States; named specifically were the USSR and all countries under its domain.

A third means of implementing an embargo on trade with Communist countries had to do with US efforts to enlist support of non-COCOM countries in the West. One way this was achieved was by incorporating into bilateral foreign aid agreements provisions that in effect coordinated export controls of the aid-receiving countries and the United States. The Battle Act, in fact, provided for sanctions, in the form of withdrawal of all military, economic, or financial assistance, against countries violating US embargo policy. In addition, language in the legislation authorizing Marshall Plan aid to Europe in 1948 stated that delivery of goods be refused to countries that used the aid to produce goods for export to Communist countries in conflict with US export control policies.

In 1951, the Trade Agreements Program was before the Congress for renewal. The Truman administration argued in favor of most-favored-nation treatment for East European countries on grounds that denial of MFN would break existing treaties with Poland and Hungary and would violate US obligations to Czechoslovakia under the GATT. Furthermore, it was argued that accordingly MFN treatment would not affect US security interests that were already well protected by other laws pertaining to export controls. Nevertheless, Congress did vote to withhold MFN treatment and to discriminate against imports from Communist-controlled countries, including the USSR. The tariff rates on imports from those countries thus reverted to the higher duties prescribed by the Smoot-Hawley Tariff Act of 1930, the so-called "column 2" duties.

In 1953, the United States moved to supplement other measures aimed at insuring foreign compliance with the COCOM embargo policy. The Transaction Control Regulations, to be administered by the Foreign Assets Control Office of the Treasury Department, were issued under the authority of the Trading with the Enemy Act (1917) as amended in 1933. Persons in the United States or any foreign firms controlled by US citizens were prohibited from purchasing, selling, or arranging the purchase or sale of COCOM-controlled goods located outside the United States for ultimate delivery to Communist countries. (The Trans-action Control Regulations applied to transactions with all Communist countries except Cuba and Yugoslavia. Transactions with Cuba were later dealt with under the Cuban Assets Control Regulations.)

In addition to COCOM, a second coordinating committee was set up in September 1952 in order to deal with a more extensive embargo on trade with Asian Communist countries. The second committee, known as CHINCOM, established a broad export control list for China and North Korea. CHINCOM was promoted by the United States, which was then involved in the Korean Conflict. Inasmuch as the United Nations was also involved in that military action, the United States was able to persuade the UN General Assembly to adopt a "China embargo" resolution that called for a cooperative effort among member nations supporting the UN force in Korea to embargo strategic exports to the Peoples' Republic of China.

The foregoing measures and laws comprised the major elements in the foundation of US policy on East-West trade. It was a strong policy of containment applied to what was regarded during the early 1950s as a more or less monolithic Communist bloc. The United States took the initiative in persuading other industrial nations to join in a cooperative enforcement of the embargo. While European nations from the outset appeared to be less disposed than the United States toward such a policy, they went along willingly, because of close ties with the United States, because of the tremendous postwar reconstruction tasks they faced, because the United States was the only country in a real position to offer much needed assistance, and because of allied unity generated by the Korean Conflict.

Upon termination of war in Korea in 1953, the historical predilections of West European countries toward Eastern Europe began to surface bit by bit, and pressure built up on the United States to agree to a reduction in the scope of the COCOM embargo; indeed, some cuts were made in the COCOM lists during the middle 1950s.[9]

But there were other forces at work undermining the Western embargo alliance. For example, there was growing awareness that a stalemate was evolving between Eastern and Western powers and that the Communist bloc was becoming more and more of a permanent feature of the world community. Economic recession in Western industrial countries underscored the economic costs of the embargo policy, particularly so for West European countries, which by the mid-1950s had overcome many postwar supply bottlenecks. Marshall Plan aid was concluded in 1953, and sanctions within the program to evoke compliance with US embargo policies ended, too. From the East, there were growing signs of Russian interest in trading with the West, especially after the death of Stalin in 1953.[10]

While there was considerable softening of attitudes within Western Europe toward East-West trade, the US position continued in the hard line vein of the very early 1950s. US unilateral export restrictions increased as the COCOM embargo list was reduced; consequently, effectiveness of the US embargo policy came to rest increasingly on a high degree of product differentiation in third countries, in order to make substitution for US embargoed products difficult, and on controls to prevent US export of embargoed products through friendly markets to Communist countries. It was during the mid-1950s, in fact, as the McCarthy hearings took place, that a strong anti-Communist movement was in progress. That development hardened US attitudes on the issue and made the contrast with West European attitudes all the more sharp.

The split between the United States and its trading partners was particularly great in respect of trade policy toward the Peoples' Republic of China. At US insistence, relaxation of the COCOM list in 1954 was not extended to China, which meant the embargo of trade with China was made relatively more severe. Other COCOM members went along initially; but in 1957, England unilaterally revoked the "China differential," and other COCOM members, save for the United States, followed suit. Thus, after five years of support from its allies, the United States stood alone in enforcing a complete embargo on trade with China.

During the late 1950s and early 1960s, there were some modifications in the US view of a monolithic Communist bloc and the need to contain it economically as well as politically. Just as Yugoslavia had been recognized earlier as being an independent satellite of the USSR, Poland was so recognized and therefore was found deserving of more favorable treatment. Changes were soon forthcoming in respect of US foreign aid restrictions, export, and import controls.[11]

Cuba, on the other hand, was the recipient of increasingly unfavorable US trade policies after Fidel Castro came to power in 1959. An embargo on US exports to Cuba was enforced in 1960, and an import embargo on Cuban products was administered under the authority of Cuban Assets Control Regulations starting in 1963. Moreover, the United States exerted pressures on its trade partners to curtail their trade with Cuba. Despite US protestations, allied members of COCOM refused to embargo the sale to Cuba of products not already on the COCOM list.

During the 1950s and early 1960s, the Communist bloc, and particularly the USSR, experienced rapid economic and military growth—considerably more rapid, in fact, than growth in the Western industrial countries. It came to be viewed as a contest of their economic system versus our own, and the other side was boasting of future supremacy. In addition to such general tensions, there occurred the U-2 incident of a downed US reconnaissance plane in Russia, the erection of the Berlin Wall, the Russian-United States confrontation over missiles in Cuba, and increased political-military tensions generally in particular quarters of the world.

Under the Kennedy administration, which took office in January 1961, Congress passed important trade-restrictive measures, including in 1962 extension and amendment of the 1949 Export Control Act. Those measures and amendments to the 1949 legislation reflected congressional concern that US national security was threatened and that the trade measures already in effect should be further tightened and their scope broadened. In regard to the Trade Expansion Act of 1962, Congress withheld presidential discretion in the application of MFN treatment and required denial of same to products imported into the United States from any country or area dominated or controlled by communism. This requirement would have forced withdrawal of MFN treatment previously extended to Poland and Yugoslavia had it not been for an affirmative finding by the president that MFN treatment promoted the independence of both countries from Communist domination.[12]

In effect, an asymmetry was emerging between American export and import policies in East-West trade: some policies, most notably those affecting exports, reflected the slightly more liberal attitude of the executive branch, which was trying to move away from the position of regarding the Communist world as monolithic; other policies pertaining more to imports bore the marks of the most recent congressional actions, which themselves arose out of new concern for national security and a determination to strengthen the old containment doctrine.

The Kennedy-Johnson administration during the 1960s made attempts to depart from the old containment policy, but they were largely frustrated by reaction to the Vietnam War. There was growing sentiment during the early 1960s within the executive branch that US isolationist policies were not only of dubious effectiveness but were also increasingly unrealistic. A new thrust was therefore designed to build bridges between West and East.

In 1965, President Johnson created a Special Committee on US Trade Relations with East European Countries and the Soviet Union. The committee's report, known as the Miller Report, emphasized the new themes of peaceful coexistence, polycentrism, and internal liberalization, all intended to be part of a new strategy aimed at broadening trade relations with Communist countries.[13] In particular, it was argued that increased trade (in nonmilitary goods) could be a most helpful device to enhance Eastern countries' receptivity to Western ideas and could be regarded as an incentive for them to institute greater economic and political decentralization.

Implementation of the new "building bridges" policy proved difficult, however, because of less liberal attitudes that continued to prevail within the Congress, because of restrictions placed on presidential authority to extend MFN treatment to Socialist nations, and because of limitations placed in 1964 on Eximbank participation in helping to finance East-West trade.

In 1966, President Johnson introduced the East-West Trade Relations Act to Congress. It was designed to give the president full discretion regarding MFN. The bill never was passed, however, and a similar bill introduced in 1969 was not voted out of the Senate Finance Committee. Thus, the Congress continued to maintain a firm hold on US import policies with respect to Communist countries. The negative result of these proposals was blamed by and large on the Vietnam War; the legislation would have allowed more liberal import policies to be extended to various Communist countries that actively supported the North Vietnamese objectives. Thus, not only did the Vietnam War impede progress toward a more liberal US posture in respect of East-West trade, it also prompted Congress to increase restrictiveness of US policies. For example, penalties for violations of regulations under the Export Control Act were increased in 1965, and presidential discretion concerning P.L. 480 sales of surplus agricultural commodities to Socialist countries was removed in 1966, as was also presidential discretion in offering Eximbank credit support for sales of goods to Communist countries.

Starting in 1965, and in spite of intensification of the Vietnam War during the latter half of the decade, there were new pressures in favor of a more liberal US East-West trade policy. One of the most important considerations in the movement for liberalization derived from the ability and willingness of American allies to trade with the Communist countries. Technological gains achieved by Japan and Western Europe made it increasingly easy for exporters of those nations to supply products unilaterally embargoed by the United States which were no longer under COCOM control. As evidence of this, the US market share of COCOM members' trade with Communist countries of Eastern Europe declined from 21 percent in 1948 (the year before COCOM was established) to 7 percent in 1957-59 and to 5 percent in 1967-69. The loss in US market share of COCOM members' trade with Communist countries of Asia was far more pronounced. These developments revealed the decreasing effectiveness of US embargo policies for a wide range of goods, and it led to growing agitation on the part of private US business interests over the fact that they were barred from competing for Communist country markets on an equal footing with other Western and Japanese exporters.

A second consideration that helped to promote the liberalization in the United States had to do with steadily worsening balance of payments difficulties then being encountered. This problem created new interest in favor of expansion of US exports—even of exports to Communist countries. Such interest was further buttressed by the employment-creating benefits that stood to be gained from such additional exports at a time when US unemployment was increasing.

Congressional hearings in 1968-69 witnessed a merging of the "building bridges" strategy of the executive branch with private business pressures. The result was a new, potent force for liberalization, which led to passage of the Export Control Act of 1969, an extension and modification of the Export Control Act of 1949.[14] Pursuant to that legislation, the Office of Export Control liberalized restrictions in a number of areas, including controls on the sale of a long list of nonmilitary goods to Communist countries in Eastern

Europe, and the standardization of forms used in the licensing approval process. Very important among the export control liberalization measures were those that opened trade relations with the Peoples' Republic of China.[1 5]

US liberalization initiatives were advanced further in 1971, when legislation was approved returning discretionary authority to the president in respect of Eximbank financial support of East-West trade. Concerning US imports from Communist countries, however, the same barriers persisted. There was no comparable domestic pressure to liberalize US import policies such as there had been for exports; and the continuing US trade and balance of payments difficulties created arguments (especially from domestic protectionist groups) for more, rather than fewer, import restrictions. Thus, while US export policies were taking on an increasingly liberal stance, there was continuing discrimination against imports from most Communist countries.[1 6]

Over the entire postwar period the United States was the leading proponent of the containment philosophy; the various measures taken and laws adopted leave little doubt that this was true in the early 1950s, and it continued to be the case during the late 1950s and early 1960s as US allies began to adopt their own more liberal trading policies with all Communist countries. Realization on the part of the United States that containment as a policy had outlived its usefulness, together with the country's mounting balance of payments pressures and a desire on the part of US business to try and keep step with its foreign competitors in bidding for Communist markets, all helped to set a new, more liberal course in respect of US trade policies with Eastern nations. Despite recent developments, many restrictive measures remain and must be substantially modified before potential benefits of East-West trade can be enjoyed more fully.

## Problems of the Developed Countries

During the late 1960s, and especially after the conclusion of the Kennedy Round in 1967, noticeable strains appeared between industrial trading nations. Many economic problems could be traced to frustrations in the realm of monetary affairs and to mounting problems encountered by the dollar as the leading international currency and primary reserve asset of the international monetary system;[1 7] other problems were particularly related to the trade area.

Following the Kennedy Round of trade negotiations, much of the existing structure of tariffs, quotas, and exchange controls that had long exerted a strong negative impact on trade between industrialized countries had been dismantled. Indeed, economic exchange and international commercial activities prospered on an ever increasing scale. Although tariffs on some items remained important, attentions were turned increasingly to nontariff barriers to trade (NTBs). The list included various subsidies to domestic producers, different customs classification practices, government procurement regulations, tax rebates on exports, and environmental controls, to name a few. Such barriers differed greatly in form, in purpose, and in their effect, but they were clearly a source of trade distortion amounting to protectionism. It was also apparent that such practices were so diverse, so slippery, that it would be virtually impossible to deal with them by the same sweeping, uniform approach that had proved so successful in reducing tariffs and eliminating quotas.[18]

Central to US foreign policy in the past quarter century has been the stabilization of relations between West European nations and promotion of their economic development into a sturdy unified force capable of standing on its own. American security interests have worked hand in glove with those foreign policy objectives; globally and in Europe, US interests were tied to a strong, cohesive bloc of European nations. In short, it was the conviction of the United States that Europe should come to play a constructive, leading role in the international economic system. As time passed and the 1960s slipped by, America's frustration over economic relations with Europe mounted. Rather than a positive multilateral effort forthcoming from Europe, the United States viewed policies on the other side of the Atlantic as increasingly discriminatory and mercantilistic; the hoped-for attention on modernization of the international monetary and trading systems was, for the most part, absent.

In the trade area, Europe's external policies developed bilaterally and tended to discriminate against the United States. From the founding of the Common Market in 1958 and thereafter, a network of special tariff preferences gradually materialized that encompassed more than fifty countries located in Africa and the Mediterranean area. (First, there were agreements with excolonies of Common Market members, then, in the 1960s, with excolonies of nonmembers, and finally in 1970 with noncolonies around the Mediterranean and certain North African countries.) It was a discriminatory network that constituted a major departure from the most-favored-nation principle accorded all members of the GATT. The EC tariff preference system worked in a manner that was doubly discriminatory to nonparticipants. First, exports of participating nations were accorded preferential duty treatment upon entry into the EC, thus placing exports of all other less developed and developed countries at a disadvantage. Second, EC exports were granted "reverse preferences," that is to say, lower tariff assessments compared to tariff rates applied to exports originating in non-EC countries. The long-run implications of this network of tariff preferences were clearly unfavorable to the United States and to other countries with global interests, since the trade bloc of EC members and affiliates tended to create an inward diversion of purchasing power and commercial activity.[19]

More serious in terms of the immediate trade effects was the inclusion of Sweden and Switzerland in the tariff preference network. This was the EC solution to special problems posed for countries formerly belonging to the European Free Trade Association (EFTA) that did not join the Common Market. Indeed, the trade coverage of the discriminatory network (both within the EC and between the EC and other designated countries in Europe, Africa, the Mediterranean and the Caribbean) increased to the point where almost one-half of the world's trade was under special arrangement.

Another bone of contention between the United States and the European Community has been the attempt to resolve problems of European political integration at the expense of foreigners. The Common Agricultural Policy has been a prime case in point. The CAP was intended to stabilize the agricultural market within the EC, especially between France and Germany, and to help harmonize national policies in what has always been a politically sensitive area.

The CAP has been operated aggressively, however, in relation to the world market. First introduced in 1966 for major commodities, the CAP was responsible for a nearly 50 percent reduction in American exports covered by the variable import levies. The purpose of the CAP has been to reduce imports, promote increased domestic production, and to dump exports abroad when excess production occurred. The success of the CAP in those terms is evidenced by the fact that the self-sufficiency rate with the original six EC members in agriculture rose from 91 percent in 1958-59 to 96 percent in 1968-69.[20]

The harmful effects of the CAP for the United States, Canada, Australia, and other agricultural exporting nations have been compounded by expansion of the EC in 1973 from six to nine members. Britain's traditional position as a net importer of foodstuffs benefits the EC producers at the expense of British consumers, who formerly enjoyed lower food prices under the program of deficiency payments to British farmers, and at the expense of foreign agricultural producers who had exported portions of their produce to England at prevailing world prices.

In respect of conflicts, such as the CAP, that exist between the United States and the EC, it is apparent that the United States has global security interests and global economic and political interests—all of which explain why this country has long advocated a global, nondiscriminatory trade system over one based on regional economic blocs. There are those in Europe, however, who argue that Europe's interests are indeed regional (that is, they lie to the south in Africa and to the eastern part of Europe) rather than global. The multilateral trade and payments system embraces rules and obligations amenable particularly to countries with global interests such as Japan and the United States, but perhaps less amenable to Europe, which might gain little from such a system. The answer to traditional American economic domination, it is asserted, is to make Europe into a more or less self-sufficient power bloc which discriminates against outsiders. Such an approach would foster growth of European corporations to the point where they could compete on an equal footing with giant US corporations.[21]

The mercantilistic, discriminatory attitudes of the European Community in the trade area constituted one important explanation of the great surge in US direct investment in Western Europe. The rationale was that by basing manufacturing operations within the EC tariff wall, greater sales could be achieved locally within the EC and to other countries participating in the network of EC tariff preferences.[22] The investment was concentrated in manufacturing and high-technology industries. US direct investment in Europe increased almost fourfold from $6.7 billion in 1960 to $24.5 billion in 1970.[23] Such investment, coupled with US direct investment in other countries (especially in Canada, where the same rationale of a relatively high tariff wall against foreign-made goods induced more US investment) generated rapidly increasing amounts of remittances and profits, which were repatriated to the United States and which offset the initial capital outflows.[24] Only a very small proportion of sales (less than 10 percent) by foreign affiliates of US firms came back to the United States as imports. Roughly 80 percent of sales were to local markets overseas and another 15 percent went to third countries.

Another factor prompting increased US fixed investment abroad during the 1960s, especially during the latter half of the decade, was the increasing overvaluation of the dollar vis-à-vis currencies of many other industrial nations. For the US investor, dollar overvaluation in effect provided a subsidy for foreign investment over domestic investment. In response to increasing capital outflows for foreign investment, the US government introduced its Foreign Direct Investment Program in 1965. It was designed to limit access to US capital markets for US firms with foreign operations; it was operated on a voluntary basis at first and, later, beginning in January 1968, on a mandatory basis. These and other controls on US capital flows imposed during the 1960s were costly to operate and proved to be largely unsuccessful when measured for their effect on over-all US balance of payments.[25] Although these results of US capital controls were anticipated by many at the time of their introduction, it seemed appropriate then from an international political standpoint to do something to indicate that the United States took its balance of payments problems seriously and was actively attempting to alleviate them. Then, too, from a domestic political standpoint, organized labor was showing its anxiety in regard to increasing US investment abroad; the assertion was made repeatedly that this was costing a loss of jobs at home.

While the United States was making such efforts to stem the leaks in its balance of payments, there was growing resistance in Europe to encroachment of US firms.[26] The strength of US business in Europe, particularly in what were regarded to be key industries of the future, was seen as a threat to European sovereignty, although there was still great receptivity to individual instances of new American investments in Europe. (Resistance to US investment in Canada did not surface until the early 1970s, while in Latin America there was only the occasional episode of discontent during the 1960s.)[27]

While the United States and Europe were experiencing growing trade problems with one another, difficulties between the United States and Japan were also on the rise. Specifically, Japan was slow to liberalize a wide array of import quotas, some which were remnants from as far back as the postwar reconstruction days of the late 1940s and early 1950s, when Japan was beset with balance of payments problems. By the latter 1960s, Japan's exceptionally high growth rate, continued increase in labor productivity, and very stable export prices brought steady improvement to her trade balance.

Roughly one-third of Japan's trade was with the United States, and the increasing flow of products into US markets began to present major challenges to producers of such products as steel, textiles, electronics, and automobiles. Pressures became so intense that Japan imposed "voluntary" controls on its steel exports to the United States in January 1969.

By the end of the 1960s and particularly after the Nixon administration took office in early 1969, tensions centering on trade issues between the United States and Japan mounted precipitously. Textiles was the hottest problem of all. On top of the already existing Long-term Agreement on cotton textiles limiting growth in trade,[28] the United States was pressing Japan, and also Taiwan, Korea and Hong Kong, for a "voluntary" agreement to limit exports of man-made fiber textiles and wool textiles to the United States. Japan resisted the US pressure, arguing that the matter should be taken up within the multilateral framework of the GATT. From the US vantage point, Japan and Europe too, as discussed already, were themselves flaunting the GATT rules with their own particular practices to limit US exports. In short, there was frustration and bitterness on all sides; the designated forums for arbitrating disputes simply were not functioning, and the shifts in the balance of economic strength which had been going on for some time—from the US to Western Europe and to Japan—meant that there was a new resistance and an unwillingness to knuckle under to US pressures.

Textiles proved to be one of the most vocal and hotly argued issues between the United States and Japan at the turn of the decade;[29] however, there were other issues of greater economic consequence for both sides. In a variety of products that Japan was exporting with great success, the secretary of the treasury ordered dumping investigations, under the Antidumping Act of 1921, against Japanese producers in order to investigate challenges that they were selling their goods to US importers at less than fair value (which was taken to mean at prices less than those charged to their own domestic wholesalers). In several cases, the dumping investigations were upheld, and the cases were forwarded to the US Tariff Commission to determine whether industries in the United States were being or were likely to be injured. When the Tariff Commission's findings were affirmative, the secretary of the treasury imposed special dumping duties on all imports of the products in question. All of these cases, including many for which no affirmative finding of dumping resulted, had to do with what US producers regarded as unfair trade practices by their Japanese counterparts.

In agriculture, an area of considerable comparative advantage to US producers, Japan persisted in enforcing extensive import quotas in order to protect its domestic producers. Such controls were of great importance for Japanese consumers in that they were forced to pay prices for food well above world prices. Of course, there were adverse consequences for US agricultural producers and for exporters of foodstuffs in other nations as well, particularly Southeast Asian countries, many of which were encountering increasing balance of payments problems as a result of the rising tide of Japanese finished products flowing into their markets. Had Japan taken a softer position in protecting its high-cost domestic agricultural sector, the balance of payments imbalance recorded during 1970-72 might have been significantly reduced.

Japan's investment policies were another source of frustration for Americans. Unlike European countries, where US entrepreneurs were able to leap over protective tariff walls and then produce and market their products within the Common Market, Japan continued to enforce strict controls on inward foreign direct investment. It was rare indeed when Americans or other nationals were allowed to gain a significant toehold inside Japan to produce for its rapidly growing market of over 100 million people, or to produce in Japan for export to other countries in the Pacific region.

The United States' single most important trade partner, Canada, is also its closest neighbor. During the early and mid-1960s, important agreements were entered into by the two countries. A Defense Production Sharing Arrangement was concluded in 1963 in order to promote defense industries in both countries and to carve out an enlarged preferential market. And in 1965, a special agreement on automobile production was established with the intention of creating a free trade area between the two countries. It is of considerable significance that the United States entered into these agreements at the time, given its long and traditional preference in favor of multilateral, nondiscriminatory trading arrangements. Perhaps the mood of creating a more efficient economic region between the United States and Canada, then being popularized in some quarters, and possibly a desire to indicate to European countries, then establishing their own regional blocs, that the United States had lucrative options of its own, lay at the bottom of US motives.

In any case, these two agreements did not lead to the kind of favorable economic conditions and opportunities that the United States had initially expected. Contrary to the spirit and the letter of the two agreements, there occurred over time a substantial, cumulative deterioration from the US standpoint in the bilateral balance of trade concerning the goods covered by the defense and auto parts. That is to say, the balance of trade in automobiles and parts and in defense goods swung substantially in favor of Canada. These developments occurred in part because of Canada's success in luring American business concerns to Canada to establish subsidiary plants, and in part because the agreements were never implemented fully to the point where free market forces could determine trade and investment flows. Ill-feeling and concern arose within the US government and within Congress, not only for the way things were going under the auto and defense agreements but for a number of other reasons related to both trade and investment.

Indeed, the number of irritations in the trade and investment areas between the two countries seemed to mount in the mid and latter 1960s as Canada's determination to create its own independent industrial economy began to take hold. With the regional approach to the economic development of North America becoming increasingly unpopular in Canada, policies were designed to promote national self-sufficiency and an industrial sector that would stand up to the international competition.[30] From the US point of view, Canada seemed to be going about its tasks in ways often injurious to US trade and domestic employment interests; Canada's continuing failure to live up to the terms of the auto and defense production agreements continued to be the major cases in point.[31]

All of these growing frictions in international trade relations among developed countries were bound up in the shifts in relative economic power that had been occurring for some time. The relative economic power of the United States had been declining, while economic strength in Europe and in Japan had been rising. The United States no longer possessed sufficient power to restore order and balance to the world economic system by itself; and neither Europe nor Japan displayed willingness to assume the burdens of leadership.

US balance of payments problems and strains on the dollar as the world's most important currency were becoming increasingly troublesome and indeed gave rise to more frequent and more severe financial crises during the latter 1960s and the start of the 1970s. US defense expenditures abroad, not only in Vietnam but elsewhere, including Europe and Japan, were becoming too great a burden in light of the over-all international economic position of the United States.

In August 1971, aware of the magnitude of monetary problems prevailing in the world and convinced that major reforms as well as a general realignment of currencies were necessary, President Nixon launched a dramatic program of New Economic Policies.[32] Those policies were aimed at improving some of the immediate problems in US trade[33] and balance of payments, but they were also intended to set the stage for negotiations dealing with long-term reform of the international economic system in all its aspects—trade, monetary and investment.

It was recognized that important international institutions, such as the International Monetary Fund and the General Agreement on Tariffs and Trade, had worked well up to a point and contributed directly to economic growth and well-being of the postwar international environment. On the other hand, important structural changes had occurred in the system and in the economic characteristics of countries comprising the system. Clearly, the time had come to make basic changes in the rules and operations of those institutions if they were to remain viable and to continue to make a positive contribution to the world economic order in the future.

# 4

## Less Developed Countries and the Current Issues

Less developed countries have multiple interests in the forthcoming multilateral trade negotiations. Indeed, the diversity of their interests reflects two factors in particular. First of all, LDCs are by no means a homogeneous group. There exist vast differences in the levels of economic development and industrialization among them, and accordingly there are equally great differences in the product composition of their trade. Thus, the least developed countries, compared to those LDCs that are more developed, have very limited capacity to produce and export even low-technology manufactured goods; indeed, they rely to a very great extent on the production and export of usually a small number of raw materials, primary products, or foodstuffs. Trade interests of some LDCs are limited pretty much to commodities, therefore, while interests of other countries reflect increasing concern over their trade opportunities in semimanufactured and manufactured products.

The second factor relevant to the LDC interest in multilateral trade negotiations is that the representation and effectiveness of less developed countries in various international forums have been rising in recent years. Large amounts of time and energy have gone toward enhancing the understanding and improving the public presentation of particular problems and concerns of less developed countries. All of this means that LDCs will be better prepared, better informed, and more ready to advance their interests at the forthcoming multilateral trade negotiations than ever before.

The major issue as far as less developed countries are concerned is likely to be generalized tariff preferences. The objective is to obtain preferential access to markets of the large industrialized countries for an increasingly wide range of products produced in and exported by LDCs. Over time, as discussed earlier in Chapter 3, the aspirations for improved trade positions, for export growth, and for general economic development have come to rest on the placement of an increasing share of LDC products in what have proved to be hard-to-enter, but potentially lucrative markets of developed market-economy countries. The various impediments encountered over the years in elevating LDCs' share of world trade and growth of exports have provided the basis for their seeking preferential treatment vis-à-vis other trading nations. Such an approach is directly at odds with the reciprocal trade, most-favored-nation approach that has characterized trade policies of the United States and other nations and multilateral trade negotiations for decades.

Another set of issues has to do with nontariff barriers, which embrace a great number of obstacles to increased LDC trade. A substantial amount of time and research has been spent recently in identifying and evaluating the importance and significance of various nontariff barriers for less developed countries.

A third area of interest has to do with international commodity trade. While world prices and quantities traded either have been recently or are presently at record high levels for many items, there is much uncertainty with respect to future trends. International commodity agreements (involving cocoa, coffee, sugar, tin and wheat) have been tried in the past, but generally with little success. But in view of present concerns in many industrial countries about future access to foreign supply, it may be that commodity agreements could provide a measure of stability and assurances about the future that LDCs—and quite possibly a number of industrial countries—might find attractive.

These three issues—generalized tariff preferences, nontariff barriers, and international commodity trade—will be discussed at some length in this chapter. Of course, there are many other issues of concern to LDCs, some of which will be dealt with more briefly. One issue of particular importance is the issue of multilateral safeguards. In the past, safeguards have been resorted to in varying forms and in emergency situations where rapidly rising imports imperiled particular domestic industries. While LDCs seek rapid change in the volume and composition of their exports to developed countries, the well-being of producers in industries affected by increasing competitiveness of LDCs will have to be considered, and changes in industrial structure will have to be achieved over time by means of orderly adjustment. Thus, from the LDC standpoint, international safeguard arrangements constitute an issue of major significance which bears directly upon the future realization of their most fundamental objectives.

**Less Developed Countries and the**
**Multilateral Trade Negotiations**

During plenary meetings held in conjunction with UNCTAD III in May 1972, discussions took place regarding multilateral trade negotiations. As a result of those discussions and ensuing consultations, all of which dealt directly with the role LDCs would play in such trade negotiations, a statement by developed countries and a resolution by less developed countries were adopted as part of the official record.

The representatives of France introduced a statement by developed countries (known as Group B countries in the UNCTAD context) on the participation of developing countries in the multilateral trade negotiations then scheduled to begin in 1973 under the auspices of GATT.[1] The statement indicated Group B countries' recognition of the need to ensure effective participation by LDCs in the trade negotiations. In addition, Group B countries promised to request that the contracting parties to GATT make adequate arrangements, in practical terms, for the full and active participation of all developing countries in the negotiations; and it was anticipated that continuation of cooperative arrangements between the secretariats of UNCTAD and GATT would continue. In the ensuing discussions, many representatives of developed countries expressed their hope of full participation by LDCs in the 1973 negotiations; but in almost every instance the nature of the negotiations then foreseen and the role to be assumed by LDCs were very much in line with what had occurred previously. Only one developed country representative referred to nonreciprocity, saying that while LDCs should not be expected to grant reciprocal trade concessions to developed countries, efforts to liberalize their trade could prove advantageous for themselves.

The adopted resolution referred to above was introduced by the representative of Ethiopia on behalf of the Group of 77, which consists of ninety-six LDCs from Latin America, Asia, the Middle East and Africa; Cyprus and Yugoslavia are also members of the group.[2] LDC members of the Group of 77 expressed their firm interest in participating in the upcoming trade negotiations "if the ground rules, techniques and modalities foreseen for the negotiations take adequately into account their interests and aspirations." Concerning the formulation of those modalities, techniques, and ground rules, the resolution requested specifically that certain principles be fully taken into account: LDCs should not suffer collectively or individually any adverse or prejudicial effects as a result of multilateral trade negotiations; indeed, LDCs should receive additional benefits that would represent substantial improvement of their position in international trade in order that they might secure an increasing share in the growth of future trade "commensurate with the needs of their economic development on the basis of non-reciprocity, non-discrimination and preferential treatment."

The key words in the resolution—non-reciprocity, non-discrimination, preferential treatment—set the tone for what LDCs hoped to achieve in the forthcoming multilateral trade negotiations. In their view, specifically stated in the resolution on behalf of the Group of 77, what they were seeking was at odds with past traditions and practices of the most-favored-nation reciprocal approach to trade.

In Tokyo on September 14, 1973, a meeting at the ministerial level was convened to declare the new multilateral trade negotiations officially open. In furtherance of the views noted above, both by developed and less developed countries, the text of the Tokyo Declaration was replete with references to less developed countries and the need to secure additional trade benefits for them.[3] Thus, all indications continue to point toward a more active role for LDCs in the current multilateral negotiations than has ever occurred previously. A more active role, so their representatives hope, will increase the likelihood that the present round of negotiations will result in significant trade benefits coming their way. Until such positive achievements have been secured in writing, however, LDCs will no doubt remain suspicious of developed countries' motives in the current trade negotiations—and not entirely without good reason, in view of the results of previous trade negotiations.

**Generalized Tariff Preferences:**
**A Recapitulation**

The concept of tariff preferences is not new. As discussed in Chapter 3, the LDCs first began to press developed countries for generalized tariff preferences at UNCTAD I in 1964. The United States initially opposed the idea, because by their very nature preferences ran contrary to the principle of most-favored-nation treatment, one of the cornerstones of US trade policy for thirty years. In 1967, US opposition to generalized trade preferences ended, primarily because a growing need was perceived to counter the proliferation of reverse preferential trade arrangements between the European Common Market and a number of developing countries in Africa and the Mediterranean area, and existing discriminatory preferential trade arrangements between Britain and its former colonies. The US aim, as announced by President Johnson at Punta del Este in 1967, was to bring to an end existing discriminatory and reverse preferential schemes, which were deemed to be of limited benefit to participating LDCs and which also served to discriminate against other developed countries, and to form instead a global preferential tariff arrangement that would afford more favorable conditions for all LDCs to export more of their goods to a much larger number of developed country markets.

During the year 1967-70, negotiations were conducted within the OECD and the UN General Assembly on particular aspects of a generalized scheme of preferences.[4] But since no single scheme could be agreed upon by the participating conferees,[5] the major trading nations decided that implementation should proceed on the basis of similar schemes which would be roughly comparable in terms of benefits accorded to LDCs. Accordingly, in October 1970, members of UNCTAD and the UN General Assembly approved the various generalized preference proposals as the basis for a "mutually acceptable" system of generalized tariff preferences. Legislative actions were necessary for a number of prospective donors, including the United States;[6] in addition, a waiver for the preference-giving countries from existing GATT obligations was sought and obtained in June 1971.

During the latter half of 1971, the European Common Market, Japan, and Norway implemented their generalized tariff preference systems, and on January 1, 1972, the United Kingdom, Ireland, Sweden, Denmark, Finland, and New Zealand followed suit. Switzerland and Austria joined ranks on March 1 and April 1, respectively. Australia continued to operate a limited system of tariff preferences as it had done since 1965. Canada, the most recent participant in generalized tariff preferences, activated its scheme in July 1974.[7]

Thus, until the Trade Act of 1974 was finally approved and signed by the president, the United States was the only remaining large industrial country that was without its own generalized tariff preference scheme. Efforts by the Nixon administration to get congressional approval for its proposed GSP were unsuccessful in 1971 and 1972 owing to strong and growing protectionist forces, which were aided and abetted by US balance of trade and payments problems, then at a peak.[8]

## Evaluation of Tariff Preference Schemes and the Scope for Enlargement

The rationale for providing tariff preferences to developing countries gives due recognition to the fact that trade is an essential part of the engine of economic growth. While LDCs must make concerted efforts domestically to bring about development, international trade offers a key link with foreign technology and economic efficiency. Proceeds from exports provide a large proportion of the financing to purchase imports essential to development efforts and to fund debt repayments. Yet, as has been discussed in earlier chapters, recent history has shown LDCs abilities to increase total exports while competing on an equal footing (i.e., on a most-favored-nation basis) with industrial countries have been poor. Therefore, by offering *preferential tariffs* to LDCs, and thus giving them advantageous access to developed countries markets, it is presumed that LDCs would be in a better position to earn more foreign exchange as a result of increased exports. It is also believed that since preferential tariff treatment provides relatively advantageous entry into developed countries' markets, it consequently creates an inducement to new investment and production of eligible products in LDCs. Indeed, advocates regard this to be the greatest strength and most potentially rewarding feature of tariff preferences.

To date, however, the tariff preference schemes implemented have offered little discernible benefit to developing countries. In the first place, of the trade flowing from LDCs to developed countries, about 39 percent is subject to tariff treatment. This is because developing countries' exports tend to be heavily concentrated in primary products and industrial raw materials, many of which are imported by industrial countries on a duty-free basis. Second, processed agricultural and fishery products, in which LDCs have been becoming increasingly competitive in recent years, are excluded for the most part from generalized tariff preference arrangements. Such products constitute about 15 percent of preference-giving countries imports from LDCs. Third, some less developed countries have demonstrated their ability to produce certain manufactured and semimanufactured products; yet the most successful producers are often the very ones excepted from general preference schemes of donor countries because of political pressure from domestic industries. The most well known of these products include textiles, leather goods, and petroleum products, all of which account for another 13 percent or so of LDC exports to donor countries. Fourth, conservative, protective mechanisms built in to existing tariff preference schemes limit the extent to which LDCs producing or capable of producing products included in those schemes can singly or collectively expand exports in any given period of time.

Thus, the conscious exclusions from generalized tariff schemes and the given configuration of production and export within LDCs combine to reduce the scope to only some 9 percent of total trade moving from beneficiaries to donors, or about one-fourth of dutiable trade.[9] Since the US scheme has not yet been implemented, the 9 percent figure is reduced to 4 percent of an annual trade flow of $234 billion in 1968.

Some quantitative estimates of benefits deriving from GSP have appeared in the literature. One writer estimates that the United States, EC, Japan and British schemes would create an expanded value of imports of $300-400 million per year, assuming a 50 percent tariff preference.[10] Another writer concludes that 100 percent preferences would result in an annual net revenue transfer of $400-500 million.[11] A third writer argues that institutional constraints reduce actual benefits to about $100 million per year.[12]

The problem with such evaluations is that they do not consider the possible dynamic effects of trade preferences. Most estimates of benefits resulting from preferences are based on static or comparative static economic analysis and look at the existing configuration of productive capacity in LDCs for those manufactured products included in GSP schemes. But advocates of tariff preferences have conceded all along that only marginal benefits would result from expansion of trade based on existing production. The real strength of preferences, however, is believed to be the incentives created for new investment. Preferential access to developed country markets will induce entrepreneurs, both domestic and foreign, to make particular investments and to establish new production facilities in those beneficiary countries. Thus, tariff preferences will provide the incentive for new production and exporting capabilities which in time will allow LDCs to realize much more substantial gains from trade with developed countries than would have been presumed on the basis of the initial manufacturing or industrial capacity. Tariff preferences can, potentially at least, provide the needed spark for an industrialization program in LDCs that is oriented to those products granted preferential tariff treatment in developed country markets which LDCs have a reasonable chance of producing on a competitive basis.[13]

Thus, if tariff preference schemes were guaranteed for an extended period of several years, rather than being subject to, say, annual review, and if the existing safeguard provisions (discussed below) were removed entirely or eased very substantially, then by the end of the 1970s, the value of LDC exports arising because of direct or indirect incentives created by tariff preferences would in all likelihood be several billions of dollars, rather than the 1980 price equivalent of $.5 billion 1968 exports.

That such a small portion of dutiable exports of beneficiaries to donor countries is covered by present preference schemes implies that a more forthcoming attitude by the donor countries could greatly broaden and increase benefits of GSP in the immediate period ahead. Existing preference schemes could be made more liberal and more inclusive of manufactured and semimanufactured products, toward which they are primarily addressed; and they could be extended much more to include agricultural products. Developing countries themselves—i.e., the beneficiaries—can also help their own cause by resorting to various policy measures in order to encourage particular kinds of new investment, which ultimately will help alter the composition of exports toward those dutiable manufactured products not excluded from GSP. But the greatest potential impetus for increasing the present level of benefits of GSP lies clearly with the preference-giving countries.

In conjunction with generalized preferential tariff schemes, donor countries instituted special safeguard arrangements in order to protect their own markets from undue disruptions. In some cases an escape-clause provision similar to that provided for already in the GATT was used. Japan and the EC, however, have resorted to a system of tariff quotas such that imports in excess of a stipulated ceiling for any given product are charged normal duties as provided under MFN agreements rather than the preferential duties accorded under GSP. Although a growth factor is included in the ceiling calculations, what has happened is that the existing generalized preference schemes have provided very little incentive to beneficiary countries to expand exports, since actual growth in exports usually exceeds annual elevation in the ceilings.[14] Not only do ceiling limitations apply to imports of a particular product from all beneficiaries combined, but they also provide for maximum imports from individual beneficiaries of 50 percent or less of the ceiling for that product. The purpose of this second ceiling provision is to ensure that GSP benefits are shared at least to some extent among recipient countries.

What is required is a modification of the Japanese and EC GSP safeguard systems so that preferential treatment is accorded to substantially expanded levels of developing-country trade. The tariff-quota safeguard presently used results in GSP being much more a form of aid rather than an incentive to increase trade.[15] This follows since ceilings are generally not set high enough to cover the level of LDC exports that would arise in the absence of the special incentives provided by preferential tariffs.

Generalized tariff preference schemes include certain rules of origin in order to guarantee that goods imported under GSP "have been 'substantially transformed' in the beneficiary country, 'directly consigned' to the preference-giving country, and documented by a validated 'certificate of origin.' "[16] Although the clear purpose of such rules is to prevent undesignated countries from benefiting from GSP, numerous problems have been caused by the application of such rules. Transformation requirements vary from one GSP scheme to the next. In some cases, they are very strict and call for complicated classification procedures. The direct consignment requirement has been found in practice to limit trade, owing to prevailing marketing and distribution techniques. Greater flexibility in the requirement might entail simply that no further processing take place after the goods in question leave the beneficiary country.

The certificate of origin, also designed to ensure that goods presented for customs clearance under GSP are entitled to such treatment, is prepared by the exporter and must be certified by an authority predesignated by the beneficiary government. A problem encountered early under this requirement was that beneficiary countries were failing to communicate to preference-giving countries the complete list of those bodies authorized to issue stamps or certificates. That difficulty has been solved, and it is apparent that a certificate of origin requirement is entirely in order so as to assure proper application of GSP. If rules of origin could be standardized for all existing tariff preference schemes, however, many of the administrative difficulties of simply meeting requirements would be overcome.

Two momentous decisions taken recently by European nations are very likely to have a negative effect on benefits accorded under generalized tariff preferences. Recognition of these effects might be used to evoke offsetting concessions in the upcoming multilateral trade negotiations. In the first place, enlargement of the EC on January 1, 1973 from six to nine countries has resulted in the operation of a new GSP for the EC-9 since January 1, 1974. The separate and more liberal schemes of Britain, Denmark, and Ireland were replaced by one closely resembling the earlier, more conservative EC scheme.

The second problem for GSP flows from the fact that EC enlargement entails free-trade agreements covering manufactured products and processed agricultural and fishery products, with former members of the European Free Trade Area who did not join the EC in 1973. The free-trade agreements will become fully effective on July 1, 1977. This will put all producers in Western Europe in an advantageous position over all outsiders in marketing their goods within the area. In practice, they will even possess advantages over GSP beneficiaries because of the limiting nature of those schemes: tariff quota or escape-clause safeguards, ceilings, exceptions lists, maximum country amounts, and the like. Indeed, GSP beneficiaries will have a preferred position over only non-European developed countries, such as the United States, Japan, Canada, Australia, and some Socialist countries. This situation compares unfavorably for GSP beneficiaries to the situation prior to EC enlargement, when a preferred position was enjoyed over several European countries as well as other nonbeneficiaries just mentioned.

The existing GSP arrangements offer comparatively fewer benefits to the group of least developed countries[17] than to developing countries as a group. A study performed by the UNCTAD secretariat indicates that only 20 percent of dutiable imports of donor countries from the least developed countries are covered by GSP. (This compares with 39 percent of dutiable donor imports from all LDCs eligible for GSP.)[18] This is hardly surprising, since the least developed countries have the smallest capability for producing and exporting manufactured and semimanufactured goods, toward which existing GSP schemes are generally oriented. (Indeed, exports of the least developed countries are largely composed of agricultural products.) Their circumstances are such, moreover, that it will be relatively more difficult for them to attract foreign investment to help them change their composition of exports in order to take advantage of GSP schemes.

Several of the least developed countries do receive some special assistance as a result of preferential access to EC markets under reverse preferences and other discriminatory trade preference agreements, including the old British Imperial Preferences. Approximately three-fourths of the least developed countries' dutiable trade is with member countries of the enlarged EC. Within the context of GSP, however, least developed countries' trade would benefit substantially if the EC were to include coffee and aluminum oxide on its list of eligible products, and if preferential tariff rates for agricultural and fishery products were substantially reduced.[19]

There is no denying, however, that the least developed countries need both trade and aid. Thus, even if the EC and other donor countries expanded their GSP schemes along the lines suggested, technical assistance and project aid would be indispensable to realizing the opportunities offered to least developed countries in the trade area.

Most important from the LDCs viewpoint and the future of generalized tariff preferences is that the United States promptly adopt its scheme. The United States is the last of eighteen donors (nineteen including Australia) to implement its program now that Canada activated its proposed scheme in July 1974. The addition of the US preference arrangements will increase from about 4-5 percent to roughly 9 percent the amount of donor country imports from beneficiaries covered by the GSP.

Early implementation of the US GSP is vital from another standpoint as well. Britain, the EC, Japan, and other countries implemented their generalized tariff plans in 1971-72, while the United States was unable to do so because of domestic economic, political, and balance of payments problems. While those countries implementing tariff preferences gained a political advantage over the United States, they also had a ready political excuse for not doing more. The political excuse was that all developed countries had to bear a fair share of the burden in making GSP available to LDCs, lest issues of equity and trade diversion be called into question. Since the United States had failed to implement its pledge on GSP, it was inappropriate for other countries to broaden and improve their already enacted schemes.

The economics of this line of reasoning do not hold much water; indeed, preferential tariffs mean that eligible imports enter at lower cost, which at least in theory implies that consumers have to pay less. To the extent a burden exists, it falls upon exporters in nonpreferred countries, since it is their trade which is displaced by exports from beneficiary countries. Domestic producers in donor countries are not adversely affected by GSP unless the level of imports rises significantly and demand is satisfied at the expense of domestic production. It is that problem for which safeguard measures are designed. Nevertheless, it must be recognized that the politics of GSP are real and that, accordingly, early implementation of the US preference scheme is prerequisite to very substantial improvements in GSP schemes already in operation. While the EC announced early in 1974 some modifications in its arrangement, as proposed, these changes do not represent any dramatic liberalization in policy.

Achieving early implementation of the US preference scheme, while it will be a significant step forward, represents only another wedge concerning what conceivably could emerge from the concept of GSP. What the LDCs have in mind was spelled out in greater detail at UNCTAD III.

On May 19, 1972, at the 118th plenary meeting, UNCTAD III adopted a resolution without dissent on trade preferences. In that resolution the conference urged prospective-giving market economy countries that had not implemented their proposed generalized tariff preference schemes (most importantly the United States) to do so as soon as possible, and exhorted Socialist countries of Eastern Europe that had not specified their preferential tariff schemes to do so at an early date. It was decided, moreover, to establish a Special Committee on Preferences as a permanent part of the machinery within UNCTAD. The purpose of the special committee is to conduct consultations with various governments for the purpose of improving and otherwise implementing preferential schemes.

In the same resolution, the developing countries sought to include all processed and semiprocessed agricultural and primary products of Chapters 1 through 24 of the Brussels Tariff Nomenclature in donor countries' schemes of generalized preferences. All products in Chapters 25 through 99 of the BTN excluded from existing arrangements, it was hoped, would be included in their schemes. In order to further broaden the preference schemes, it was suggested that duty-free and quota-free entry be provided to imports from all developing countries by preference-giving countries. Simplified formulation and application of rules of origin under generalized preferences were recommended in order to achieve maximum harmonization of the various schemes. Preference-giving countries were requested not to resort to escape-clause or safeguard actions except in extraordinary circumstances, which should be subject to prior international consultation and approval. As a final request, donor countries were asked to eliminate, on a preferential and nonreciprocal basis in favor of all LDCs, all nontariff barriers on products covered by the generalized system of preferences.

In the context of what has been realized, these proposals would entail a major departure from past traditions in commercial policy: reciprocity and the MFN principle of nondiscrimination. Although a start has clearly been achieved by the several GSP arrangements already in effect, it may be sometime before GSP can begin to approach what has just been outlined above. And by that time the relevance of generalized preferences may well have been overtaken by other events. Certainly the developed countries are not going to suspend efforts to reduce trade barriers on an MFN basis simply to assure GSP greater longevity. GSP must be regarded as a medium-term device to give LDCs improved access to developed countries markets while significant tariff barriers to entry persist. But in the course of the present and succeeding trade negotiations, further reduction in such barriers are expected; hence, the relevance and significance will diminish accordingly. Over the long term, trade policies discriminating in favor of LDCs will have to look beyond modifications of the present GSP schemes. Nevertheless, in the current multilateral trade negotiations, some further significant progress in modifications may be hoped for.

In terms of evaluating the results of GSP, it will be several years before the dynamic effects, as well as the more immediate effects, will have had a chance to run their course. Unless the tight safeguard mechanisms incorporated into the existing GSP arrangements are very substantially relaxed, however, the dynamic benefits resulting from induced investment and industrialization within LDCs will be neutralized in large measure.

## Nontariff Barriers

Nontariff barriers have constituted an area of continuing interest and concern for UNCTAD and its members for several years.[20] Indeed, numerous studies and intergovernmental consultations have been conducted with a view to the relaxation and progressive elimination of such nontariff barriers affecting trade in manufactures and semimanufactures that are of interest to developing countries. In the context of the forthcoming multilateral trade negotiations, progress in removing or in alleviating the impacts of NTBs is certain to be a major objective of the developing countries.

In broadest terms, nontariff barriers (NTBs) refer to governmental policies and practices that operate in such a way as to distort the volume, direction or product-composition of international trade.[21] While nontariff barriers most frequently affect imports, some affect exports. Some NTBs are used as instruments of commercial policy and may take the form of quota licensing, variable levies, or subsidies to import competing groups, for example. There are other NTBs used from time to time in order to restrict trade. This category would include a wide variety of requirements pertaining to packaging, marking, classification, and customs valuation regulations. Third, there are NTBs whose trade effects are a by-product of policy objectives not directly related to trade. Included in this category are various taxes on consumption and government monopolies.

In relation to all three types of NTBs, some may affect specific products, in which case their reduction would be most susceptible to the kind of bargaining solutions used in the past to reduce tariffs under the Reciprocal Trade Agreements Program. Other NTBs affecting broad categories of products lend themselves to international standardization as a liberalization method. Measures in the third category cited above are most difficult to alleviate, because their enforcement has to do with non-trade-related goals.[22]

The type of nontariff barriers encountered most frequently is discretionary licensing (applied alone or in conjunction with other restrictions). Global or bilateral import quotas are found next in order of frequency and are used about evenly between items in agricultural product categories (BTN, Chapters 1-24) and those in manufactured product categories (BTN, Chapters 25-99). Variable import levies are applied mainly to imports of processed agricultural products by EC countries, Austria, Sweden, Switzerland, and Finland. In the past, import restraints have been applied mainly in connection with textile products other than cotton by the EC countries and Canada; more recently, their use has spread to other countries and to a number of products such as leather and leather goods, ceramic products, and woolen goods.

Up to the present, efforts to relax and progressively eliminate nontariff barriers have given rise to much consideration and discussion at the international level. Discussions within UNCTAD over the years have led to some of the most forceful and specific recommendations as far as the interests of less developed countries were concerned.[23] Other international bodies as well, however, were addressing the question of nontariff barriers. For instance, reports and discussions were taking place periodically within the General Agreement on Tariffs and Trade on particular aspects of the more general question of how to deal effectively with existing nontariff barriers. In 1971, the GATT Committee on Trade and Development decided to establish a "Group of Three" to present proposals for action that might be taken to deal with trade problems of developing countries. None of these discussions, recommendations, or other efforts in UNCTAD, in GATT, in the OECD or elsewhere, however, have proved especially fruitful or have led to any significant international progress in alleviating the preponderance of NTBs generally or of those in particular applied by developed market-economy countries on imports from LDCs.

At the national level and within particular economic blocs, some progress was made in liberalizing or removing nontariff barriers of export interest to less developed countries. In Japan, in New Zealand, and in various member countries of the EC and EFTA, some restrictions were eased, although other policy actions tended in the opposite direction.[24] All in all, progress at the multilateral and national levels has been limited indeed, and the need for establishing a consistent program for the liberalization of NTBs has become the more important.

The impacts of nontariff barriers, on relative prices and costs and on the value and pattern of trade, have been found to vary widely; accordingly, evaluation of such trade distorting impacts has proved difficult. In some instances, the effects are similar to effects caused by tariffs, while in other cases, the effects are more analogous to those generated by quotas.

Nontariff barriers administered in industrial countries tend to be complex; some are based on existing legislation, others on policies of executive agencies. All in all, there tends to be little if any central coordination or systematic regulation. Partly for these reasons, but for others as well, it has been maintained that NTBs imposed by industrial countries create a greater burden on LDCs than on other developed countries.[25] The essential points in the arguments are stated and analyzed in a paper by Ingo Walter, presented to the 1970 Annual Meetings of the American Economic Association.[26]

The alleged de facto discrimination caused by developed countries' application of NTBs is attributed to two sources. First, the variety of NTBs is greater on imports from less developed countries than is the case on imports from competing developed countries. This follows for several reasons. First, industrial countries impose especially rigorous standards or procedures for importation of certain products from LDCs; the basis for this is usually health and quality control efforts, which are part of a broader effort to raise specific standards. Second, LDC exporters are less capable of dealing effectively with NTB measures than exporters of industrial countries, both in an operational sense and in the sense of influencing the outcome of decisions bearing on their interests. In addition, alternative production possibilities for LDC suppliers are less readily available as a means of bypassing NTBs. Then, too, LDC suppliers generally do not possess the in-depth knowledge of industrial countries' markets and the nature of existing NTBs relevant to them. This results allegedly in uncertainty, miscalculation of supply responses, and a dampened export performance. A final reason concerns the fact that, as in past trade negotiations that dealt primarily with tariff reductions, LDC interests have assumed a role of secondary importance in various intergovernmental attempts to reduce nontariff barriers. (Thus, it is claimed that GATT procedures place LDCs at a disadvantage, both because notification must be made by member countries in respect of measures affecting their exports, and also because many LDCs are not contracting members of GATT, or if they are, they often begin from weak bargaining positions.)

The second source of de facto discrimination is that identifiable nontariff barriers pertain more frequently to products or to product groups that are of particular interest to exporters in LDCs than to manufactured and semimanufactured products whose supply is largely within the domain of industrial country exporters. Moreover, the semimanufactured and manufactured products in which LDCs are establishing or are likely to establish a comparative advantage in international markets are often the very same products subject to nontariff barriers.

The first source of alleged discrimination (that LDCs are burdened to a disproportionate extent by the impact of NTBs because of more limited adjustment capability, more vulnerability to uncertainty, and more limited understanding of the nature and impact of NTBs) rests very heavily on qualitative and subjective evaluation.[27] On that account, it is unlikely that LDCs will be able to construct a case convincing enough to industrial countries that they should be granted *preferential* relief from specific NTBs.

Even so, results of a series of six product studies by Allen and Walter suggest there may well be disproportionate impacts on LDC exporters compared to developed country competitors.[28] Their findings are positive for quantitative import restrictions, for relatively liberal or quasi-automatic licensing procedures, for public and quasi-public procurement, indirect tax and border adjustments—in short, for nontariff barriers falling in all three of the categories identified earlier. Indeed, Allen and Walter estimate that in the absence of NTBs bearing on the six product groups studied, the 1968 trade base of $486 million would have been increased by 54 to 68 percent. Although qualifying their results, they suggest that such figures should be interpreted as "an indication of the order of magnitude that may be involved in estimates of the restrictiveness of NTBs, particularly in such important and highly sensitive sectors as processed agricultural products."[29]

The task of establishing the coincidence of manufactured and semimanufactured product groups affected by NTBs and corresponding product groups of special interest to exporters in LDCs can be done with somewhat greater objectivity than can the first source of alleged discrimination just discussed. In 1968, developed market-economy countries imported some $128 billion of manufactured and semimanufactured products. Of that amount, 28 percent was subject to NTBs. One-sixth of that total import figure, or $21 billion, were products originating in less developed countries, and of that amount, 33 percent entered under NTBs.[30] If one accepts the earlier proposition that NTBs bear disproportionately on suppliers in LDCs as opposed to suppliers in developed countries, and therefore that the developing countries' share of industrial markets is biased downward, then the differential incidence of NTBs implied by the above figures for 1968 is also understated.[31]

Other evidence contained in a report by the UNCTAD secretariat was consistent with the findings of Allen and Walter, that nontariff barriers on semiprocessed agricultural products imported in 1968 by developed countries from LDCs were numerous.[32] Indeed, the report by the UNCTAD secretariat found that the incidence of NTBs was greater for products in those areas, that is, for products falling within BTN Chapters 1 through 24, than was the incidence of NTBs applied to manufactured and semimanufactured products falling within BTN Chapters 25 through 99. While processed agricultural products comprised one-third of the total number of products included in an UNCTAD inventory of products of particular interest to LDCs that are subject to restrictive measures, they accounted for nearly two-thirds of the total frequency of restrictions on all products in the inventory. Within the categories of manufactured and semimanufactured products, the greatest frequency of nontariff obstacles was found for such items as textile products not covered by the Long-Term Arrangement on trade of cotton textiles,[33] petroleum products,[34] ferro-alloys and ceramic products, jute products, leather and leather goods, and woolen goods.

The report by the UNCTAD secretariat referred to above found that in 1968 there was a good deal of variation between the developed market-economy countries concerning the number of nontariff obstacles applied to products of particular interest to less developed countries. France, West Germany, Italy, and Japan appeared to be applying the largest number of such restrictive measures, followed by Denmark, Finland, and the Benelux countries. Austria, Ireland, Norway, the United Kingdom, Sweden, the United States, and Switzerland were found to be maintaining relatively few restrictions, while Australia and Canada were maintaining the fewest of all.

Nontariff barriers applied to imports of developed market-economy countries affect a number of products covered by generalized tariff preference schemes. Where this occurs, the effectiveness of GSP tends to be undercut depending upon the restrictive degree of the nontariff barriers. About one-half of the forty processed agricultural products in the UNCTAD secretariat's inventory were included in one or more of the GSP schemes. Of the ninety manufactured and semimanufactured products within BTN chapters 25 through 99 that were included in the inventory of the UNCTAD secretariat, seventy-four were included in GSP schemes in operation or in the generalized preference schemes proposed but not then implemented by the United States and Canada. Another five out of the ninety products were already accorded MFN duty-free treatment but were nonetheless confronted with various nontariff obstacles.[35]

In the face of these nontariff impediments confronting less developed countries, and the lack of progress to date in reducing or removing them, the question arises, What is to be done in the context of the forthcoming trade negotiations? Nontariff barriers per se are sure to be a topic of major interest for industrial countries as well as for less developed countries.

One proposal has to do with a standstill on the imposition of new barriers and on the intensification of existing barriers. It was first put forth in the recommendation in annex A.III.4 to the Final Act of the first session of UNCTAD in 1964; it was subsequently reaffirmed in a decision of the Committee on Manufactures and in the United Nations' International Development Strategy for the Second Development Decade.[36] Adherence to a standstill would have to be carefully observed, and there would have to be instituted within UNCTAD, or perhaps more appropriately in the GATT, consultation procedures in order to establish criteria by which departures from the standstill might be permitted, and to ensure that such departures were justified and only of temporary duration.

Another proposal concerns the elimination of discriminatory aspects of existing nontariff barriers. Quantitative restrictions and licensing enforced by some developed countries still retain discriminatory features that result in imports of certain products from some LDCs being treated less favorably than similar imports from other developing countries and from some developed countries. As an individual step in the liberalization of quantitative restrictions, such discriminatory features of country import classifications might be eliminated. Sometimes it is suggested that only discriminatory aspects affecting LDCs be eliminated. But a most-favored-nation approach to this problem might generate greater support in the present context.

Since nontariff barriers have been shown to interfere with existing and proposed generalized tariff preference schemes, consideration should be given to the early elimination of obstacles confronting products covered by the GSP. LDCs should be able to make a substantial case along such lines, possibly with the objective of winning modifications in the language of generalized preferences so as to exclude the application of NTBs on those products in question. Even for products or product groups excluded from preferences on grounds of their "sensitive" nature, it may be argued that their exclusion and continued protection at MFN tariff levels undercuts the rationale for their also being protected by nontariff restrictions.

A variety of other proposals have been offered for reducing or eliminating various types of nontariff barriers.[37] In general, it seems that a multilateral approach, either on a product-by-product or product group basis, is more likely to lead to substantial liberalization. A key question arising in the multilateral bargaining approach, wherein developed and less developed countries would all participate together, is whether LDCs should band together and push for preferential or discriminatory liberalization of NTBs, just as they lobbied for tariff preferences as a unified body in 1968.

That approach may not be the most promising for LDCs to take. Although there is considerable evidence to suggest that developing countries suffer from the existing structure of NTBs to a greater extent that developed countries, the evidence is still preliminary, and it may very well be that the differential incidence of NTBs is largely unintentional on the part of developed countries. As Harold Malmgren has pointed out, a great many NTBs result from differing national standards, differing tax systems, labeling requirements, customs and administrative procedures, and therefore are closely related to domestic social objectives, laws and policies.[38] Thus, for the LDCs to argue long and hard in favor of preferential treatment could lead to an endless debate with charges of discriminatory trade barriers coming from all sides and with no substantive progress in achieving positive results. In the end, LDC interests might be served better if the evidence concerning the special NTB problems they are confronted with were used to bargain for broader, more liberal generalized tariff preference schemes. Then in multilateral negotiations to reduce NTBs, the less developed countries would give maximum cooperation feasible to developed countries and to their efforts to proceed on a nondiscriminatory basis, except where willingness to extend nonreciprocal concessions to LDCs was indicated.

At this juncture, a promising approach in the liberalization of NTBs is for all countries to work toward harmonizing national policies by first establishing improved international rules and consultative procedures. The objective should be to prevent the costs of domestic policies from being passed to foreign interests, or if such passing of costs take place, there should be some sort of compensation. Approaching the problem in such a manner should allow for establishment of a new multilateral framework for liberalizing nontariff barriers and for the development of guidelines to control or police potential emergency exceptions.

## International Commodity Agreements
## and Access to Foreign Supply

International commodity policies have been of long-standing interest to less developed countries. Not only has the production of raw materials and semiprocessed and processed commodities comprised the great bulk of economic activity in LDCs, but, also, such commodities have constituted the largest proportion of LDC exports. The dependence on commodity trade, both domestic and external, has been aggravated by a variety of short-term and long-term problems, all of which have prompted a search for international measures to bring greater price stability and more rapid growth of both production and trade in commodities. At UNCTAD II, an action program was elaborated covering some twenty individual commodities of export interest to developing countries, but with very little resulting success.[39]

At least for the time being, much of the interest in improving access for primary commodities produced in LDCs to the markets of industrialized countries, and in arresting the historically declining or stagnant price trends for many agricultural products, tropical foods and beverages, has been overtaken by recent international developments of rising international demand and short supply. The high level of international trade and production that persisted in nearly all major countries in the early 1970s until 1974 created a surge in demand for a number of important primary commodities, both agricultural and mineral, the likes of which have not been experienced before except during wartime. Shortages of supply became commonplace, and prices spiraled upward. For some less developed countries, the last two or three years have been a time of prosperity created by rapidly increasing foreign exchange earnings from exports of primary products. However, offsetting a substantial part of increased foreign exchange earnings from rising world demand for and increasing prices of LDCs exports was the fact that LDCs were having to pay much higher prices for their own imports of foodstuffs, capital equipment, and fuels.

During 1973, the Organization of Petroleum Exporting Countries (OPEC), acting more or less in concert, imposed a quadrupling of crude-oil prices on importing countries and for a time curtailed world exports by embargoing sales of crude oil to certain importing countries whose political policies were judged not to meet minimum standards laid down by Middle East oil-producing countries. This cartel-like action by a group of primary commodity producing countries was unique in its success, and its ramifications for the world economy have been pervasive.

Certainly the example of OPEC is something which other primary-commodity-producing countries would like to emulate as a means to dramatically improve their terms of trade and thereby to lift themselves out of the seeming morass of economic ills that have plagued them in the past. For the present, there exists a wide diversity of opinion as to how successful other OPEC-like cartels are likely to be, or, to put it another way, how much of a problem groups of primary-commodity-producing countries will be able to create for developed countries in their exercise of cartel arrangements with each other.[40]

The rising cost of oil and of many other primary products, indeed the increasing rate of worldwide inflation, cuts many ways. Some LDCs have expressed interest in indexing the prices charged for their exports on the basis of prices they are obliged to pay for capital goods and other products imported from abroad. Such countries are among the less fortunate LDCs in that their export products are not among those whose prices have been rising most rapidly; yet, the cost of their imports, including oil, have gone on rising, and they find themselves hard pressed indeed to find means to pay for those items.

But attempts to foist on other countries either the burdens of inflation via indexation or the more traditional burdens of less developed, primary-producing countries[41] via cartel arrangements are neither sensible nor likely to be durable. Higher oil prices will yield oil-producing countries large profits for a few years. But by adding significantly to world inflationary pressures, OPEC members are contributing directly to the higher costs of the very commodities they wish to import, all of which erodes in a real sense their apparent windfall profits. Moreover, in a few years time and with the continuation of oil prices anywhere near recent levels, alternative sources of oil supply and alternative sources of energy will become available commercially, both of which will work to subtract from the temporary advantage enjoyed by OPEC. Hence, the exercise of cartel activity as a means of altering the relative distribution of wealth in the world may have merit for short periods of time, but it is of dubious merit indeed in the long run.

So, too, are other related attempts to shift the burden of inflation to other countries by boosting the price of exports. The international trade community comprises a true network whereby inflationary and deflationary trends, expansionary and contractionary measures, are transmitted from country to country. The responsible approach to controlling that mechanism and its destabilizing tendencies is to attempt to reach a multilateral accord whereby countries will agree to certain rules pertaining both to the conduct of domestic economic policies and to the conduct of external commercial policies and balance of payments measures. The remedy for worldwide inflation is something each nation must swallow; and the tensions between the have and the have-not nations of the world must be resolved in a forum appropriately created for such a task. If expedient measures in a time of inflation or if the exercise of international cartels can propel the nations of the world toward more determined efforts to come to grips with long-standing problems, then they will have served a purpose; but they do not constitute a means to an end in themselves.

In this spirit, a number of experts maintain that a fresh look at the international commodity scene is particularly appropriate at the present juncture and quite possibly more promising than at any time in the recent past. On the one hand, primary producers in LDCs are enjoying high world demand and record prices for many of their commodities; yet, they are uncertain as to the long-term outlook, and many are aware that efforts on their part to form cartels and to increase their returns in the near term could backfire by causing reduced demand and the production of substitutes elsewhere. Accordingly, the attractions of industrialization and greater diversity of economic activity remain high. On the other hand, many developed countries are greatly concerned about the issues of access to foreign supplies, and some believe strongly that new trade rules must be drawn up during the current multilateral trade negotiations that would set down precise rules governing the use of export controls.

Out of these concerns could be born a comprehensive arrangement benefiting all sides. Renewed efforts to negotiate commodity agreements, buffer stock schemes, and the like could reduce uncertainty with respect to future trade volumes and price ranges of commodities involved. Those agreements could be buttressed by nonreciprocal reductions in tariff and nontariff barriers of special interest to LDC primary producers, or by government-to-government agreements pledging increased aid for ongoing industrialization efforts. In return, developed countries would receive assurances of access to commodity supplies in the future, along with support of LDCs for new rules to govern export controls and other amendments to the GATT that may be negotiated in the current round.[42]

In the long run, the issues of short supply, if left unresolved, could pose problems for all countries, not just industrial nations. Thus, the long-outstanding issues created by previously unsuccessful international commodity agreements might receive more satisfactory treatment if they are considered simultaneously with the problem of access to foreign supply.

## Other Issues of Concern to Less Developed Countries

Tropical products, and the need to treat them as a special priority sector in the multilateral trade negotiations, are twice mentioned in the text of the Tokyo

Declaration. This emphasis is a purely practical attempt at the outset of the negotiations to select and spotlight an area of unambiguous interest to LDCs in order to see precisely what sorts of trade concessions developed countries could offer that would significantly increase trade in such products. For developing countries whose major exports are tropical fruits and like products, these efforts could lead to a significant breakthrough. But for other LDCs in tropical zones whose exports may include other commodities or products, there may also be some side benefits in view of the fact tropical products, loosely defined, could embrace a large number of items.

Safeguard measures, which restrict the flow of imports when competing domestic interests are adversely affected, have been of concern to less developed countries for years. In various forums, LDC spokesmen have repeatedly gone on record as favoring arrangements within developed countries to assist the adaptation and adjustment of industries and workers threatened or adversely affected by increased imports from developing countries, especially imports of manufactures and semimanufactures.[43] (This means, of course, that LDCs would greatly prefer safeguard measures in the form of adjustment assistance rather than escape clauses, since the former would not have deleterious effects on the levels of imports.)

The rationale for adjustment assistance is that it facilitates realization of the benefits of trade liberalization from the expansion of exports in which LDCs possess a comparative advantage. Adjustment assistance, it may be argued, promotes more effective resource allocation in both developed and developing countries and accordingly leads to greater world productivity. Adjustment assistance implies that resources are reallocated out of declining industries threatened or injured by rising imports, and into industries characterized by rapid growth and increasing productivity. Many adjustment assistance programs as operated to date in major developed countries, however, tend to provide for the modernization and rehabilitation of productive factors which then continue in the same lines of production, as well as for their reallocation into entirely new pursuits.[44]

In the long run, there is probably no single issue of greater importance to LDC interests than international safeguards. What kinds of safeguard standards and procedures are ultimately adopted will bear directly on LDCs' ability to sell increasing amounts of an ever widening range of export products in developed countries' markets. Indeed, the resolution of the safeguard issue will go a long way in determining LDCs' access to foreign markets in the future, and that in turn will be of major importance to investors who may be considering establishment of manufacturing or processing operations in LDCs. Clearly, the safeguard issue and how it is handled will be of very considerable significance to LDCs' long-run development prospects; accordingly, some preferential treatment for developing countries in international safeguard arrangements may entail potential benefits that could transcend the dreams envisaged by proponents of GSP—the reason being that preferential treatment in the area of safeguards would more fully resolve the ultimate problem of assured access to markets than tariff preferences ever could have done alone.

# 5

## Developed Countries and the Current Issues

History reveals that commercial policies of nations tend to become either more liberal or more protectionist over time. Such policies are therefore inherently unstable. In order that world trade continue to evolve within a cooperative, increasingly more liberal framework in the 1970s, as was indeed the case on balance during the 1960s, it is widely accepted that international negotiations on a scale similar to, and even exceeding, the Kennedy Round are required.

Much has been written concerning the growing economic interdependence of nations and the role of international trade in helping the world achieve a more efficient allocation of resources and higher levels of well-being. Not only are multilateral trade negotiations at this current juncture essential to protect the benefits of freer trade obtained through past efforts, but negotiations are of potential, direct relevance to resolving or helping resolve many of the world's current economic difficulties, which, if left otherwise unattended, could easily lead to a regression of commercial policies on a wide scale.

In September 1973, in Tokyo, over one hundred sovereign nations agreed to a new round of multilateral negotiations to be held under the auspices of the General Agreement on Tariffs and Trade. Circumstances and events prevailing then, and developments in the one year since then, make this round of negotiations perhaps the most important and certainly the most wide-ranging ever to be held. This chapter is addressed to the major problems and issues posed for the industrial nations on the eve of the Tokyo Round of trade negotiations. Some are familiar problems and issues of preceding trade negotiations, such as tariffs on manufactured goods, commodity trade agreements and nontariff barriers. Other issues are more novel, including protection against international supply disruptions of raw materials and goods as opposed to the more traditional questions involving access to markets. Still other issues considered in past rounds of GATT negotiations, but likely to be more prominent in the current round, include international trade in agricultural commodities, safeguards against import disruption, trade relations with the less developed countries, and reform of the General Agreement on Tariffs and Trade.

### Security of Foreign Supply

In rather sudden, and certainly in dramatic, fashion the trade policy issue uppermost in people's minds turned recently from the time-honored interest in access to foreign markets to access to foreign supplies. Indeed, neither had the full impact been felt, nor had the potential significance of the security of supply issue been assessed by the time of the Tokyo conference in September 1973. Accordingly, such concerns are not mentioned in the text of the Tokyo Declaration.

The principal events that brought about this change included: the oil embargo of late 1973 and early 1974 imposed by Arab oil-exporting nations against particular countries whose political postures vis-à-vis the Arab-Israeli War of October 1973 were not deemed sufficiently sympathetic to the Arab cause; increasing scarcities and multiple price increases in a number of basic foodstuffs, minerals, fibers and other materials, all of which resulted in the main from many large industrial countries simultaneously experiencing rapid increases in domestic economic activity; and the interaction of rising domestic and export prices in a number of industrial countries, which exacerbated inflationary problems throughout the world. The sum total of the developments underscored as had never been done before a need to broaden the traditional scope of international trade policy to provide it with a balance or symmetry so that there would be ground rules for exports and their restraint, just as there has developed over the years a body of rules pertaining to imports and their restraint.

The scarcities of foodstuffs, raw materials, and other products experienced recently signal at least a temporary departure from the sorts of economic policy issues that have challenged authorities and preoccupied economists since the early 1930s; namely, how to generate sufficient aggregate demand in order to keep the labor force as close to full employment as possible, but without resorting to exchange-rate depreciation, protectionist commercial policies, or other beggar-thy-neighbor measures, all regarded as contrary to the dictates of classical economics, the promotion of free trade, and the principles underlying the reciprocal trade approach. Not long ago the major policy objectives were the promotion of rapid economic growth and of high levels of employment; today the major economic concerns are how to stem the tide of inflation—both domestic and worldwide—and how to alleviate bottlenecks and supply deficiencies in particular sectors. (In Western Europe and in Britain, there is at least as much concern that efforts to throttle inflation could lead to serious, worldwide depression. These concerns are shared in part but to a lesser degree by the United States.) These preoccupations imply domestic requirements in a number of countries today which again pose a potential conflict with the liberal trade policies and orientations of the past. In the present context, trade policy could be misused in ways that would result in the export of domestic inflation or in ways that would deny other countries' access to products or commodities through the normal course of international trade. This threat to international trade order should thus be viewed in many respects as the mirror image of the more traditional threat to foreign market access.

A divergence of opinion exists concerning the possible long-run implications of the scarcity problem. There are those who maintain that we have just entered a new era in which population and economic growth will outstrip new resource development and the discovery and production of substitute materials, synthetic or otherwise; accordingly, it is maintained that cost structures are changing in ways that will profoundly affect competitive relations between industries and even between countries. The other point of view is that many of the recent or current shortages are temporary and are simply the consequence of worldwide demand pressures converging simultaneously and aggravated by unanticipated supply shortages and by arbitrary restraints imposed on the international sale of particular commodities. According to this thesis, the scarcity problem is likely to abate almost as fast as it first arose; the play of free market forces will cause new production capacity to be built, will stimulate development of new supplies of resources and foodstuffs, and will create new incentives for entrepreneurial activity and technological innovation.

But whether one believes the world economy has indeed entered a new age of scarcity or that the interplay of free market forces will soon bring relief, the problems of inflation and shortages pose a major new issue for trade policy and for the upcoming multilateral trade negotiations. In an interdependent world such as exists today, nations cannot afford to allow market forces to run their course without additional stabilizing devices. The sacrifices in terms of private and social welfare are too high, and when there are measures available that, if adopted, might help to reduce those costs, it would be foolish indeed not to opt for them. Thus, even if recent events are interpreted as a short-run or medium-term phenomenon, it would be prudent to supplement and bolster existing international trade rules and regulations in order to possibly speed the end of such disturbances and certainly to offset, cushion, or otherwise control the possible occurrence of similar problems at some point in the future. International rules were adopted in the past to deal with problems of short supply, but the problems were then relatively minor in scope. The regulations as formulated seem vague and are presently believed to be inadequate in the face of existing shortages.[1]

Before considering what means there are to cope with the shortage problem in the context of trade negotiations, it is first of all helpful to identify and distinguish between the various motivations for the recent use of export controls. One motivation is political and the clearest example derives from the Arab nations' curtailment of oil shipments (and for some countries an outright embargo of oil exports to individual nations) as a lever to force international opinion over to their side in the ongoing Arab-Israeli conflict. A second motivation, and again oil serves as the most successful example to date, is to force up international prices by cartel action of producer nations—to improve the terms of trade through extraction of a monopoly surcharge. Another motivation has to do with attempts to transfer inflationary pressures from domestic to foreign consumers through a diversion of exports back onto the domestic market.[2] Examples here include controls on steel scrap and on cereals, which are imposed by a number of countries at present, and restrictions on US exports of soybeans of 1973.

Both political boycotts and cartel actions represent critical challenges to the world economic order. The threat is that a few suppliers, by taking coordinated decisions in their immediate self-interest, can disrupt economic activity in large parts of the world. At this point, there is no consensus as to the ultimate scope of this threat.[3] But the cartel idea is not a new one, and its attempted application in the past proved unsuccessful—that is, until the episode of the major oil-exporting countries in 1973. Meanwhile, efforts are going forward to reduce unnecessary oil consumption in many countries in the hope that a more financially tolerable short-run balance will emerge. In addition, the Energy Coordinating Group, composed of leading industrial nations, has been meeting in Brussels at regular intervals since its inception at the Washington Energy Conference in early 1974 to work out ways in which trading nations acting cooperatively can deal more effectively with future threats of supply disruption.[4]

As for what may be done to address the security of supply issue at the forthcoming trade negotiations, much hinges on the attitudes displayed by some of the leading industrial nations. (For example, Canada and South Africa are major suppliers of critical imports to the United States, while Western Europe, Britain, and Japan rely heavily on the flow of goods and foodstuffs from the United States and Australia.) If they affirm a strong interest in creating order out of chaos now emerging in respect of individual countries' export control policies, for example, then a number of alternative courses of action might be considered. First of all, Article XI of the GATT prohibits quotas or other restrictions on both exports and imports, but it exempts export restrictions applied temporarily to prevent or alleviate shortages of foodstuffs or other products essential to the exporting country. No mention is made concerning the use of export restrictions as an anti-inflationary device, nor is the possibility foreseen that export controls might be used to further political objectives. One area of concern, therefore, should be how to expand or elaborate Article XI so that it might better deal with and bring an order to the now growing resort to export restrictions.[5]

In conjunction with such negotiations, consideration would need to be given to the desirability of including the principles of nondiscrimination and minimum interference with free market forces in order that they might serve to help define those exceptional conditions where resort to export restrictions should be allowed. There might also need to be periodic multilateral consultation and reviews, either under GATT auspices or perhaps within the OECD, to insure that national policies were consistent with the general objectives of alleviating supply shortages and ensuring maximum possible access to foreign supplies. Indeed, consultations might well be required to precede use of trade measures designed to deal with domestic or international shortages; and if their use were deemed appropriate, it might also prove helpful and desirable that nations enforcing them be required to consult with a review body in order to justify their continuation or to agree to a timetable for their removal. In many respects, the principles and procedures for dealing with shortages, and the forum for consultation and review, might parallel the approach to import problems and access to foreign markets.[6]

Another way in which the pressing issues of scarcity might be addressed in the multilateral trade negotiations is through commodity agreements,[7] although this might also be viewed as a more long-term solution to present problems, should they persist, and therefore one whose full elaboration might extend beyond the time frame of the current negotiations. It is entirely possible, however, that commodity agreements could be treated as a quid pro quo for meaningful assurances of future access.[8] The argument offered by Fred Bergsten is that access to supply can be checked by controls over domestic production as well as by controls over exports; therefore, commodity agreements are offered, in conjunction with rules governing the use of export controls, as a policy measure that would preclude the use of such production controls.

In any case, security of supply is an important issue which will challenge the abilities and willingness of key industrial nations to find workable solutions in an increasingly interdependent world. But it is also an issue that potentially pits the financially rich industrial nations against the resource-rich LDCs, whose trade and development aspirations have expanded rapidly.[9] For both reasons, but particularly the second, the security of supply issue must be given top priority in the trade negotiations, It is impossible to tell at this juncture, however, whether the sudden appearance of shortages and export controls on the world scene just prior to the start of such negotiations will be an asset or a hindrance in producing solutions. No doubt more work will remain to be done once the trade negotiations have concluded; but it is to be hoped that despite the present lack of extensive experience and study in this area (in contrast to exhaustive efforts already spent on tariffs and nontariff barriers, for example) meaningful progress can be made.

## Access to Foreign Markets: Tariffs

The Tokyo Declaration cites negotiations on tariffs as the first aim of the forthcoming multilateral trade talks. As reiterated in earlier chapters, discussions and bargaining on tariff reductions consumed the greatest proportion of the time and energies of those involved in the six preceding rounds of postwar trade negotiations. Despite the great progress made in dismantling the existing tariff structure between the United States, Western Europe and Japan, tariffs are still applied to some 60 percent of international trade in industrial goods. Average levels of industrial tariffs for the large developed countries range from 8.1 to 12.6 percent,[10] but are higher for many other countries not quite so advanced. (Spain, for example, has an average tariff level of about 15 percent.) Average tariff levels obscure the fact that many duties on individual goods are substantially higher. Moreover, effective tariffs, or the duty assessed on the value added by manufacture, are often significantly higher than the nominal tariff rates.[11] All in all, therefore, tariffs must continue to be regarded as a significant deterrent to international trade. That fact, together with the historical susceptibility of tariffs to negotiated reduction or elimination on political and technical grounds, suggests strongly that tariffs will again emerge as a central issue for industrial nations in the present multilateral trade negotiations.

For the United States, tariff reduction or elimination on a broad range of industrial products must be at the top of the list of major issues. Earlier in Chapter 3, there was a discussion of the increasing competitive challenges posed for US traders as a result of enlargement of the Common Market and also as a result of the decisions taken to expand the EC's free-trade area to include former European Free Trade Association (EFTA) nations which did not join the European Common Market. Once the phased tariff reductions between those European countries have been effected on July 1, 1977, and a common external tariff has been established for all trade outside the area, the commercially discriminatory impact for nonmember industrial nations will be considerably greater than in years past when there was free trade among EFTA nations and free trade within the EC, but not between the two areas. In anticipation of such developments, the United States—and also Japan, Canada and Australia, which have vital trade links as well with Europe—will want to offset what is otherwise certain to be increased European discrimination against their products.

For its own part, Europe is unlikely to exhibit great enthusiasm for wide-scale elimination of tariffs on industrial products. It has been the argument of the Common Market members all along, and no doubt there will also be some support from the non-EC members now in the process of affiliating with the wider free-trade area, that a common external tariff wall of some consequence is one of the essential elements that binds together the nations of the European Community. It may be countered, however, that the EC could remain strong and viable without a common external tariff as it currently exists, or alternatively, that substantial selective tariff reductions could be achieved without seriously eroding the free-trade area future.

The major issue with respect to tariffs and the multilateral trade negotiations is that the momentum of liberalization established in previous negotiations not be allowed to lapse. The ultimate threat of the free-trade area, be it in Europe or in one of the developing areas, is that it could result in the fragmentation of the international trade community into rival trading blocs. While there has been some drift away from the one-world concept of trading nations, recent momentous events such as the oil crisis have brought home the idea once again that the world is comprised of nations whose economies are very closely interconnected with one another and that such interdependence and economic well-being will be served far better by more open trading arrangements. Thus, in the current period there is likely to be a consensus among industrial nations in support of negotiations to reduce tariff barriers on a selective product category or perhaps even industrywide basis.

## Access to Markets: Nontariff Barriers

As the relative importance of tariff barriers to trade have been reduced through negotiations over the years, the importance of nontariff barriers (NTBs) has increased.[12] The Tokyo Declaration took note of this fact and stated specifically that the next round of trade negotiations should aim to "reduce or eliminate nontariff measures or, where this is not appropriate, to reduce or eliminate their trade restricting or distorting effects, and to bring such measures under more effective international discipline."[13]

NTBs are not only sometimes subtle and often complex, they are also very numerous. They include import quotas, discriminatory government procurement policies, standards for products which discriminate in favor of domestic-made goods, and a large number of customs and other administrative provisions that may be applied in a discriminatory manner to restrict imports. NTBs are also taken to include special government measures extended to domestic producers such as export subsidies, investment subsidies, and easy access to financing. Some NTBs are geared to protect certain industries. Some are clearly protectionist by intent, while others are not. All NTBs, however, tend to impede imports to one degree or another.

Previous attempts to negotiate reductions in NTBs bogged down and ultimately ended in failure; the most recent example occurred during the Kennedy Round in the 1960s. Partly for that reason, but also because of the proliferation of NTBs and the reduced relative importance of tariffs, many experts believe the most important negotiations in terms of impact on trade at the current juncture will have to do with nontariff barriers.[14]

Fortunately, much necessary study and assembling of data in respect of NTBs has taken place since the end of the Kennedy Round. The GATT undertook a comprehensive compilation of nontariff barriers and emerged with a list of over eight hundred policies or practices of governments considered by other governments to be NTBs.[15] And efforts have been made in the Organization for Economic Cooperation and Development (OECD) for more than a decade to try and resolve discriminatory government procurement policies in member countries. By building on such information already assembled, a successful negotiation of NTBs could lead to a substantial improvement of international trade conditions.

No one underestimates the difficulties involved in such negotiations, but studies in recent years have led to a heightened awareness of the importance for all countries that nontariff barriers be controlled and be made subject to tighter regulation. Only a few NTBs are thought to lend themselves to reduction or elimination in the manner that tariff reductions were negotiated in reciprocal fashion in the past. Some NTBs will require further definition and interpretation at the bargaining table prior to establishment of procedures to deal with them. Many NTBs are believed more susceptible to restraint according to codes of conduct that might be appended to nontariff articles already contained in the GATT Agreement. Indeed, the NTB area is seen as one that will benefit from a strengthening or a tightening of international rules and regulations rather than a simple tradeoff of one country's NTB for that of another.[16]

A key question in the negotiations concerning NTBs, especially in relation to principles embraced in negotiations of years past, is whether concessions, codes of conduct, or other forms of agreement reached should be subject to unconditional most-favored-nation treatment. In some cases, such as customs valuation procedures or various administrative practices, it may prove that MFN treatment is the only practicable approach. In other cases, however, it may be that only those willing to participate in a given agreement or commitment should enjoy its application; in that case, participation could be widened at future dates as other nations pledged willingness to abide by the rules as stated.[17] Perhaps such selective application, at least at the outset, will greatly facilitate the NTB negotiations. If so, however, it would be an important break with the nondiscrimination principle that proved to be such a strong guiding light in the past.

### Access to Foreign Markets: Multilateral Safeguards

The Tokyo Declaration urges that the forthcoming multilateral trade negotiations "include an examination of the adequacy of the multilateral safeguard system, considering particularly the modalities of application of Article XIX, with a view to furthering trade liberalization and preserving its results." The term "safeguards" in this context has to do with the search for a formula that would at one and the same time allow countries to contain imports, regarded in some sense as "disruptive," and enforce limits on national freedom to raise and maintain trade restrictions in what would presumably be billed as an emergency situation.

The very considerable interest in safeguards stems from adjustment problems encountered by different industries in a number of countries in the wake of several years of rapid world export growth in manufactured products and the particularly sharp growth in manufactures exports of Japan and certain less developed countries.[18] Indeed, some contend that a stronger safeguard system is prerequisite to a successful outcome of the trade negotiations now pending, in that many governments might not otherwise be willing to commit their countries to a schedule of tariff cuts or other concessions extending over a number of years.[19]

In essence, GATT Article XIX, the safeguard provision, provides that a member country may impose temporary import restrictions if imports are the cause of "serious injury" to domestic producers. The same article provides also that other members may seek recompense by obtaining equivalent new concessions or, in the case of no compensations, by retaliation and enforcement of their own equivalent import restrictions. Many believe that in neither respect, but particularly the second provision concerning retaliation, has the existing safeguard clause proved adequate.

At the root of Article XIX are the long-hallowed principles of most-favored-nation treatment and reciprocity. If, however, a large number of exporting countries are involved, or if large volumes of imports are in question, reciprocity may be neither feasible nor desirable, even if the option is to retaliate. In part for this reason, the Long-term Arrangement in cotton textiles, which was renegotiated at the end of 1973 to include all textiles, was worked out originally in order to evade the GATT retaliation-compensation provision. But also, the LTA recognized that the disruption of textile markets was caused largely by extremely rapid export growth of the low-wage countries—not by all exporters—and therefore, the nondiscrimination principle was inappropriate.[20]

Still another problem encountered with Article XIX is that no review process is called for. Once a restriction has been imposed, there is no language requiring its periodic review, nor is there any clause requiring that concessions taken away be reinstated at some point in time or when deemed appropriate by an impartial body. If compensating arrangements are negotiated to the satisfaction of the parties concerned, then the matter is regarded as having been settled. Alternatively, claims not settled within three months are considered to have been waived.

While all countries agree that each government must be entitled to some form of emergency protection, modifications in the provisions of the present multilateral safeguard system are necessary in order that further trade liberalization not be jeopardized. To that end, a number of suggested changes have been offered, ranging from a kind of two-track safeguard system whereby a country faced with injury from imports could act either with or without approval of an international review group (the difference being that equivalent compensation or retaliation would be deemed justified in the latter case)[21] to an interpretive note or protocol subscribed to by the contracting parties of GATT and added to the existing Article XIX. The purpose of the note would be to recommit participants to a multilateral escape-clause procedure with explicit preestablished time limits for emergency protection and to provide for a permanent review group in the GATT to oversee operations.[22]

**Trade in Agricultural Products**

Trade in agricultural products is one of the few obvious areas in which postwar liberalization efforts have failed. Increasing income to farmers and maximization of domestic food supplies have been strong political issues in many countries, and the political response has most often been to limit imports and to raise domestic prices. When overproduction arose, government subsidies were applied in order that exporters could compéte successfully with foreign producers for existing export markets. Such has been the case in the past for the United States, Canada, Japan, and the members of the European Community.

During 1972-73, and again to some extent in 1974, a world shortage of grains and foodstuffs gave rise to sharply higher prices. Foreign demand for US supplies was so great in 1973 that export controls had to be imposed temporarily on soybeans and its substitutes to ensure adequate domestic supplies. Moreover, the once vast US inventories of various grains and other agricultural produce have for the most part been exhausted, and toward the close of 1973, the US government was obliged to remove all restrictions on lands that could be cultivated in the coming crop season.

Many experts view the worldwide shortage in agricultural products as a short-lived phenomenon; others see the present situation as the beginning of a longer-range problem of short food supplies generally, and protein shortages in particular. In either case, recent developments could not have put into better focus the need to improve the present international agricultural system, which has become so distorted by both domestic and external policies. Whereas in the past, domestic political considerations in several key countries were ultimately the undoing of promising agricultural negotiations, it appears more likely at the current juncture that the political and economic motivations for placing agricultural trade barriers as well as domestic agricultural programs in a more rational, more flexible framework will not falter.

In order to be successful, agricultural negotiations will need to take into account and provide solutions for three related concerns.[23] First, there is the social and political problem of improving farmers' income. Their incomes have tended to rise more slowly than incomes of other people in a wide range of occupations in all of the industrialized countries. Accordingly, and because farm groups remain a strong political force, various supportive measures have been used, but at the cost of creating trade barriers which seriously distort agricultural trade. Reduction or removal of those trade barriers must realistically entail some alternative measures for a period of time so that the income prospects of farmers in many countries will not be immediately threatened in a major way.

Second, there is the national security and the human problem of ensuring enough food for the domestic population. Possibly more than in other areas, increased national dependence on foreign sources for foodstuffs kindles a nation's sensitivity to the possibility of insufficient supplies for reasons quite beyond its control. But increased self-sufficiency in the agricultural area usually entails inefficient production and higher costs. The problem to be reckoned with in the forthcoming trade negotiations is, therefore, how to create a system that will ensure adequate supplies of agricultural products for the world and will also allow the most inefficient, high-cost farm areas to be used for other more productive purposes.

Third, there is the economic problem of achieving and maintaining reasonable levels of food prices at the consumer level. In the past, consumers' interests have usually taken third place to the political considerations of farm income and national self-sufficiency. The momentum of the consumer movement in the United States and in other industrial nations is on the upbeat, however, and more than ever before, fulfillment of rising public demand for meats and other livestock products as part of an everyday diet is gaining new prominence among the long list of national objectives.

This economic problem is, of course, a modern-day manifestation of the terms of trade issue so prominent during the 1950s and in other periods as far as less developed countries were concerned.[24] In their own national interest, countries want to import goods and services at low prices and export their own goods and services at high prices. What with the recent very sharp increases in prices of foodstuffs, industrial countries that have to import from abroad are expressing their concern about their deteriorating terms of trade; food has become expensive relative to a variety of other products. For countries that are large producers and exporters of agricultural commodities, these circumstances are viewed favorably and as a long overdue reversal of their own worsening terms of trade in years gone by. International negotiations in the agricultural area will be directly concerned with the terms of trade issue; but it must be recognized that a pair of scissors has two blades. The struggle over agricultural prices has two sides and how one views the present problem depends importantly upon where one's own national interests lie.

In addition to domestic considerations just noted which in the past have obstructed efforts to liberalize agricultural trade, there have been important differences in philosophical approach of the two leading protagonists: the United States and the European Common Market. For the most part, the United States has long sought trade liberalization in the form of reduced tariff and other trade barriers and through adjustment of domestic agricultural policies so as to promote efficient, low-cost world production. Plainly enough, the US approach was motivated by the great comparative advantage it held in agricultural production. The EC, on the other hand, placed emphasis on international commodity agreements to stabilize world prices and to help establish orderly markets wherein there would be greater assurances for adequate producer income along with better regulation of the flow of foodstuffs. The EC approach not only was tailored to meet domestic political needs of member countries, which were dictated by influential but economically inefficient farmers; the EC approach also reflected an important unwillingness to trust in, and abide by, the workings of the free-market mechanism. These fundamental differences in approach to international agricultural negotiations went unresolved during the Kennedy Round. In order for successful results to occur in the forthcoming negotiations, there will have to be compromises on both sides.

Still another agricultural consideration germane to the current setting is the widened scope for international trade in foodstuffs as a result of vast markets beginning to open up in Russia and in the Peoples' Republic of China. These new markets must be taken into account both by exporting nations and by nations that have been traditional importers of agricultural products from the free world.

The attitudes of the United States, members of the European Common Market, and other leading industrial nations may be inferred, at least in part, from the just discussed philosophical differences. The United States is a very efficient producer of a large number of agricultural products, has enjoyed a strong comparative advantage in this area vis-à-vis other nations, and certainly it hopes that successful negotiations will result in US agricultural exports providing a continuing and increasingly positive contribution to the US balance of payments. All of this implies opening overseas markets to increased competition in agricultural trade.

To be balanced against that traditional attitude, however, is the experience in the most recent past when crop failures in some key agricultural-producing countries caused a rise in world demand that outstripped available supplies in the chief exporting nations, including the United States. That experience has created substantial concern in various quarters as regards scarcity of supply. In order for the United States and other exporting nations such as Canada, Argentina, Australia, and New Zealand to obtain increased access to markets of nations that are comparatively inefficient producers of agricultural products, there will have to be substantial, but reasonable, assurances that those exporting nations will be able to meet the rising needs of importing countries. While this does not at all suggest an easy solution (indeed, negotiations are likely to be extremely difficult and complex), it does imply that the elements of a bargain do in fact exist.[25] If import barriers that have kept potential world efficiency in this area unrealized for so long are to be reduced, it appears that agriculture must be dealt with as a self-contained negotiation, separate from negotiations on other matters or having to do with industrial products. In the past, this has not been tried; instead, concessions in the industrial area have been offered in exchange for concessions in agriculture, or agricultural products and industrial products were not distinguished in the process of bargaining for the reduction or removal of tariffs and other forms of protection.

The official attitude of the Common Market has been that agriculture is a matter replete with social, political, and economic considerations and that agricultural systems do not constitute an appropriate topic for multilateral trade negotiations. The Common Agricultural Policy (CAP), about which so much has been written, involves a system of variable levies used to insulate a relatively inefficient agricultural sector from world markets, at the expense of high food prices for consumers. But the CAP, once viewed as an essential pillar of European unity, has not worked well; indeed, it has been a focal point of bitter internal dispute, and the need for reform has been growing.[26] The addition of Britain to the EC may facilitate a more accommodating EC position in the forthcoming negotiations. Britain, as a net food importer, paid dearly in the area of higher food prices when she joined the Common Market, and she has a strong interest in promoting more liberal policies in world agricultural trade.

Japan's attitude toward agricultural negotiations has not been spelled out in full. However, Japan already imports substantial amounts of foodstuffs and is the largest single market for US agricultural exports. Japan does maintain a substantial farm sector but at a high cost both in terms of food prices Japanese consumers must bear and in the sense that use of precious land for high-cost agricultural pursuits takes place at the expense of more productive industrial or recreational pursuits. But the cultural and historical traditions of an agricultural rice society run deep, and Japan cannot be expected to depart quickly or easily from the ways of the past.

There are, nevertheless, reasons to believe that Japan will support efforts to negotiate a more liberal structure of world agricultural trade. First, largely as a result of some recent, difficult experiences with short-supply problems and ensuing US export controls, Japan has been prompted to seek greater diversity in its overseas sources of food supplies. She has been doing so by investing in overseas farm land and by concluding long-term contracts for foreign production of basic agricultural products. In the end, however, such assurances of future supply will depend not only on the physical availability of the produce contracted for, but also on a liberal trade structure which will permit Japan and other net food importing countries to bid for supplies possibly produced even more efficiently in still other countries.

Second, Japan's pattern of food consumption has been changing gradually over time. Now that her per capita income has reached a level equivalent to those in Western Europe, possibly a more rapid expansion in demand for meat and meat products and other relatively expensive food items will occur during the next few years. Such changes in food consumption habits will depend greatly on the prices of those meat products and that of other food items Japanese consumers will face; and those prices will be influenced to a large extent by the trade policies the Japanese government endorses at the present juncture. If the authorities move away from their past position of protecting the high-cost domestic agriculture sector, remove import barriers, and allow foreign distributors greater latitude of operation in Japanese markets, the relative cost of food will probably decline, and by a significant amount.

A third and important reason to believe Japan will come out in general support of more liberal agricultural trade has to do with her commercial position in the world. Japan, truly a world-trading nation, will be materially affected by the outcome of multilateral trade negotiations. A more liberal trading system that permits Japanese exporters greater ease of entry to foreign markets is crucial to the future well-being of Japan. In return for that kind of a trading environment, Japan will have to give ground to her competitors by permitting them easier access to Japanese markets; and in that regard, increasing freedom of foreign nations to sell more agricultural commodities to Japan will be very important.

Although the lead in agricultural trade negotiations is sure to be taken by the United States and certain other industrial countries, many less developed countries produce basic commodities and livestock for export and have a vital interest in obtaining easier access to foreign markets. Those countries, too, are desirous of sharing in the foreign exchange proceeds that will result from higher demand due to rising incomes of consumers and a possible further expansion in demand due to lower product prices if more liberal world trade in agriculture can be realized. In all of this, however, LDCs will have to be willing to share some responsibility for, and help work out, arrangements that will provide reasonable assurances of future supply to importing nations.

**Trade with Less Developed Countries
and Communist Countries**

The text of the Tokyo Declaration makes frequent and detailed reference to less developed countries and to their particular needs and desires regarding multilateral trade negotiations.[27] The need for "stable, equitable and remunerative prices for primary products" is singled out. Products of export interest to LDCs, including "tropical products and raw materials" should be covered in the negotiations with a view toward relieving impediments to trade. "The developed countries do not expect reciprocity for commitments made by them in the negotiations to reduce ... barriers to the trade of developing countries.... The importance of maintaining and improving the Generalized System of Preferences" is recognized. Moreover, the need to give special treatment and consideration to "the least developed among the developing countries" during the negotiations is specifically mentioned.

Indeed, the need for special attention and particular measures in order to improve the long-term deterioration in the trade position of LDCs has become widely recognized in recent years since the start of the last multilateral trade negotiations in 1963. The GATT, of course, was drawn up on the principle of equal treatment—that is to say, on the principles of most-favored-nation treatment and reciprocity in trade negotiations. In 1957, a major turning point occurred in efforts of LDCs to obtain greater understanding in GATT for their special problems. Three disturbing elements in the international trade system were singled out for careful investigation by a panel of experts appointed by the Contracting Parties to GATT. The three problems were the prevalence of agricultural protectionism, sharp changes in primary product prices over time, and the failure of LDCs' export trade to expand at a rate commensurate with their growing import needs.[28] The report of the panel, published in 1958 and better known as the Haberler Report,[29] helped pave the way later on in 1965 for the addition of three special articles added to the General Agreement as Part IV.[30]

Much of what is covered in the Tokyo Declaration in regard to LDCs is included already in that section of the agreement. Thus, the present multilateral trade negotiations represent the first major opportunity for the developed countries to take substantive actions now that the claims of the less developed and least developed countries in the world have been recognized and their legitimacy accepted. To be sure, however, an unrelenting, conscientious effort by both sides, both the developed and less developed, must be made to provide feasible solutions to what are indeed difficult problems. (The grand-stand debating sessions that have characterized some of the earlier UNCTAD meetings and have led to little more than a stand-off should be avoided at all costs.)

Concrete measures could be adopted during the forthcoming negotiations to alleviate the problems of LDCs and to help improve their international trade positions: reduction or elimination of tariffs and nontariff barriers on products of special interest to LDCs is one broad and ripe area. There should also be serious consideration of improvement and expansion of generalized tariff preferences, including early implementation of the US scheme that is part of the Trade Act of 1974. GSP is, of course, a device regarded as temporary, in the sense that its applicability would be relevant for perhaps a decade or so. The point is that GSP is something designed to improve LDCs' access to developed countries' markets in the present and immediate future; but GSP should not be allowed to retard further MFN reductions in tariffs and other trade barriers (either in the current negotiations or in subsequent bargaining sessions) that will serve the interests of both the developing and the developed world. Such concessions have proved long lasting in the past, are likely to be so in the future; and they represent improvements in the world trading community that can provide catalytic action for traders and investors everywhere, including those in LDCs.

Possibly, commodity agreements and price stabilization efforts may prove more beneficial and more durable now than they have in the past. (In this regard, the EC preference for better management of international trade through greater use of commodity agreements should be noted. The US preference in the past has been to allow free market forces to do the job to the maximum extent possible.) Prices of many commodities—oil, bauxite, sugar, for example—have reached record peaks recently. Prices of some commodities have started to decline in mid-1974, and there may be valuable opportunities for all concerned, both exporting and importing countries, to concur on supply access and floor price issues.[31] Such agreements might help to achieve the kind of stability everyone has been seeking.

In regard to the problem of world food reserves, and particularly reserves for LDCs, the Food and Agriculture Organization has made a strong case for developing foodstocks to be held against the threat of potential famine. Much more on these and related issues may be expected to evolve from the resolutions taken during the World Food Conference held in Rome in November 1974. There are matters here, however, that are the appropriate concern of GATT and the current multilateral trade negotiations, especially as they become concerned with agricultural trade.

Trade between free world nations and Communist countries in Europe and Asia is still in its infancy at the present time. The volume of trade took a significant quantum jump upward in 1972 and 1973 as a result of large grain shipments from the US and other countries to Russia and China. The "normal" levels of East-West trade have yet to be discerned, and certainly many factors, political, financial, as well as major differences in economic systems, must be overcome in large measure before the great potential of international trade envisaged by many observers can be realized to the mutual benefit of both sides.[32]

For the United States, for other Western nations, and for Japan, potential benefits include reductions in political tensions (hence diminished need for military spending); improved balances of trade (for it is believed that Eastern demand for Western goods exceeds and will continue to exceed Western demand for Eastern goods, the difference being made up by a flow of capital and technology from West to East); and possible access at some future date to substantial supplies of energy and raw materials known to exist in Russia and perhaps to be discovered in other Communist countries. On the other hand, the Eastern nations would gain greater access to advanced Western technology and capital equipment, denied them for so many years; to the extent Communist governments were interested, they could purchase large new supplies of consumer goods and, to a lesser extent, agricultural goods in order to meet the growing demands of their consumers.

In the context of the forthcoming multilateral trade negotiations, there is not a great deal to be done to further facilitate East-West trade. Most free world nations already grant most-favored-nation status to Communist countries. The major exception, of course, is the United States, although that is now almost certain to be modified in view of the provisions contained in the Trade Act of 1974, which President Ford signed into law January 3, 1975. (See Chapter 6.)

As for liberalizing exports from Western countries to Communist nations, private and public pressures in recent years to reduce the COCOM list of embargoed goods have been substantial and have cleared the way for trade in many products that only a few years ago would have been unthinkable. A slimmed-down COCOM list of products, sensitive for their military value or for their high technological content, will of course remain; even so, the over-all impact on potential East-West trade should not be great and certainly will be minuscule compared to the COCOM and CHINCOM product lists of the early 1950s. Beyond those considerations, some countries, including the US, may still carry on their books trade legislation relevant to another era. To the extent those pieces of legislation significantly restrict countries' ability to compete with their trading partners for available markets of Eastern countries, amendments will be required and no doubt will be soon forthcoming. The more interesting and complex questions confronting East-West trade, particularly eventual changes in the existing framework of international institutions, are likely to be addressed not at the forthcoming multilateral trade negotiations, but at some time further in the future. (See Chapter 7.)

## Reform of the Institutional Structure

The General Agreement on Tariffs and Trade was born out of a process of consolidating and multilateralizing the network of bilateral trade agreements that had come into being under the reciprocal trade agreements program. Embodied in the GATT articles was a set of multilateral trading rules and policies, some of which had originally been drafted for the ultimately stillborn sister organization, the International Trade Organization. Viewed originally and even throughout the 1950s as a rich man's club, its contracting parties remained unchanged for the most part until the 1960s, when a growing number of less developed countries began to join; the original membership of twenty-three countries has now grown to one hundred.

Two glaring faults of the General Agreement need to be remedied in order to pave the way for other necessary changes. In the first place, GATT is based upon executive agreements. Accordingly, its Articles have no power to override national legislation that may be inconsistent with an individual member's GATT obligations. The GATT should be given legislative endorsement of its contracting parties in order that its authority may be enhanced and its rules and regulations as well as its benefits may be administered to all members in a fair and just manner.

Second, unlike the International Monetary Fund, the voting principle in GATT is one country-one vote. Each nation has the same influence in GATT decision taking, even though many of the smaller and more recent members do not or cannot abide by the rules and regulations of GATT.[33] To make matters still more difficult, amendments to the Articles require a two-thirds or sometimes even a unanimous vote. Such voting procedures give strong endorsement to the status quo, but they provide all too little scope for pragmatic, yet responsible management of evolving trade problems, and they do not reflect the new realities of the present day world economy.

In addition to those two general areas, other shortcomings and inadequacies of GATT that are functional in nature have grown increasingly apparent in recent years, and matters have reached the point where a substantial number of reforms must be achieved if GATT is to effectively meet the current and future needs of the international trading community.[34] Procedures and mechanisms for settling disputes are absent, and many important issues have been left unattended. Earlier in this chapter, in the discussion of particular issues, references were made to needed modification or revision of existing GATT Articles. Those areas where GATT reform is needed include export controls, nontariff barriers, international safeguard provisions, agricultural trade, and application of quantitative import restrictions under the GATT.

Unless the voting procedure is altered, it is conceivable but not realistic to expect that a sufficient number of contracting parties would vote for or accept the obligations entailed in such reforms. This poses a major dilemma for international trade policy and the future of international trade itself. On the one hand, either the majority or a sufficient minority of GATT contracting parties would decide against most substantive reforms; thus, future problems of international trade policy would have to be settled increasingly on an ad hoc basis, to the extent they could be settled at all. On the other hand, due recognition might be made of the fact that whatever else happens, the traditional principles of nondiscrimination and reciprocity are going to be compromised more rather than less in the years ahead. If that were done, the way might well be cleared for creation of a special arrangement within GATT, presumably made up at first of the large industrial nations but open to others willing to abide by the commitments laid down, which would build upon the previous strengths of the GATT Articles, but would modify them in ways deemed appropriate by its members in order to form an instrument more responsive to present needs and circumstances.[35] The success of such an approach to reform would depend not only upon a substantial degree of determination on the part of the large trading nations, it would also be necessary for those countries to assure nonsubscribing countries, particularly the less developed countries, that their interests would be served at least as well if not better than before.

A second area of reform is bound up in what many observers have come to view since 1971 as the need for closer cooperation and coordination between international agencies.[36] For example, trade measures applied for balance of payments reasons would normally come under the jurisdiction of the GATT for "consultation-after-the-fact," whereas foreign exchange measures applied for balance of payments reasons would usually fall to the International Monetary Fund for "consultation-before-the-fact." It has been proposed, therefore, that trade and foreign exchange measures designed for similar purposes be treated on the same basis. Thus, the IMF might be granted the authority to evaluate and approve or disapprove the financial basis of both trade and exchange measures designed to deal with balance of payments problems, and the GATT would retain responsibility for reviewing the commercial aspects of trade measures as well. Such changes would eliminate what now amounts to overlapping responsibility between the two institutions in this area.[37]

Another area in which existing international institutions could and should cooperate more fully concerns scarcity problems and the issue of access to foreign supplies. The Organization for Economic Cooperation and Development is a most likely institution to study current and future problems in the resource area; its members bear primary responsibility for the rapid increases in consumption of basic materials and at the same time are sure to be the major sources of technology and investment capital that will have to be devoted to increasing future supplies. The work already going on within the OECD may well provide important insights into the kinds of GATT reforms most appropriate for dealing with short supply and security of supply problems as they are likely to arise in the international trade context.

# Formulation of US Trade Policy: The Trade Act of 1974

United States trade policy encompasses a wide range of economic and political interests. Business, labor, agriculture, and other private forces on the one hand, the Congress and the executive branch on the other, together with a variety of foreign policy considerations, all help to determine the shape of US trade policy. The process that has been going on intensively for three years, 1972-74, to produce a comprehensive, coherent trade bill, has involved a major overhaul of US positions on various key issues.

The complexity of issues and interests involved and the great amount of time consumed can be attributed in part to what at times appeared to be intractable political problems. First, there were the domestic political preoccupations of 1973-1974 that diverted congressional attentions and energies away from matters at hand, including the pending trade legislation. Second, there was great political difficulty in resolving US trade policy toward Communist countries not enjoying most-favored-nation treatment. In particular, the emigration policies of the Soviet Union became a focal point of attention; some relaxation of those policies became for particularly key politicians a quid pro quo for their agreement to extend MFN treatment to Russia. Third, within the Congress and important groups such as organized labor, there was a hangover from the protectionist philosophy and thinking that had been expressed so strongly during 1971-72 and had nearly succeeded in the passage of trade legislation that would have caused a severe setback in US international economic interests.

The great significance of the Trade Act of 1974 (known as the Trade Reform Act until it was finally approved by the Congress on December 19, 1974) is that it will enable the United States to undertake comprehensive negotiations with other nations. The timeliness and the need for such negotiations has been the subject of earlier chapters. But without US legislation, which provides the president with a mandate to negotiate with other nations and reach agreement within broadly prescribed limits on various trade topics, other countries would be extremely reluctant to enter serious negotiations of the scope envisaged in the MTN. Despite structural changes within the world economy of the past several years, the United States is still the largest single trading nation in the world. Its policies and its positions on the major issues therefore continue to carry great weight, and the ability of the United States to participate actively in the MTN is a necessary prerequisite to the holding of those negotiations, as well as to any successful achievements that may result from them.

This chapter is addressed to the major influences on US trade policy, to the

93

emergence of strong protectionist forces that reflected both the political pressures prevailing and various economic adjustments occurring in the early 1970s, all of which had to be surmounted before the Nixon administration was able to introduce its Trade Reform Act to the Congress in April 1973. The general purposes and features of the trade bill that emerged from all that turmoil and ensuing congressional debate at the close of 1974 are discussed in the latter half of the chapter.

## The Influences on US Trade Policy

The forces that determine US trade policy have been experiencing more than the usual amount of flux in recent years. For a long period of time there had been a broad base of support for liberal trade policies, both on economic and foreign policy grounds.

The economic arguments for liberal trade as discussed earlier had their origins in classical economic theory; the main idea was that improvements in a nation's wealth and income would result from an exchange of those goods it could produce most efficiently for goods that other countries were able to produce most efficiently. Related arguments were concerned with beneficial effects that derived from liberal trade. The foreign policy argument for liberal trade was predicated on a desire to forge a strong alliance between the United States and free world nations, and on a desire to keep less developed countries in the camp of Western countries. In recent years, however, the broad support for liberal trade policy has been eroding, again on economic and foreign policy grounds.[1]

US trade policy is constantly being shaped and reshaped by various private interest groups as well as by the public sector—that is to say, both the administration and the congress. The most influential of all private interests is organized labor, and particularly the American Federation of Labor-Congress of Industrial Organizations. Other private interest groups able to influence trade policy include organized agriculture, represented in Washington by farm lobbyists, and organized business, spokesmen for which include the US Chamber of Commerce, the National Association of Manufacturers, and a host of individual trade associations. Private consumer groups could quite conceivably have an impact on trade policy, although in the past they have not effectively mobilized their potential influence.

Labor's influence on US trade policy is largely transmitted through labor lobbyists working on the Congress. For years, labor tended to give strong support for liberal policies; however, since the early 1960s there has been an increasing shift toward protectionism. One consideration in explanation of this development has been the rising level of unemployment from 1970 to the present. But other factors were clearly at work, since unemployment was dropping throughout most of the 1960s. Another consideration is complacency growing out of increasing affluence. Labor's income has reached such high levels that organized workers have become more interested in avoiding the costs of dislocation and other changes, whereas in an earlier period those costs were accepted as the price of increasing national output more rapidly and enhancing workers' own welfare. Labor's support for protectionist trade policies may be viewed as perhaps inevitable in a highly developed country such as the United States where foreign trade accounts for a relatively small share of total economic activity, and given the increasingly tough competition from foreign producers in areas of US industry where organized labor has become well entrenched.[2]

Another consideration that sheds light on labor's changed stance toward US trade policies is the often heard view that technological change is transmitted faster and more effectively as a result of international trade and investment. Economic and geographic dislocations caused by technological change may be acceptable, therefore, only up to some point in any given period. Indeed, multinational corporations (MNCs), which have done much to facilitate change and growth internationally, have been singled out by organized labor as detrimental to US national interests and to labor's interests in particular because of their alleged negative impact on domestic employment. MNCs hire other factors of production—capital and management—which tend to be very mobile internationally, much more so in fact than labor; and decisions to locate production plants overseas appear from labor's viewpoint to be at the expense of domestic employment.

Still another factor underlying labor's increasingly protectionist stance on US trade policy derives from the fact that organized labor has been and continues to be concentrated in the goods-producing sector.[3] Nonunionized workers are concentrated in the service sector, the very area that has been growing most rapidly in the United States in recent years. Since service workers by the nature of their product clearly have everything to gain and nothing to lose from free trade, as opposed to workers in goods-producing fields, labor's tougher position on trade policy has become decreasingly representative of US labor interests over all. This development is of considerable importance to what may be a significant distortion in the tone of US trade policy.[4]

A somewhat related consideration is that labor has been slow to organize in the rapidly developing, high-technology industries. Since these industries are among the most competitive of any in the United States and since they have done extremely well in international trade, more active support by their workers could help to reinforce a liberal US trade policy. Representative or not, it is a fact that organized labor, the most powerful private interest group that influences trade policy, has turned away from a liberal position and has embraced a protectionist trade policy.

Organized agriculture also wields substantial influence over US trade policy. Indeed, in terms of the small farm population (about 5 percent) and the relative size of its annual production (some 3 percent or less of GNP), it is somewhat surprising that agriculture's influence is as great as it is. But farm income and the welfare of farmers have broad implications for rural America generally, and this helps explain agriculture's considerable influence.[5]

In certain notable areas and at critical junctures, farm lobbyists have won protectionist measures. For example, dairy products, sugar, wool, wheat, and peanuts have been subject to special restrictive import controls. The importation of meat was subject to quotas until early 1974. And probably of greatest significance, in 1955 it was the United States which insisted on a waiver by the GATT for US import restrictions on any farm product included under a domestic agricultural program of price support.

Despite such instances of success for protectionism, the interest of organized agriculture appears to have been generally in the liberal trade camp. In the production of major crops such as feed grains and soy beans, American farmers have a comparative advantage over foreign producers. In fact, all the land rendered idle by US government price support programs has been returned to cultivation in light of the world shortage of many foodstuffs during 1973-74 and consequent rising prices.

Another major influence on US trade policy is that exerted by organized business. The US Chamber of Commerce and National Association of Manufacturers have already been mentioned as important national bodies. The International Chamber of Commerce and the Committee for Economic Development rank on the same level. Another important organization has been the Emergency Committee for American Trade. It was established by several leading multinational corporations to work against the protectionist Mills Bill in 1970. Although a wide variety of attitudes toward trade policy may be found among US business, support for internationalism rather than protectionism has prevailed over time. This has been true in particular for firms with important business interests outside the United States. In recent years, however, there have been some key exceptions to this attitude within US industries. For example, the textile and shoe industries and certain lines of the electronics industry have turned sharply protectionist in the face of exceptionally strong competition from producers overseas.

Consumers of all income brackets have a great stake in liberal trade policy, since protectionist measures can only have a detrimental effect on prices and on the range of choices available. Yet, consumer groups have not exerted any major influence on national trade policy. Consumer action groups have made progress on issues of domestic importance. But either the consumer movement is too diffuse in its present state, or trade policy remains too broad, or perhaps it is not easily dramatized, for consumerism has a long way to go in realizing its potential impact on trade policy.

The US Congress is influenced by private interest groups as described above, and of course it is also influenced by the executive branch, which has traditionally proposed trade legislation. The view of the executive branch has been that decision-making authority rests with the president and with principal members of his staff. Some interesting work done recently by I.M. Destler suggests that the officials and particular organizational structures within the executive branch which have access to, and influence on, the president have an important bearing on the tone of decision-making in trade policy.[6] If the principals involved have responsibility for foreign economic policy alone, they will tend to give different counsel than other principals who hold political, national security, and foreign policy responsibilities. In the Nixon administration, it seemed that the latter group of advisors often played an important if not always decisive role in the determination of foreign economic policy.

In respect of the Congress itself, it must be recognized that it is not only influenced by various interests in its national decision-making tasks, but also is to some extent an independent force with a very important say on the general direction of trade policy and on many of the details of any legislation. In the past, Congress has indeed played a key role in the formulation of trade policy. One clear implication of the Trade Reform Act proposed by President Nixon in 1973, discussed at greater length below, was that some of the authority and influence on US trade policy would be relinquished by the Congress to the executive branch. In its deliberations, however, the Congress made clear on different occasions and through various modifications in the language of the trade bill that it was not about to bestow unlimited authority upon the executive branch in this important area. In fact, congressional authority and responsibility for reviewing and passing judgment on trade agreements entered into by the executive branch is greater in the current trade bill than it has been for many years.

Much of this tug of war between the Congress and the executive branch, at least as far as the trade bill was concerned, served a public relations purpose. The administration never expected to get from the Congress the kind of blanket authority it initially proposed; yet it was mutually understood that the administration would offer a bill tending toward the grandiose and then the House Committee on Ways and Means and the Senate Finance Committee would pare it down to proportions and authority more in keeping with past trade legislation. Such a scenario would satisfy the executive branch, since it would still get its trade bill and would have the authority to enter into the new round of trade negotiations; and it would satisfy the Congress, which would be able to state publicly it had been doing its job in tempering the zeal of the executive branch while at the same time providing the United States with a forward-looking, imaginative trade bill.


## Protectionist Forces Gather Momentum

Since passage of Trade Expansion Act of 1962, US trade policy has moved away from the liberal trade approach that generally was its most prominent characteristic for more than a quarter century. The shift was very much in evidence by 1968, when the Johnson administration submitted to the Congress a trade bill whose only strong liberal feature was its request for repeal of the American Selling Price system of customs valuation. The bill never got beyond the Ways and Means Committee. As a reflection of the protectionist trend within the executive branch, but perhaps more particularly a reflection of congressional and private pressures on it, a number of agreements of "voluntary restraint" by foreign suppliers were concluded. Examples included steel and meat imports at the end of the decade. And when it took office in 1969, the Nixon administration sought agreement with the Japanese government and other countries that would have imposed "voluntary restraints" on exportation of synthetic and woolen textiles to the United States.

In late 1969 the Nixon administration proposed its first piece of trade legislation to Congress. It offered improvements in existing laws according to which industries might obtain relief from injurious import competition; it relaxed the criteria already contained in the Trade Expansion Act for providing adjustment assistance to individual firms and workers; it provided the president with new but limited authority to negotiate new trade agreements and to reduce tariffs; it proposed elimination of the American Selling Price system of customs valuation (a US nontariff barrier according to which the value of imports for tariff purposes is set by the price of competitive American products rather than the price of the foreign product); it expanded the authority of the president to impose duties or other restrictions on products exported by a country that placed "unjustifiable" restrictions on US exports; it provided for the establishment of Domestic International Sales Corporations (DISC) in order to encourage (by means of an income tax deferral) domestic companies to establish export subsidiaries abroad; it called for acceptance of mandatory quotas on textiles because of unsuccessful efforts (with Japan) in negotiating a system of voluntary restraints which would have provided for more orderly expansion of synthetic and woolen textile imports.

On November 19, 1969, the bill, which had then become known as the Mills bill, was adopted by the House. It contained several provisions proposed and endorsed by the administration, but it also contained important provisions to which the executive branch was opposed: quotas on footwear and tariff quotas on mink skins and glycine; major relaxation of standards for escape-clause relief, plus new criteria that reduced presidential discretion in providing remedies in escape-clause cases; and restriction of presidential discretionary authority to regulate imports under the national security provisions of the Trade Expansion Act. At the end of November, the Senate Finance Committee reported out a bill containing several more protectionist features unacceptable to the administration. However, no further action was taken by the Senate, and the Mills bill, clearly protectionist both in form as well as substance, died when the Ninety-First Congress adjourned.

The next major piece of trade legislation proposed was the Foreign Trade and Investment Act of 1972, sponsored by Representative James A. Burke of Massachusetts and Senator Vance Hartke of Indiana.[7] It was a bill introduced against the backdrop of seriously worsening US trade with the world and continuing erosion of confidence in the dollar.[8]

Proponents of the Burke-Hartke bill thought they had the solution to these ongoing and alarming developments concerning US trade and the international competitive position. Their objective was to curtail imports, since in their view imports undermined jobs and incomes of American workers employed in import-competing industries, threatened the profitability of firms in those same industries, and drained dollars out of the United States. The bill proposed regulation of multinational corporations in respect of their exports of US technology and capital; it suggested removing tax considerations or such incentives that encouraged US companies to set up foreign subsidiary operations; it called for mandatory import quotas on a wide range of manufactured products whenever an industry could claim to be hurt by excessive foreign competition. The bill had the aggressive support of George Meany, president of the American Federation of Labor-Congress of Industrial Organizations, and leaders of certain large industries with political influence.

The Burke-Hartke bill, opposed from the outset by the Nixon administration, had to be taken seriously because of the surprising amount of support awaiting it in Congress if it ever got out of the Ways and Means Committee. Such support was indicative of how far protectionism had advanced in the United States in recent years. For some, the bill appeared to be the most restrictive trade legislation introduced since the Embargo Act of 1807; certainly it was the most protectionist trade bill since the Smoot-Hawley Tariff Act of 1931. According to one authoritative estimate, the welfare costs, that is, in terms of income foregone, of the Burke-Hartke bill would have come to an amount somewhere between $6.9 billion and $10.4 billion.[9] Clearly, the time was ripe for a major counteroffensive by the Nixon administration, since it was not prepared to let the new protectionist movement develop into a logrolling process, as had happened forty years earlier in the case of the Smoot-Hawley Act, with disastrous consequences for US foreign economic policy.

## Laying the Groundwork for New Trade Legislation and the MTN

The Burke-Hartke bill should have been sufficient cause in itself for the Nixon administration to propose its own more forward looking trade program. In actual fact, however, a more complicated movement was afoot, and the administration's trade bill, submitted to Congress in April 1973, was only one part of a larger effort that embraced the whole range of foreign economic policy making. A series of events in 1971-72 revealed how comprehensive in scope the administration's intentions were in respect of reshaping the international economic and financial system.

In May 1970 the president appointed a Commission on International Trade and Investment Policy, better known as the Williams Commission after its chairman, Albert L. Williams of IBM. The president requested the commission to study the major problems facing the United States in the fields of foreign trade and investment in order to assess prevailing US policies, and to make recommendations for the 1970s which would take into full account changes that had taken place in the world economy since World War II. The commission's report recommended a program of measures, both immediate and long term, to be undertaken in trade, monetary, investment, and environmental policy areas, with special focus on those policies dealing with the European Community, Japan, Canada, less developed countries, and Communist countries.[10] On the international front, it was recommended that negotiations begin in order to prepare for elimination of all barriers to international trade and capital movements within twenty-five years through a joint initiative by the United States, Western Europe, and Japan.[11]

As the Williams Commission was still preparing its report, the president established under his chairmanship a new Council on International Economic Policy.[12] This was an administrative step designed to improve and better coordinate the machinery in the field of international economic policy. The belief was that foreign economic policy in the 1970s would require new and different approaches to better reflect the interrelationships between trade, monetary, investment, and other areas of international economic relations. The purposes of the council were ones everyone could applaud:

1. to achieve consistency between domestic and foreign economic policy;
2. to provide a clear top-level focus for the full range of international economic policy issues; deal with international economic policies—including trade, investment, balance of payments, finance—as a coherent whole; and consider the international economic aspects of essentially foreign policy issues, such as foreign aid and defense, under the general policy guidance of the National Security Council; and
3. to maintain close coordination with basic foreign policy objectives.

CIEP as the council quickly became known, could thus be regarded as an important rallying point for both the high-minded and the practical. By keeping a focus on other US international economic interests as well as those interests of a particular industry or firm, it was hoped that the task of preventing trade policy from veering too far in either a protectionist or liberal direction would prove both easier and more successful. In that endeavor, CIEP was to play a major role in framing the administration's Trade Reform Act, which was sent to Congress in April 1973.

By its actions during 1970-73, the Nixon administration demonstrated it was moving forward, attempting to launch multilateral negotiations in matters concerning international trade on the one hand and on the international monetary system on the other. It had become increasingly clear that major changes in the rules and procedures governing the international monetary system were necessary, and that the existing machinery was simply inadequate to prevent large and persistent payments imbalances from arising.

The administration's initial act to set in motion a thorough reform of the international economic system concerned a set of bold initiatives introduced by President Nixon on August 15, 1971. The two principal measures in the international phase of the president's program were suspension of the convertibility of the dollar into gold, a key pillar of the Bretton Woods international monetary system, and a surcharge of 10 percent on dutiable imports into the United States. Those and other measures taken at that time led to prompt initiation of international negotiations among the major industrial countries. Although the immediate interest concerned a general realignment of exchange rates, the United States made clear its views from the outset that improvements in the monetary system were closely linked to reform in the international trade system.

On December 18, 1971, the Group of Ten concluded the Smithsonian Accord, which provided for a realignment of exchange rates for the leading currencies and an increase in the dollar price of gold. Before the Smithsonian Accord was formally endorsed by the Congress, a matter necessary in order to change the official US gold price, intensive trade negotiations were under way with Canada, Japan, and the European Community for the purpose of reducing or eliminating a number of specific barriers to US exports.

As important as it was in dealing with certain of the most pressing international financial problems, the Smithsonian Agreement was not a definitive solution to the problem of international monetary reform. The agreement, however, did set the stage for subsequent negotiations on broader reform issues encompassing trade as well as monetary relations.

Monetary reform negotiations were the first to be launched, and this was done within the Committee of Twenty under the aegis of the International Monetary Fund in July 1972. A package of reform proposals was put forth at the 1972 annual meeting of the IMF-IBRD by President Nixon and Treasury Secretary Shultz. Among other things, the US proposals again stressed the interrelationships between monetary arrangements, trade, investment, and economic assistance. It was agreed that monetary reform negotiations would be supplemented by other negotiations to achieve greater equity and uniformity concerning the use of subsidies and fiscal or administrative pressures on trade and investment transactions.

Multilateral trade negotiations received their initial impetus from joint US-EC and US-Japan declarations in February 1972, just after the Smithsonian Accord. In those declarations, it was recognized that a comprehensive review of international economic relations was needed and that substantive improvements were necessary in light of structural changes that had occurred in the world economy in the past quarter century. The review was to include all facets of international trade, and especially those measures that tended to impede or distort trade in agricultural, raw materials, and industrial products. It was agreed, too, that special attention should be accorded to problems of less developed countries. In addition, the signatories to the above declarations undertook to initiate and actively support comprehensive multilateral negotiations under the auspices of the GATT, beginning in 1973. Further, it was agreed that such negotiations should be conducted on the basis of mutual advantage and mutual commitment, with over-all reciprocity as the guiding theme. The negotiations were intended to be as comprehensive as possible, both in respect of inclusion of countries and also coverage of agricultural and industrial products.

Other industrial countries recorded their support for multilateral trade negotiations in March of 1972, and by the time the annual GATT session was held in November, many more countries had confirmed their affirmative stance that negotiations begin in 1973. Those intentions were realized at a ministerial meeting in Tokyo on September 14, 1973, at which over one hundred countries joined in declaring the negotiations officially open. The objectives agreed upon at the Toky meetings were to

... achieve the expansion and even greater liberalization of world trade ... through the progressive dismantling of obstacles to trade and the improvement of the international framework for the conduct of world trade; and ... secure additional benefits for the international trade of developing countries.[13]

A critical prerequisite for meaningful trade negotiations is that representatives of participating countries be given necessary authority by their governments to enter into negotiations, and that in some cases national legislatures provide the designated trade negotiators with sufficient bargaining authority as a clear gesture that substantive negotiations leading ultimately to agreements will stand a good chance of being upheld in the ratification stage. This internal authorization is especially important for the United States, where traditionally the Congress has first approved legislation that gives the president a mandate to bargain with US trading partners and enter into agreements within broadly defined limits as set forth in the legislation itself. In view of that tradition, the president asked Congress to enact new and comprehensive trade legislation in April 1973. His proposals were based on deliberations within government and on discussions with the private sector.

## The Nixon Administration's Trade Reform Act

On April 10, 1973, President Nixon sent to Congress a comprehensive trade bill designed to give him sweeping authority to raise and to lower US tariffs and other trade barriers. The Trade Reform Act of 1973, as it was named initially, was designed to give US negotiators the necessary tools with which to enter into negotiations and reach agreements with other trading nations, and also to modify domestic laws in order that they might better reflect the new realities in the international economic world. On the surface, the trade bill was to be sold on the traditional grounds that enhanced trade liberalization would serve economic growth and well-being in the United States. But the real purposes and issues in the bill were more complex, and they reflected some of the new realities and transitions occurring in international trade policy.

The Trade Reform Act as proposed by the president had five major purposes. The *first* was to give the president the necessary authority to negotiate a more open trading world which would benefit the economic well-being of the United States. This authority either to reduce or raise tariffs as part of a negotiated package was to last for five years from the date of enactment of the bill. Any tariff changes could result only after specific studies had been performed by the Tariff Commission, and in any case, changes were to be phased in over a period of five years or longer. In respect of nontariff barriers, President Nixon requested a mandate from the Congress permitting him to negotiate changes in the nontariff barriers deemed to be in the US interest; and concerning certain well-identified customs barriers, such as methods of customs valuation and marking requirements, the president asked for advance authority to negotiate agreements providing for their reciprocal reduction. In addition, a new optional procedure was requested to deal with the agreements to change nontariff barriers. Under the procedure, ninety days prior to entering into an agreement to change a nontariff barrier, it would be put before the Congress for any reaction they might wish to make. Then, for ninety days after the agreement had taken effect, either body of Congress could veto the particular change in the nontariff barrier by a simple majority vote.

A *second* major purpose of the trade bill was to achieve a more equitable environment for American goods to compete fairly with foreign-made substitutes at home and abroad. Concerning competition abroad, the trade bill requested authority to permit retaliation against unjustifiable and unreasonable barriers to US goods or against such practices and policies of foreign countries that inhibited the sale of US goods abroad. As for assuring fair competition domestically, the president requested that the countervailing duty and anti-dumping laws be strengthened. Countervailing duty action by the Treasury

Department would have to be completed within twelve months, and authority to countervail would be expanded to include nondutiable goods.

The *third* major purpose of the trade bill was to provide more liberal import relief in the case of serious injury to domestic producers and easier adjustment assistance to workers affected by changes in tariffs and other barriers. The bill would allow the president to extend import relief for a maximum of five years where injury from increased imports was found to be the primary cause of a firm's difficulties. A market disruption formula also proposed was designed to offer prima facie evidence that injury did indeed come from imports. For workers who lost their jobs because of imports, a new unemployment and pension system was proposed. Also, permanent authority was requested to provide for job training and job relocation allowances.

The *fourth* purpose of the trade bill was to enable the United States to respond better and more quickly to imbalances in the international economic system and economic imbalances at home. In order to help deal with balance of payments imbalances, the president proposed that he be empowered to raise or reduce trade barriers both across the board and selectively with respect to countries. A second request was for authority to effect temporary reductions in tariff barriers as a means to counteracting domestic inflation. Third, the president requested greater latitude in the management of the US trade program to allow him to make full use of alternative courses of action as provided under the General Agreement on Tariffs and Trade. GATT rules permitted certain responses by member countries to commercial policy measures of other countries, but US domestic law did not allow them. Additionally, limited authority was requested to enable the president to negotiate trade agreements after the initial five-year period had elapsed. The idea was that agreements beneficial to US interests might be negotiable at any time and that, accordingly, the president should have some authority to bring them to fruition.

The *fifth* major purpose of the Trade Reform Act was to expand US trade opportunities. Specifically, the president requested authority to put into effect generalized preferences for less developed countries. Preferential tariff treatment would apply largely to manufactured and semimanufactured goods, although some agricultural goods might be included as well. It was suggested that generalized preferences be limited in duration to ten years, and that other constraints in addition to a list of products excluded from GSP be imposed. For example, the administration proposed that generalized preferences not be offered to any country that continued to grant preferences in their own markets to major developed countries that were competitors of the United States.

A major initiative concerning expansion of US trade opportunities had to do with the request to grant most-favored-nation authority to Communist countries. The request asked that veto power be accorded either body of Congress for ninety days after such agreements were concluded. In a related action, the administration also proposed certain changes be made in the Webb-Pomerance

Act to allow associations of exporters to act in concert with one another when bidding on major foreign proposals, without their running the risk of antitrust action. The purpose of this proposal was to remove an important constraint so that US exporters might compete more equally with their largest international competitors.

The Trade Reform Act was passed first by the House of Representatives in December 1973 and then by the Senate just twelve months later. After a conference of House-Senate members to resolve differences in the two versions, the amended bill, then known as the Trade Act of 1974, was passed by the Congress on December 19, 1974. Finally, on January 3, 1975, President Ford signed the Trade Act into law.[14]

The balance of this chapter deals with some of the most important features of the trade bill.

### Extending MFN Treatment to Communist Countries

There has been no greater issue for proponents of the administration's trade bill to surmount than the issue of trade relations with countries not enjoying nondiscriminatory treatment, i.e., the Communist countries. Here was an issue that other industrial countries had already put behind them, and it was simply a matter of the United States recognizing one of the new realities of the international trade order, dropping its outmoded policies of the Cold War era, and extending most-favored-nation treatment in principle to Communist nations. But while the United States was belatedly gearing itself for legislative action that would quite possibly have a substantial impact on future US trade relations, the issue of Soviet emigration policies toward its minority groups was interjected into the midst of the congressional debate.

For many months certain key members of the House and Senate insisted that the United States offer of MFN treatment hinge on Russia's relaxation of its emigration laws. Indeed, the House version of the trade bill contained specific provisions relating to emigration procedures that had to be met before the president could grant MFN treatment to that country. The House also required the president to make periodic determinations that the provisions were being adhered to and to request renewal of MFN every three years for countries receiving nondiscriminatory treatment under those provisions. Until the closing months of 1974, it appeared that the intransigence of the Congress and the unwillingness of the administration to concede to such conditions would, in fact, lead either to no trade bill at all or to a presidential veto if a trade bill with such provisions were passed by the Congress.

This burning issue acquired a new complexion when Gerald Ford assumed the office of president in August 1974. Mr. Ford immediately and forcefully stressed the importance of passing the trade bill before year's end and of seeing to it that multilateral trade negotiations got underway thereafter as promptly as possible. Accordingly, and as a direct result of the efforts put forth by President Ford and Secretary of State Henry Kissinger, a compromise solution was worked out involving Russian negotiators, the Congress, and the administration. In the end, some concessions by the Russian authorities on their strict emigration policies persuaded the Congress to grant the president somewhat greater discretion in according MFN treatment to the Soviet Union or to other nations that limit the right of their citizens to emigrate.

For US trade policy and for international trade policy in general, it is of major importance that a compromise be achieved and that the United States advance to a position where it can negotiate trade concessions in the form of MFN tariff treatment and trade credits with Russia and with other Communist countries. There is concern, however, that the compromise solution may reserve authority to the Congress to countermand at some later date trade concessions exchanged between the president and the authorities of leading Communist countries. Thus, until the implications of the compromise become more clear, negotiators on both sides are likely to move cautiously, and certainly investors and business interests in the United States and other countries concerned will await further clarification of US policy and the intentions of the Congress before making any major commitments.

The significance of US willingness to negotiate trade concessions with Communist countries must not be missed, for this is a substantive change in US trade policies that have prevailed since the end of World War II. Ultimately, it could lead to the development of Russia's untapped reserves of oil and gas and other natural resources; it could open up new markets for US products, including possibly a wide range of consumers goods and more certainly a large number of products in the category of industrial plant and machinery; it could mean alternative sources of US imports of competitively priced manufactured products, which would help combat present domestic and international inflationary trends. In short, extending MFN treatment to Communist countries is a first step toward opening up an important potential for international exchange that promises substantial benefits to all parties concerned.

**Relief from Import Competition: Adjustment
Assistance vs. Escape-Clause Relief**

As recounted in Chapter 2, the adjustment assistance provisions to workers and firms injured by import competition under the Trade Expansion Act were more symbolic than functional. The eligibility criteria were too strict, there were serious flaws in the administration of the program, and the level of benefits was inadequate. To the dismay of organized labor, the Trade Reform Act as originally introduced by President Nixon would actually have weakened the existing adjustment assistance measures. The eligibility criteria were indeed relaxed, but the duration and level of benefits were measurably reduced. According to observers, the administration was placing heavy emphasis on escape-clause measures, on antidumping and countervailing duties to provide import relief.[15]

Both the House and the Senate made extensive changes in the administration's trade bill as it pertained to relief from injury caused by import competition. Those changes had the effect of making adjustment assistance, rather than escape-clause relief, play the major defensive role. In essence, Congress tightened access to escape-clause relief to make it more like the terms prevailing under the 1962 act, and it made the duration and levels of benefit under adjustment assistance equal to, if not slightly better than, those prevailing under the previous legislation. The adjustment assistance program for firms, which the Nixon administration had proposed to eliminate, was restored, and the eligibility criteria were substantially relaxed.[16] Guy Erb and Charles Frank have estimated that the House version of adjustment assistance—including readjustment for some 35,000 workers, other benefits such as training, placement, relocation, health, and assistance to firms—would cost about $150 million per year. If their figures are accurate, then the adjustment assistance program in the trade bill will be both inexpensive and therefore not very helpful in relieving adjustment problems that are bound to arise in the course of the next several years. A more adequate adjustment assistance program might cost on the order of $350 million per year.[17]

All in all, the Trade Act of 1974 does provide for a rather more enlightened adjustment assistance program than the program contained in any previous legislation. And while many believed Congress should have gone substantially further than it did in this area,[18] the provisions of the bill do signal another transition in US trade policy—a slow but significant move away from escape-clause relief toward greater reliance on adjustment assistance.

The more comprehensive the adjustment assistance programs, the more the United States can afford an open trade policy and the greater will be the gains from trade for the country as a whole. Resort to escape-clause relief is costly to American consumers; it and other restrictive trade practices cost American consumers billions of dollars per year, according to Erb and Frank. It also wipes out trade benefits for other trading countries, since it is their exports that are prevented from entering US markets. Adjustment assistance, on the other hand, permits gains to both the domestic economy and foreign economies to be realized, while providing for relief at the origin of the problem for workers or firms adversely affected by the superior competition of imports.

## Generalized Tariff Preferences

The Trade Act of 1974 provides for a scheme of generalized tariff preferences. This provision, which makes good on a commitment made by President Johnson in 1967 to consider trade preferences for LDCs, allows the United States to join the eighteen other industrial countries that have already made tariff preferences available.

As has been true for the preference schemes of other nations, the US GSP is limited by various provisions that water down its potential benefits. Eligible products are mainly those in the manufactured categories; with some exceptions, primary products and semiprocessed agricultural items will not be included, and there will be a list of exceptions for particular manufactured products deemed sensitive. Another limitation pertaining to competitive need is that GSP will not be extended to a country that supplies more than half of all US imports of an eligible item, or more than a total absolute amount of $25 million in any given year. Furthermore, the president, under the terms of the legislation, may withdraw, suspend, or limit preferences with only sixty days prior notice. The US preference scheme has a time limit of ten years.

Based on the House version of the trade bill and the GSP included therein, Erb and Frank have compiled some estimates of the potential impact on US imports.[19] These estimates, however, like other estimates of trade effects resulting from tariff preferences, are static and take no account of possible dynamic effects that some observers contend to be the most important consideration of all. In 1971, US imports from LDCs amounted to $11.5 billion, and of that total, $7.1 billion were dutiable and hence potentially eligible for inclusion in GSP. But taking into consideration the various commodities and products that are excluded, the total import value of remaining items comes to $2.8 billion, or approximately 40 percent of dutiable imports from LDCs. If exclusions of items under the competitive need criteria are excluded, then the total eligible imports from LDCs is reduced to about $1.1 billion, or about 10 percent of all US imports from LDCs.[20] Other provisions of GSP could limit still further the total of US imports subject to GSP. (For example, some countries could be declared ineligible because they might refuse to give up their reverse preference agreements.) These calculations suggest that the US GSP scheme is in line with what other countries have made available to LDCs in the form of their own preference schemes.

Although the scope of the US preference scheme is limited, other effects resulting from preferential access to US markets may lead to a substantial increase in imports. One aspect of this question has been addressed by various experts; some of the estimates prepared by Christopher Clague and others by Tracy Murray were discussed in Chapter 4. Other estimates have been compiled by the US Tariff Commission[21] and by the State Department.[22] All of these projections are rather close in their estimates of trade effects, even though the assumptions and methodologies vary. The results suggest that the impact of the US preference scheme will be to increase imports of eligible commodities within a range of 30 to 50 percent. Some of the additional imports will be at the expense of other countries ineligible for GSP; in other words, there will be a trade diversion effect perhaps amounting to one-half of the total increase; another portion of the new imports will occur at the expense of domestic production. The US Tariff Commission study estimates that this latter amount may be about one-sixth of the total.

The problem with all these studies is that they take as given existing demand and supply functions. The contention of tariff preference advocates is that international investment, prompted by an improved generalized scheme of preferences, would structurally shift the supply schedules for eligible products produced in LDCs. Thus, the ability of beneficiary countries to satisfy potential demand in the developed countries could increase several times over in the course of a few years. Similarly, with respect to the donor countries' demand functions for eligible products, factors in addition to price could cause an upward shift to occur in their demand for imports and this would widen still further LDCs' markets in those countries.

All in all, however, the available projections based on static or comparative static analysis imply that the impact of preferences on US trade flows, on the present pattern of US production, and on improving LDCs' access to US markets will be marginal. Thus, the widely held impression that generalized preferences more than anything else are a symbolic gesture to LDCs' is unlikely to be disturbed as a consequence of the US scheme.

But perhaps the major reasons why preferences as a mechanism for improving LDCs' international trade shares and world trade positions will never amount to very much include the following: First, the United States and other preference-giving countries are unlikely to broaden the product coverage of their schemes to include categories of goods attractive or potentially attractive to LDC production. Second, the same countries are unlikely to loosen, let alone abolish, the quantitative limits or escape-clause provisions that severely contain imports of eligible items from expanding rapidly. Third, preferences have not, and are not likely to be, made permanent features of developed countries' trade policies, a step that would almost have to be made in order for investors and entrepreneurs to go into LDCs and commit their capital, their time, and their technology and establish a significant production base for eligible products. Neither the US scheme of preferences nor any foreseeable changes in those existing schemes of the nations are likely to shed new light on this issue of the potential dynamic forces underlying tariff preferences.

## Provisions Relating to Short-Supply Problems

Once the trade reform bill had been passed by the House of Representatives in December 1973 and as it came before the Senate Finance Committee in March 1974, the issue of access to supplies of internationally traded commodities had become as important a focal point of attention as the more traditional issue of access to overseas markets. Major questions of scarcity arose in 1973 and early 1974, especially in the areas of fuels, basic raw materials, and foodstuffs. (The House version of the trade bill offered very little guidance or suggestion as to how the president should proceed in trade negotiations that might relate to short-supply issues, since representatives working on the bill had completed the bulk of their task before the international oil crisis commenced in late 1973.)

The arrival of these new problems and issues on the scene, if they had to come, was well timed as far as US interests were concerned. There was still plenty of chance for the Congress and the administration to work together to reorient the trade bill in order that it might better reflect the new realities. Indeed, there was an excellent opportunity at hand to add new provisions or to modify already existing language in the House version that would direct the president to deal with scarcity problems in the forthcoming multilateral trade negotiations.

On behalf of the administration, the president's special trade representative, William D. Eberle, proposed modifications in the House trade bill that were designed to reflect the new concerns. In particular, it was requested that the Congress empower the president with authority to retaliate against countries that might impose "illegal or unreasonable" restraints on their exports to the United States. Retaliation was to consist of withheld trade concessions that would otherwise give US foreign competitors easier access to US markets. Ambassador Eberle also proposed certain changes in the negotiating authority that pertained to nontariff barriers, for export restraints could just as easily be applied in the form of quotas, for example, as in the form of duties imposed on exports. Third, the administration sought a mandate from the Congress to negotiate a new set of rules that would provide for nondiscriminatory export sales and equitable access to foreign supplies and that would also set up procedures or sanctions to be applied to countries not abiding by the new international codes.

Within the Congress, a series of amendments were offered by Senators Walter Mondale and Abraham Ribicoff and others. First, there were proposals for promoting negotiations on new international rules that would restrict the use of export controls. Other amendments would have provided the president with the necessary authority to help develop and participate in multilateral sanctions against export embargoes. Some of the suggestions in respect of retaliation were far-reaching indeed, in that they would have bestowed upon the president the authority to cut off economic and technical assistance, to suspend credits and investment guarantees, and to curtail foreign investment by US firms. Ultimately, however, the proposed amendments that provided for sweeping retaliation were not included in the trade bill.

Over all, the Trade Act of 1974 presents a balance between access to markets and access to supplies that has not been evident in previous trade legislation. A number of the act's provisions will take into account the various supply issues; but it is not possible to discern from the Trade Act itself whether the US emphasis in trade negotiations will be weighted in favor of supply problems or not. From the tone of comments from both the administration and from the Congress, it may be safely inferred that the United States will actively push for negotiations on supply matters as prescribed in the NTB negotiating authority, and that there will be serious efforts to try and work out with other nations some set of rules governing the use of export controls. Those endeavors will lend a counterbalance to negotiations concerned with access to markets issues, but they do not appear likely to detract from US efforts in respect to the latter.

The basic US statute on export controls remains the Export Administration Act of 1969, which was modified and extended in late 1974. It has provided the president with authority to control exports for reasons pertaining to foreign policy, national security, and domestic shortage. It has been invoked rarely and then for short periods of time. In the 1974 review, both the administration and the Congress considered various changes in the act; but in the end, the new law was basically an extension of its predecessor.

One set of changes ultimately adopted was offered by Senator Chiles. His approach paralleled the administration's proposals in the trade reform bill. Specifically, his amendments gave the United States authority to respond to injurious foreign export controls with controls of its own, and provided a clear expression of congressional support for negotiations either to strengthen existing rules and institutions responsible for problems of access to supplies, or to develop new ones. In a sense, these changes did move the Export Administration Act from essentially an instrument of domestic policy to one of foreign policy, and they reinforced the provisions being written into the trade bill.[23]

In the new Export Administration Act and in its deliberations on the trade bill, the Congress made clear its unwillingness to delegate sweeping authority to the president in respect of the use of export controls, or in respect of the United States becoming involved in negotiations that could lead to long-term commitments guaranteeing access to supplies at prices that might prove disadvantageous in the future. Instead, the Congress registered its support for a middle approach that would on the one hand authorize the president to respond to harmful export controls imposed by foreign countries, and at the same time would direct the president to improve and develop international rules pertaining to export controls. This middle approach also appears to be the one most generally favored within the administration.

These major features of the Trade Act of 1974 support the view that US trade policy in particular, along with international trade policy more generally, are in transition. New areas of US concern have opened up and have emerged as major issues for this country in the context of the forthcoming multilateral trade negotiations; in addition, some of the old areas of concern have been modified in light of recent circumstances or have faded from the forefront of attention.

The negotiating authority of the Trade Act, which gives the president a legislative mandate to enter into trade agreements for the next five years, together with the four features described briefly above, mean that the president has been given the necessary tools to make substantial progress in cooperation with other countries in resolving the major problems and issues now confronting the international trade order. The task will be most difficult and time-consuming; but if reasonable success is the result of those labors, then benefits lasting for years to come will duly reward all participating nations.

# 7 Some Remaining Issues of International Trade Policy

The agenda for the present multilateral trade negotiations is lengthy and complex. Even though bargaining sessions will continue for a considerable period of time, it is unlikely that all issues will receive sufficient attention or that the governments involved will be prepared to commit themselves to binding resolutions in each instance. Some of the current issues, therefore, will be carried over into the future, including the profound question of how international trade, investment, and monetary policies are to interact and help correct balance of payments maladjustments as they occur. This issue cannot be reckoned with until at least such time as a new monetary system can be agreed upon and fully implemented.

Accordingly, it must be expected that further negotiations on particular aspects of some current issues will be required at a later date. For example, it cannot be reasonably hoped that the imposing number of nontariff barriers already identified will be fully and completely laid to rest at this juncture. A significant start may well be made in the resolution of the more serious NTBs; and thereafter, the information gained from implementation and operation of those agreements will provide valuable insights into the alternative means of coping with such existing trade barriers. In a real sense, the current negotiations having to do with nontariff barriers will be breaking new ground. Similarly, progress in resolving the long-standing issues of agricultural trade will be a major step forward into an uncharted territory; yet a complete settlement of the many complex issues involved in that area cannot be reasonably hoped for at the present time, and further work will remain for future negotiations.

An important question that cannot be answered at this stage is whether the issue of access to foreign supply which has captured widespread interest will remain alive for the longer term. If it turns out to be essentially a short-run problem, then some agreement on the sorts of rules governing the use of export controls that have been proposed by various experts should go a long way toward relieving what is more of a potential than a realized difficulty for international trade policy. If the issue is more persistent, then other policy measures will have to be devised in order to augment world supplies.

Another issue virtually certain to remain active in the years ahead will be the evolving treatment of LDC access to markets of developed countries. Assuming further MFN tariff reductions are successfully negotiated in the current round, the generalized tariff preference schemes will have a diminishing effect as such tariff reductions are phased into operation. Thus, new measures must be evaluated as to their potential for increasing the pace of industrialization in LDCs and for facilitating the exportation of a growing share of future LDC production of manufactured goods to foreign markets.

For many years, the major interests of trade policy centered on improving access to foreign markets. It is entirely possible that those interests will reoccur in the not-too-distant future, but in a new context. Thus, as East-West trade increases in the years ahead, it is not unlikely that primary producers and producers of light manufactured products in Communist countries on the one hand, and their counterparts in LDCs on the other, will be competing directly with one another over the placement of their products in industrial countries' markets.

Olivier Long, the director general of GATT, once said that a person who does not advance moves backwards. This certainly applies to international trade policy, which is constantly faced with the challenge of moving forward to meet new issues in order to keep the liberalization movement on course. Some of those issues just touched upon above, which now appear likely to be among the difficult problems to be addressed in the future, are the subject of this chapter.

**Access to Foreign Markets:**
**Old Problem, New Context**

In the years ahead, expansion of trade between developed, market-oriented economies on the one hand and Communist countries in Eastern Europe and in Asia on the other offers a considerable potential benefit to all concerned. A strong possibility exists, however, that a number of the products and categories of products that will dominate the composition of Communist country exports to the West will overlap with many of the same products that less developed countries are now beginning to export on an increasing scale to industrial countries. This potential for future conflict could raise a host of new policy questions having to do with an old and familiar theme, access to markets—but in a new context. The manner in which those questions are resolved will have a direct bearing not only on the composition and direction of world trade but also on the evolving industrial structures in countries belonging to each of the three groups.

Extension of most-favored-nation treatment to exports of Communist countries has already been achieved by most developed countries in the West. With the likely addition of the United States to this long list now that passage of the Trade Act of 1974 has been secured, East European countries, and particularly those that are relatively more industrialized, stand to benefit from a substantial improvement in the categories and quantitites of goods that can be sold abroad, especially to the United States. In addition to the benefit of lower tariffs on those goods, for which there exist relatively high elasticities of demand and supply, there will also be significant political and psychological benefits represented by MFN treatment. Planners in East European countries and elsewhere will be increasingly willing to bear the high costs associated with entry into the US market in order to sell a widening range of manufactured products. Considerable importance is placed, therefore, on the dynamic effects of good-will as a result of the shortly expected US action and earlier steps taken by other Western countries, all of which constitute an essential precondition to changes in existing trade patterns.[1]

The extent and speed with which East European countries will be able to increase their exports of manufactured products to the West, and particularly to the United States, is difficult to predict at the present time. They may enjoy very considerable success for reasons just enumerated. On the other hand, other existing problems will have to be successfully overcome, including past reputations for poor quality, unreliability, lack of servicing, and poor packaging of products. Much more effort will need to be spent in order to assure that products are modern and kept up to date with substitutes produced in the West and in less developed countries; and a major advertising and distribution offensive will be required just to break into the US and other Western markets on a significant scale.

Although there were clear signals from the Soviet Union during the months of debate in the Congress over the Trade Act[2] that provision of MFN treatment was indeed an important political and economic prerequisite for further brightening East-West trade prospects, it may well be that the past absence of MFN has not seriously impeded Russian exports to the United States. To the extent Soviet exports were discriminated against, it is judged to be substantially less than in the case of East European exports.[3] Indeed, manufactured and semimanufactured products are not categories likely to figure importantly in the composition of future Russian exports. Instead, exports to the United States, Europe, and Japan are likely to consist to a very large extent of oil and gas and other raw materials.[4]

With the United States not granting most-favored-nation treatment to the Peoples' Republic of China, no doubt some diversion of trade occurred toward West European nations and Great Britain, all of which were moving to extend MFN status to China and other Communist nations during the latter 1960s. The extent of the diversion, however, is not estimated to have been large in the sense that it would have had a significant impact on the US market or on the US-PRC trade balance in 1973.[5] But here again, the symbolic significance of MFN—to say nothing of the possible dynamic economic effects that are difficult to project with accuracy—may or may not be of important political and psychological significance for future levels of trade. Despite the difficulty in assessing such factors, with the US MFN barrier to PRC imports now likely to be removed, and assuming any other remaining discriminatory obstacles to trade between the PRC and the West are also removed soon, what changes in quantity and composition of PRC exports may be anticipated in the years ahead?

Projections compiled by Eckstein and Reynolds suggest that some portion of exports now flowing to Western Europe will flow instead to the US market.[6] Even so, the level of US imports from the PRC is expected to be just below $400 million in 1980 (compared to $50 million in 1973), which would mean an export-import ratio in the favor of the United States of 4:1 or 5:1. Eckstein and Reynolds look forward to a greater share of China's exports being comprised of manufactured goods, perhaps 30 percent or so by the end of the 1970s, but the share of raw materials and commodities is expected to remain close to 50 percent.

A major unknown factor at this time concerns China's crude-oil resources and her ability and willingness to become a large-scale exporter over the course of the next several years. To the extent this possibility materializes, Eckstein and Reynolds regard Japan as an important recipient, although quite possibly the United States might also be in that category. Thus, the complexion of China's trade in the future is likely to bear a considerable resemblance to recent trade trends, unless she becomes an important exporter of oil and oil products.

The opening up of East-West trade is likely to pose some interesting problems in the future. One potentially difficult and troublesome problem concerns the rising competition between Communist nations and less developed countries for industrial countries' markets.[7] On the one hand, the more industrialized Communist countries of Eastern Europe are in a position to offer a challenge to producers and suppliers of semimanufactured and manufactured products in LDCs who themselves are now attempting to make significant inroads in Western markets with the assistance of generalized tariff preference schemes. But with the further reduction in MFN tariff duties hoped for in the current multilateral trade negotiations, the marginal benefit accorded LDCs under GSP will be diminished, while the degree of competition they face will have been enhanced.

These prospects could pose problems for developed countries on two points. First, a question may arise as to whether a portion of their import markets in the manufactured goods areas ought to be allocated to LDCs and to Communist countries according to some set of noneconomic criteria in order to help assure them all of a means of future expansion in export earnings. An important consideration here for developed countries would be the extent to which such concessions on their part would increase access of their producers and exporters to LDC and Communist country markets. Second (and related to this first question), the enlarged and growing potential supply of light manufactured products from countries outside the industrialized West is sure to bring increased political pressure on governments to implement economic policies that will help effect faster, yet orderly structural transition of their domestic industry. This will call forth expansion of adjustment assistance programs and diminished resort to escape-clause measures as the declining industries of the West are consciously phased out rather than protected still further from foreign competition.

Turning to another facet of future East-West trade, production and export of raw materials and fuels by Communist countries could offer significant additional sources of needed supplies to industrialized nations. Should this potential materialize, then sufficient price competition might result in various commodity and fuel categories between LDC producers and Communist producers in their competition for foreign markets so that the threat of cartel-type activities to extract a monopoly surcharge and pressing problems of short supply would be thwarted. Although these possibilities cannot be forecast with any certainty, the fact that they do exist means that there may be fairer weather on the horizon in respect of future prices and quantities of world trade in certain basic commodities and fuels.

## Short-Supply Problems in the Long Run

Unlike the case of import controls in an earlier period, no great legacy remains to future trade negotiations in the area of export controls. Export controls have not become at all widespread. On the other hand, import controls had become so prolific by the early 1930s that their systematic removal was looked upon as prerequisite to any significant widening in the scope of international trade. The current interest centers on the negotiation of new rules to regulate or to prevent future use of export controls, not on finding ways to liberalize existing controls, although that would no doubt follow in the future for those comparatively few export controls that proved to be a source of serious trade disruption.

Present short-supply problems and some of their proposed remedies, however, do entail important implications for the long term. Along with the negotiation of rules to govern export controls, it has been argued that comprehensive agreements should be negotiated for the purpose of assuring future access to foreign supplies. Such agreements might include or be based upon various international commodity agreements.[8] The argument is that the problem of winning assurances of supply transcends rules limiting the use of export controls and goes directly to controls over domestic production. It is maintained that commodity agreements can provide assurances that such domestic production controls will not be employed to create or exacerbate international short supply situations in the future. Whereas establishment of rules governing use of export controls is largely preventative and entails practically no negative long-term ramifications for international trade order, widespread resort to international commodity agreements, encompassing buffer stocks, production levels, and other arrangements to protect both the volume of trade and the prices of commodities traded, would mark an attempt to systematically manage on a long-run basis a large element of international trade.

The early negotiation of such commitments to such sources of commodity and raw materials supplies as now exist may later on prove to have been premature and unwise. Some of the great uncertainties born out of recent experiences of shortages and rising prices for fuels, basic commodities, and foodstuffs concern the response of the market mechanism in prompting development of alternative sources of supply and in stimulating research for new technology and discovery of competitive substitutes. Another major uncertainty, discussed in the preceding section of this chapter, has to do with the possible opening up of new sources of raw materials supply in Russia and in other Communist lands as East-West trade begins to flourish. If such developments do indeed create significant new commodity supplies, then there would be mounting pressures to abrogate binding, long-term commodity agreements negotiated at an earlier date; if that were to occur, it would provide a sure-fire basis for a new wave of resentment and ill-feeling on the part of primary-producing countries toward the rich industrial nations.

The considerable uncertainties as to the relative abundance or scarcity of future supplies of commodities, fuels, and raw materials argue in favor of a cautious attitude in the current multilateral trade negotiations concerning negotiations of any comprehensive, long-term commodity agreements. Some might argue that the presence of such agreements, and the price guarantees provided therein, might be necessary to evoke production and export of commodities from new sources. But the absence of such agreements may also be looked upon as a stimulus for the development of such new sources of supply as well as a retarding agent for countries currently supplying commodities and fuels which might contemplate domestic production controls in order to increase international prices still further.

On the one hand, increasing world population, long-run prospects for economic growth and trade, and the rising need for fuels, foodstuffs and basic commodities implied therein, offer major incentives for opening up and developing new sources of supply on a commercial basis. On the other hand, the exercise of domestic production controls, export controls, or other measures designed to substantially increase international prices of commodities supplied from existing sources can easily have detrimental impacts for primary-producing countries. In the case of bauxite, for example, substantially higher world prices will in all likelihood cause US clay mines to be developed in the Rocky Mountains and in Georgia as substitutes for bauxite imports. Eventually, bauxite-producing countries might be tempted to lower prices, and that could prompt the US Congress to resort to escape-clause action to protect its domestic producers. Thus, the bauxite-producing nations would be left worse off than before, with reduced access to foreign markets and with the consequent erosion of their ability to earn much-needed foreign exchange through exports.[9] Such examples as this can be multiplied for other commodities and for other countries that are presently actual or potential producers as well as consumers of such commodities in question.

What the present circumstances and prevailing uncertainties call for are caution, patience, and a wait-and-see attitude on the part of all countries. A rush to negotiate binding commodity agreements on the basis of what has transpired during the past two years could all too soon be overtaken by a different set of world demand and supply conditions that would threaten the relevance of those agreements and quite possibly would be the basis for a much higher level of discontent and ill-feeling between the current resource-rich and the resource-poor, the haves and the have-nots.

If, indeed, after a few years present conditions have not basically changed and new alternative supply sources are not sufficiently forthcoming, there will be time enough, and certainly a backlog of greater information and much less uncertainty about what the world demand-supply situations are with respect to fuels, raw materials and basic commodities, so that commodity agreements satisfactory to all parties can be negotiated. In the end, the mutual interdependence for both supplies and markets must be recognized and accepted. But the ultimate common objective of creating a stable world trading order will not be well served by precipitous negotiations designed to ensure a measure of stability on the basis of circumstances that are only beginning to unfold and cannot be fully evaluated at the present juncture.

Should problems of scarcity persist in the future on a high level, measures over and above commodity agreements would be required. There would need to be policies designed to augment world supply as well as those tailored to check wasteful world demand. Coordinated efforts between nations, involving new initiatives to develop substitute materials and products, and to achieve major new technological breakthroughs, would have to be developed. All in all, the extent of such commitments would go beyond anything yet considered, and there would be far-flung involvements not only in the area of international trade policy but also in the related areas of international finance and investment policies. For the present and near future, however, it will continue to be more difficult to perceive the nature of the short-supply issue beyond the current multilateral trade negotiations than to evaluate the importance and nature of some other trade policy issues.

## Trade Interests of Less Developed Countries

In the current round of multilateral trade negotiations, less developed countries stand together in pursuit of a variety of objectives, including prompt adoption by the United States of its generalized tariff preference scheme, expansion of generalized preference arrangements already in operation, and nonreciprocity in the reduction of trade barriers. While representatives of less developed countries are stressing the importance of generalized tariff preferences as the key policy measure by which they hope to gain greater access to developed country markets, and thereby improve their foreign exchange earnings in order to help finance their domestic economic development programs, it must be stressed that the potential benefits of tariff preferences can be looked upon as having little more than medium-term significance. (The term "potential" benefits from trade preferences is to be distinguished from "actual" benefits, the difference between the two resulting from the many restrictive characteristics of the existing preference schemes.) Accordingly, it is by no means too early to give increasingly active consideration to what course LDCs might pursue after generalized preferences.

The average level of tariff duties for industrial countries, after implementation of the reductions agreed to in the previous Kennedy Round, was about 9 percent. Should the current round of trade negotiations be successful in producing agreements to reduce tariffs on an MFN basis by a similar percentage amount, then the average tariff duties of the major countries after staged reductions spanning a few years time might be around the 5 percent level by 1980. In the process, the list of goods traded on a duty-free basis would be lengthened significantly, and the higher effective duties applicable to labor-intensive goods could be reduced quite substantially. Unless present efforts to focus on industrial tariffs and to achieve another round of reductions end in unexpected failure, the major potential benefits to be accrued from generalized tariff preferences will become history within five to ten years time.

The declining significance of generalized preferences as a direct consequence of further MFN tariff reductions should by no means give less developed countries cause for lament. Such concessions and the eventual elimination of tariff barriers to international trade will mark a very major achievement for all countries in the never-ending battle to overcome expedient, protectionist pressures of the present in order to bring a more economically efficient world economic order closer to realization. Such progress will be most important for the developing world as a whole, for MFN tariff concessions in the past have proven their durability. For producers, exporters, and investors in developing countries, further tariff reductions may prove to be of greater psychological importance than incentives offered currently under GSP, which are subject to modification or safeguard action on short notice.

After GSP, therefore, what measures are likely to assume foremost importance in LDC trade policy? The increasing disparity of economic development and well-being within the ranks of LDCs must be acknowledged in first addressing this question. At the same time, the growing attention that such disparity is currently being accorded suggests the emergence of two distinct trade policy themes: one for the least developed LDCs, a second for other LDCs, among which are included several that have been transmitting signs of having reached the "take off stage" of economic growth.[10]

The least developed countries are among those hit hardest by rising prices of imported oil, foodstuffs, and other basic commodities. Substantial bilateral and multilateral assistance on a grant basis or on concessional terms will be required over and above normal aid flows if these countries are to avert major financial collapse. For such countries and for the least developed countries in general, special trade measures that embrace the principles of nonreciprocity, nondiscrimination, and preferential treatment should be given serious consideration as one method of trying to come to grips with major economic problems that threaten their continued survival. Such unprecedented trade concessions should be conceived along side, and in conjunction with, more comprehensive economic assistance programs.

In effect, the regional multilateral development banks, the World Bank, the United Nations, UNCTAD, GATT, the International Monetary Fund, and the OECD will all need to be involved at one stage or another, in addition to representatives of the various national governments participating in providing trade concessions or other forms of aid. In many cases, nothing less than a wholesale effort will be required; and even then, some of the least developed countries may not survive as sovereign states but may have to revert to special political status with stronger neighbors or perhaps even become territories of other countries willing and able to assume some of the major economic burdens involved.

Special treatment for the least developed countries is gaining worldwide recognition as a necessity; but such treatment will have to be sold to other less developed countries, many of which do not yet accept the idea in principle or in fact. Thus, Latin American countries, which, with the single exception of Haiti, have no least developed countries as such in their region, have previously taken a hard line against special procedures for meeting the problems involved.

Other LDCs also face difficult times as a result of world inflation and rising import costs; yet in many instances, world prices of their major exports have been rising rapidly, and this factor has offset at least part of their balance of payments difficulties. Their outlook, taking into consideration the special lending facilities recently created within the International Monetary Fund, as well as other multilateral and bilateral sources of financial assistance, is substantially more optimistic than that for the least developed. For a number of these countries, significant economic growth in real terms, even after allowance for population increases, has become the rule rather than the exception in recent years. Some of their new industries that manufacture low-technology products are proving to be stiff competitors for their counterparts in Italy, Japan, and certain other developed countries. These LDCs cannot realistically expect to gain nonreciprocal, preferential trade concessions from developed countries in the years to come after the current round of trade negotiations; nevertheless, they might pursue a variety of policies in order to continue realizing their economic development ambitions.

Particularly for the group of LDCs that is relatively well off, national policies should be formulated with a view toward attracting foreign investors, entrepreneurs, and multinational corporations who might be considering establishment of manufacturing plants and business operations within their boundaries. In order to avoid excessive competition in this regard between LDCs, common rules and procedures should be established as much as possible, with negotiations taking place in an appropriate multilateral forum. LDCs should recognize it is in their best interests to work out guarantees with governments of developed countries regarding compensation in case of nationalization or expropriation and to establish adequate procedures to handle grievances of host country residents or host governments as well as of the foreign representatives doing business.

The potential for LDCs attracting direct investment from industrial countries is great in the long run if the precautions just touched upon can be met. Some of the specific attractions LDCs have to offer include low-cost labor, few if any problems of industrial overcrowding, such as exist in Japan, for example, fewer constraints in the area of environmental controls because of the lack of industrial concentration to date. Moreover, looking to the not so distant future when tariff barriers will have for the most part lost their meaning, impediments to exporting a substantial portion of the production from such new plants will be less than ever before. And that, of course, is another important benefit (in addition to increasing domestic employment) this course of action offers— i.e., another means of increasing foreign-exchange earnings.

If such efforts to systematically improve the environment for foreign investment in LDCs are to succeed, it is prerequisite almost that the recent confrontation atmosphere that has characterized some of the UNCTAD sessions become a thing of the past and that a more conciliatory attitude be adopted by all sides. This does not suggest that the spirit of competition, even strong competition, underlying tough negotiations be shelved. Greater cooperation will be necessary, however, to help establish confidence in the minds of potential investors and to enlist the needed support of industrial country governments in promoting substantially increased amounts of mainly private but also some public foreign investment in less developed countries.

## Multinational Corporations and International Trade Policy

At a time when international institutions bearing responsibility for the orderly conduct of trade and commercial policies have come under increasing criticism for their failure to deal with evolving circumstances, it is quite possible to look into the future and to perceive new conditions that will require those institutions to be modified and buttressed with new regulative authority. One such cause for this belief stems from the behavior and growth of multinational corporations on the world scene.

Thus far in their development, multinational corporations (MNCs) have appeared primarily in industries that are dominated by a few large firms and that are characterized by substantial barriers to entry.[11] Problems of competition policy connected with MNCs are those associated with oligopoly behavior, but for two important and distinguishing features. First, the leadership within the oligopoly includes firms that operate from different national bases. Second, the interaction of the leaders transcends national jurisdiction.[12]

During the postwar period, linkages between trade and investment increased for most developed nations. It was during the middle and latter half of the 1960s, in fact, that European concern arose regarding the increasing extent to which segments of their major growth industries as well as mature industries (for example, automobiles, petroleum, pulp and paper) were controlled and managed by US firms with far-flung business interests. Some European firms were prompted to pursue a strategy of counter penetration, and indeed, by 1971 about 125 manufacturing subsidiaries within the United States were reported to be controlled by multinational enterprises with headquarters in foreign countries. Japanese involvement in this sort of exercise has only just begun but seems likely to follow a similar path in the years ahead. A pattern has thus been established whereby many national oligopolies have been turning into multinational oligopolies.

In many respects, these new multinational oligopolies resemble their predecessors. According to Vernon, both have a "common capacity for mutual destruction, a common concern over new entrants, and a common need to find some form of cooperative behavior."[13] But when it comes to protecting themselves, the leaders of the new oligopolies can no longer simply agree to divide their markets according to some geographical division. Instead, they have sought to establish joint ventures with one another, to follow each other into new locales, and otherwise to establish a foothold in each other's major markets. These efforts provide opportunities to learn about each other's cost structures, to share the strengths of other leading firms, and to enhance cooperation. Rather than causing competition to decline, the new multinational oligopolies have resulted in reduced concentration in industrial structure and growing competition. Vernon attributes this somewhat unexpected phenomenon to the expansion of world markets and to the greater number of firms able to overcome barriers to entry.

The continuing evolution and growth of multinational oligopolies in both the mature industries and also in innovation-based industries, such as chemicals, pharmaceuticals and computers, pose problems for international competitiveness that may soon need to be addressed in a multilateral forum. Many developed and less developed countries have found that traditional fact-finding processes and corrective policy measures are only partially effective, sometimes even counterproductive, when applied at the national level; and this has led individual countries to avoid actions altogether. Events may be leading, therefore, to consideration of an international body that would be responsible for fact finding, adjudicating, and prescribing rules and regulations relative to the practices and operations of multinational oligopolies.[14] Important differences exist between antitrust programs operated by the United States and other countries, notably those in Western Europe and Japan. Yet, a basis exists for an international approach that potentially at least would offer a better framework for resolving problems of competition and monopoly than present national laws.[15] The existence, operation, and enforcement of such an international antitrust convention would help to reduce some of the national economic concerns relating both to access to foreign markets and access to foreign supplies, in that the latitude would be reduced for leaders of an oligopoly, or national governments acting in concert with the leaders, to pursue a course of action that would benefit one party or country at the expense of another.

To be sure, many of the problems and issues concerning multinational corporations pertain to international investment policy. But given the already great and rapidly increasing role of the MNCs in international trade, it would not be at all surprising if issues concerning MNCs directly were found on the agenda of some future round of trade negotiations.

### GATT: Responsive to Future International Trade Requirements?

The capacity to respond to unfolding events and to new requirements is the hallmark of any body that successfully withstands the rigors of time. In the past, the primary concerns of the General Agreement on Tariffs and Trade have had to do with a limited range of trade policy issues that had greatest relevance for the developed, market-economy countries. That tradition has been giving way to new concerns in more recent years. For example, during the 1960s the GATT Articles of Agreement were expanded to include a new chapter on trade and development, and a considerable number of less developed countries, many of whom enjoyed ample endowments of natural resources, sought membership in GATT.

More recently, some of the state-trading countries of Eastern Europe have joined GATT. Poland became something of a test case as she first sought membership in 1957. The dilemma for GATT concerned the application of the basic principles of MFN, reciprocity in negotiations and tariffs as the basis for regulating trade, to a state-trading country. In such an economic system, the volume and direction of trade is determined by a domestic economic plan. Prices on the home market are fixed, and accordingly there is no allowance for import prices or tariffs to influence either the volume of imports or domestic prices. The fact that Poland ultimately acceded to GATT membership indicates that the contracting parties "are ready to accept a new definition of the concept of reciprocity, namely, that tariff reductions can be 'paid for' by guarantees for an increased volume of trade."[16] Thus, years of intense investigation and negotiation passed before that country was finally accepted as a full member in October 1967.

Thereafter, other East European countries applied for GATT membership and subsequently were admitted. The only East European nations that are not presently contracting parties to GATT are Albania, Bulgaria, and East Germany.

Both the developments concerning the LDCs and those concerning East European countries evidence a pragmatic attitude on the part of GATT's contracting parties toward evolving issues related to but not covered previously by the rules of the General Agreement. Certainly a great deal more of that pragmatism will be necessary in the future if GATT's relevance to present international trade circumstances is to continue.

The current issues concerning improvement of the GATT, as discussed in Chapter 5, include how and in what manner rules governing export controls can best be added to the present General Agreement, and the alternative means by which needed modifications in the existing safeguard provision might be achieved. Hopefully, the contracting parties will prove themselves equal to the formidable tasks of negotiating workable compromises in these matters. Even if they do, other challenging questions lie ahead.

First, in connection with the issues of short supply, the case of petroleum has been much celebrated for its uniqueness. Indeed, more than anything else, events having to do with curtailed oil exports and the quadrupling of oil prices during the closing months of 1973 and the start of 1974 (all precipitated by the Organization of Petroleum Exporting Countries, better known as OPEC) focused attention and concern on the issue of access to foreign supply. Such concern spread to other primary goods as excess world demand led to sharply higher prices and as other primary-producing countries began to talk publicly of emulating the example set by OPEC.

But while industrial countries, and possibly some of the primary-producing less developed countries, try to come to grips with an acceptable set of rules for export controls, practically all of the important oil-producing countries remain nonmembers of GATT. (Kuwait is the only exception at present.) In order for ground rules governing export controls to be effective, they must, of course, be accepted by all those who might otherwise cause disruption and chaos in world markets by exercising freedom of action. Thus, it is crucial that the major oil-exporting countries, and for that matter other primary-producing LDCs whose commodities have figured in the short-supply controversy, be drawn into an agreement governing use of export controls, and preferably that they be drawn into full GATT membership. Observance of responsible international trade policy and acceptance of limits on freedom of national action are responsibilities to be born not just by industrial countries but by all countries if order in the international trading community is to prevail. Thus, in addition to diplomatic efforts already afoot to get those countries to reduce oil prices and increase output,[17] oil-consuming countries and other contracting parties to GATT should begin early consideration of ways to include those nations and other primary-producing countries among their ranks.

A second and less immediate challenge concerns the question of whether Russia and China may seek GATT membership at some point. A few years ago such a question would have been unthinkable. But today, with the rising tempo of trade between market-economy countries on the one hand and Russia and China on the other, such a development merits consideration and study. The relatively recent accession of East European state-trading countries to GATT speaks a great deal of their belief that GATT serves a useful purpose. Eventually, and as a pragmatic means to resolving problems that will arise as their trade expands with the West, Russia and China may find such problems more easily settled within GATT and on terms more favorable to them than could be obtained through bilateral agreements. Looked at from the other side, it would be far easier and more acceptable to Western trading nations as a group if their interests in respect of trade with Russia or China could be taken care of in such a multilateral forum as the GATT, for there the likelihood of maintaining equity and order in trade relations would be greatly enhanced.

As suggested earlier in this chapter, the future may bring forth new problems of access to foreign markets involving not only the present less developed countries, many of whom are already GATT members, but also China, Russia, and the major oil-exporting countries. Should there be a common forum such as GATT to which all countries belong before such problems surface, then indeed their resolution should prove far easier.

In addressing the question of Russia's or China's membership in GATT, consideration will have to be given to the possible addition to the General Agreement of new rules on state trading. While no additions of this sort were made in the cases of Eastern European nations that have already become members, some new rules, or modifications of existing rules, might offer a basis for face-saving compromise and thus clear the way for all major world economic powers to belong to a common multilateral institution dedicated to, among other things, "developing the full use of the resources of the world and expanding the production and exchange of goods."[18]


## NTBs, Agricultural Trade, and
## Other Continuing Issues

As suggested in the introduction to this chapter, some trade issues now on the agenda for negotiation will be carried over, at least in part, to future talks. This has been the case in previous multilateral trade negotiations, which yielded substantial progress in the field of tariff reduction but which always left something for future negotiations. It is especially significant, therefore, that successful bargaining in current negotiations may all but eliminate tariff barriers as a meaningful topic for the future. There are sure to be more than adequate replacements to fill that void, however.

A GATT study of existing nontariff barriers following the Kennedy Round uncovered some eight hundred distinct practices. Their number and their wide variety alone are enough to ensure NTBs a space on the agendas of several trade negotiations yet to come. More important than their sheer number is the fact that negotiations to reduce and eliminate some of the existing nontariff barriers will entail new solutions substantially different from the kind of agreements worked out previously in respect of tariff reductions. Those requiring arrangement of codes of conduct will benefit from a trial period of perhaps a few years. In that time there may be some light shed on amendments or modifications that would strengthen such codes or make them palatable to a larger number of trading nations. All in all, it is probable that the issue of nontariff barriers will be active for many years to come.

Another issue equally certain to command attention in the future negotiations concerns agricultural trade. Differing philosophical views as well as strong protectionist motivations on the part of all participants have successfully impeded liberalization efforts in the past, and it is realistic to expect that they again will be retarding agents in the current negotiations. Whether the *"montant de soutien"* approach advocated by Trezise and other experts, a sectoral approach, or some other means to a balanced agricultural settlement is adopted, there will need to be follow-up negotiations in order to look after the settlement and if necessary to modify it in view of changing circumstances.[19] Moreover, any agricultural settlement struck in the current negotiations is likely to be rather narrow in respect of commodity coverage. Thus, it will be up to future sessions to broaden the base of any agreement reached at this juncture. This could mean participation by a greater number of agricultural exporting and importing countries, or it could mean elaboration of buffer stock schemes or commodity agreements yet to be established.

Another set of issues ripe for future negotiations has to do with amendments and additions to the existing GATT articles. Many experts presently speak with trepidation about the prospects for achieving already overdue reforms in view of the diverse country representation in GATT, the one country-one vote principle, and the fact that amendments require a two-thirds or in some cases a unanimous vote. Accordingly, the suggestion has been made that the major trading nations get together on their own and agree to abide by supplementary codes or articles, which then might be broadened at future dates to include more countries as they indicated a willingness to accept commitments and obligations entailed therein.

But whether or not reforms of the GATT Articles come about through such backdoor approaches or by more traditional means, or whether an entirely new institution is born out of some unforseen impasse to GATT's continuation as a responsive instrument to prevailing circumstances, is not so important for the long term. What is important is that a world of increasingly interdependent nations requires an institution of universal and dedicated membership empowered with broad policy responsibilities. GATT has not reached that stage, even though national interdependence has already attained a considerable level. Thus, unless the world reverts to an earlier and simpler (but less rewarding) era of much reduced international commercial activity, modifications in the existing institutional framework and in its regulatory powers must be achieved. Sooner or later the GATT, or an agreement establishing some successor body, will have to be ratified by national legislatures so that what is now and has been for twenty-six years a provisional treaty may become permanent, and so that its articles, rather than national laws, will serve as the ultimate basis for resolving disputes of international trade policy.

Earlier in Chapter 5, the multilateral safeguard provision of GATT was discussed, and the basis for belief that its modification is necessary in the current multilateral trade negotiations was presented. But such consideration of a stronger safeguard mechanism is predicated on the expectation that negotiated reductions in trade barriers will quite possibly exacerbate the sorts of adjustment problems that have confronted various industries in recent years. The proposition considered earlier in this chapter was that access to foreign markets could once again become the overriding issue of international trade policy as Communist countries and less developed countries all attempt to export increasing amounts of raw materials and light manufactured products to industrial countries. In that event, the world could be headed toward a much more extensive level of specialization between nations. The circumstances that would facilitate such a development would be continued reductions in existing trade barriers, low-cost transportation, and a mechanism whose purpose would be to promote long-run integration of national economies and the relocation of industry from one area or one country to another.

What this suggests is that future reoccurrence of the access to markets issue could not only revive safeguard concerns, but it could very well be that the approach to the problem would take the form of establishing multilateral measures to *promote* orderly adjustment of industries, firms, labor and capital, rather than the old approach, which has been to establish measures to protect interests, impede imports, and thereby retard the adjustment process. Thus, it may be that the safeguard issue as now presented will emerge again in the future, but couched in much more positive terms.

## Trade Policy and Its Role in
## the New World Economic Order

In January 1974 it was decided that because of major uncertainties affecting the world economic outlook, including the energy crisis, higher oil prices, virulent inflation affecting virtually all countries, and other unsettled conditions, the Committee of Twenty should immediately change its emphasis from all aspects of international monetary reform to those particular considerations that bore upon the immediate financial situation. It was recognized that there would have to be an interim period before a reformed system could be fully agreed and finally implemented. During that period, it was hoped that the major changes in world balance of payments structure would be completed or at least that the positions of individual countries on how adjustments could be achieved would become clarified.

With international monetary reform now an evolutionary process, the major issues concerning what roles should be assumed by trade, monetary, and investment policies in the new world economic order cannot be resolved until such time as economic and financial situations in leading countries have become more settled and nations are prepared to move toward a more structured basis for international activity. In the new world economic order now gradually being constructed, careful thought and attention must be given to the roles of respective policy instruments and how and under what sorts of circumstances each is to be applied in order to deal with balance of payments maladjustments. Thus, to what extent will exchange-rate adjustment be relied on in the future and under what sets of conditions should use of this policy instrument be deemed acceptable? And how flexible will commercial policies be in the future world economic order? Will nations look rather more often than before to trade accounts of deficit or surplus countries to bear the brunt of short- and medium-term disturbances, or will the burden fall instead on the capital accounts and on accommodating capital flows of one sort or another? In view of the growing strength of commitments made by the large industrial countries vis-à-vis transferring an increased share of their real resources to less developed countries, how are these commitments to be met in the face of normal or even extraordinary economic disturbances occurring in the world economy over time? And what will be the relative responsibilities for trade, monetary, and investment policies to facilitate the continuing flow of resource transfer under adverse as well as under favorable conditions?

All of these and other related questions are of critical importance in shaping the new world economic order and in ensuring its operation in ways that meet the needs and objectives of participating nations. None of them can be finally resolved, however, nor should they be, until countries are prepared to move toward the kinds of binding commitments entailed in implementing a reformed monetary system and a reformed trading system. In order to close the circle, there will also need to be new understandings and agreements in the area of international investment policy.

At a later stage in time, negotiations between nations will have to occur more or less simultaneously in all three areas. Actions or policies in trade, monetary, and investment interact with one another, and to create the kind of world economic order that countries wish to create, it will be necessary simultaneously to determine the substantive roles each one is to play. Thus, it lies to some future date for trade policy experts to look beyond the issues commanding immediate attention in this current round of negotiations and to devise, in conjunction with their counterparts in the monetary and investment areas, the appropriate jurisdiction and the desired role for trade policy in the new economic order.

This chapter has offered a glimpse of some of the issues of international trade policy that can be expected to attract attention and study in the future and that are likely to be the subject of subsequent multilateral trade negotiations. Other issues may well, and no doubt will, introduce themselves in the years to come.

# 8 Summary and Perspective

The timeliness of multilateral trade negotiations is proving to be greater than imagined when the wheels were first set in motion in early 1972, or when ministers of the nations destined to participate convened in Tokyo in September 1973 and formally declared the negotiations open. This seventh round of negotiations to be held under the General Agreement on Tariffs and Trade is precisely relevant to prevailing world economic problems. Some of those problems have been on the scene for some time and were among the leading considerations that led the United States and other countries to undertake jointly a new round of negotiations; other problems have only just recently, and in some ways dramatically, made their presence known.

During the 1960s, balance of payments disequilibria of several major trading nations increased. For the United States, long accustomed to a surplus in goods traded with the rest of the world, a protracted deterioration in its trade position occurred during the latter half of the decade and, indeed, gave rise to substantial deficits in 1971 and 1972 for the first time in this century. Moreover, the divergence between developed and less developed countries in terms of economic performance and in terms of sharing the benefits from international trade had widened rather than diminished. These developments were of importance and concern to many countries in as much as they reflected major changes that had been occurring in international trade. By the start of the new decade, however, it began to be more and more apparent that the focus and attentions of trade policy in the past would require substantial modification. Indeed, trade policy was entering an era of transition.

Structural changes in the world economy have been occurring for years. But since the mid-1960s, changes that were quietly taking place beneath the surface began to emerge in ways that posed increasing dilemmas for existing international trade and monetary systems. The paramount economic strength of the United States, so striking after World War II, had declined in relative terms as a consequence of long-sustained and rapid economic growth in European countries and in Japan. Those up-and-coming industrial nations proved themselves capable of competing with US producers in a growing number of areas, a development that helped to strengthen their international trade positions.

The international monetary system had functioned smoothly when the US economy and the dollar were strong and healthy. But as the world's leading economy gave ground relative to Europe and Japan, and as the key currency became increasingly overvalued, the system was unable to correct itself; instead,

131

it became outmoded, inequitable, and a source of financial instability and disorder. Increasingly severe and ever more frequent exchange-market crises led to the demise of the international monetary system in 1971, an event that uncapped a host of fundamental distortions in the world economy and heightened uncertainties that had been simmering for some time.

Problems for the international trade system also arose out of the structural changes occurring; countries failed to abide judiciously by international rules and regulations set down or neglected to replace them with ones better tailored to meet new circumstances. Instead, a number of discriminatory or restrictive trade measures were adopted by different countries, a development prompted both by the diminished relevance of the prevailing rules and by the upsurge of protectionist sentiment in the United States and elsewhere.

The trade and monetary measures initiated by the United States in August 1971 signalled a change in foreign economic policies and marked official recognition of the need for fundamental reforms in both trade and monetary areas. In trade, the most prominent aspect of the new US policies was a 10 percent surcharge on imports of dutiable goods (a direct violation of US obligations under the GATT) and an announcement of a 10 percent investment tax credit that would have discriminated against imported machinery and equipment. These and other measures in the trade area, along with initiatives on the monetary side that included termination of dollar convertibility into gold and other reserve assets, were adopted on the one hand to help US firms become more competitive in the production and trade of goods produced abroad and, on the other hand, to precipitate a realignment of exchange rates for the leading currencies. A major objective of the United States was to dramatize the need for overhaul of the world's trade and monetary systems and to win support of other countries so that international negotiations on reform might soon be started.

The drama and suddenness surrounding those changes in US foreign economic policies represented a calculated risk, which, fortunately enough for all concerned, proved accurate. Other countries with good reason might have decided to retaliate against the US initiatives that violated existing GATT and IMF obligations. But retaliation could easily have led to still other restrictions and discriminatory practices of more lasting duration; moreover, such a course of action by other nations would have jeopardized chances for peacefully resolving the problems that lay beneath US initiatives. The absence of retaliation at the time might also have been interpreted as implicit recognition on the part of other countries that no better alternative means was available to achieve the recasting of what was an increasingly unsustainable US role in the world economic order.

Thus, in several respects recent international economic initiatives and responses to them have already achieved or have set the stage for improvements in the circumstances that had prevailed before. Exchange rates were realigned formally according to the Smithsonian Agreement of 1971 and the monetary agreements of February 1973. Since March of that same year, however, exchange rates of leading currencies have floated continuously and more or less freely, although there have been close intergovernmental consultations and occasional instances of exchange-market intervention to smooth out abrupt movements in rates. In 1973, the US trade balance exhibited a substantial improvement of over $8 billion compared to the previous year by realizing a surplus of $1.7 billion. Efforts to bring about long-term basic reforms in the institutions, rules and principles governing the international monetary system were begun, and an outline of a new system, together with a package of interim measures to serve until a reformed system could be finally and fully implemented, was announced in June 1974. Multilateral trade negotiations for reforming the international trading system were launched in September 1973, and with passage of the US Trade Act at the end of 1974, trade negotiations appear likely to begin in earnest in early 1975.

For a period of over thirty years, that is, during the reign of the Reciprocal Trade Agreements Program and including the Kennedy Round of trade negotiations that ended in mid-1967, the general perception of international trade and the approach to trade policy remained essentially unaltered. Trade among nations should be as free of governmental interference as possible; when interference was resorted to, it should only be in the form of tariff duties; tariffs were to be applied on a nondiscriminatory basis; negotiations for conceding reductions in tariff barriers should be based on the principle of reciprocity, and the resulting benefits of trade agreements should be extended to all trading partners on a most-favored-nation basis. The long period of continuity in international trade policy began in the early 1930s, when tariffs were at record-high levels. Tariffs were far and away the overriding issue for trade policy, and in recognition of classical economic doctrine, nations negotiated first bilaterally and then, after the passage of some years and the formation of the GATT, on a multilateral basis for the principal purpose of lowering tariff barriers.

By the end of the Kennedy Round, the overall significance of tariff barriers had largely diminished as a result of the many successful negotiating sessions that had gone before. Tariffs still afforded significant protection for a number of individual products; but as for most trade in manufactured products, tariff levels of the industrial nations had been cut to an average of about 9 percent.

In recent times, tariffs as the focal point of trade policy have been replaced by a host of other trade barriers and other trade-distorting measures commonly and conveniently given the rubric of nontariff barriers. NTBs are often applied unilaterally and in discriminatory fashion; some restrict imports, while others stimulate exports. Many NTBs have come into existence as a result of governmental efforts to raise product standards or to establish health and safety codes. Thus, their raison d'etre is essentially domestic, although there are often important side effects for international trade. The shift in attention from tariffs to nontariff barriers has served as one early indication that trade policy was in transition.

After several years of independent studies in various international and national forums concerning the applications and effects of NTBs, it has become clear that methods other than the reciprocal approach customary in previous tariff negotiations must be developed and tested if world trading nations are to be successful in their efforts "to reduce or eliminate nontariff measures or, where this is not appropriate, to reduce or eliminate their trade restricting or distorting effects, and to bring such measures under more effective international discipline," as called for in the Tokyo Declaration of 1973. Negotiations in the NTB area will be for the most part an exercise in developing a stronger, tighter set of international rules or codes of conduct to be applied by the agreeing parties. Thus, better and more active management of arising problems is another feature of the current transition in trade policy.

Another problem area of traditional trade policy that has been undergoing important changes since the end of the Kennedy Round concerns less developed countries. For years in GATT and in UNCTAD conferences, developed countries have recognized and agreed with the necessity of promoting economic development of LDCs, and they have stressed their willingness to cooperate to that end. But time has shown developed countries to have been dilatory in implementing decisions or resolutions accepted in those forums. (Indeed, in some cases such as textiles, mounting competition by LDC producers against producers in developed countries led to the adoption of measures to systematically control imports from LDCs.) This has been substantially true in previous multilateral trade negotiations, wherein LDCs benefited primarily from an MFN application of tariff concessions exchanged between principal trading nations or between those developed nations and themselves, rather than from any overt preferential treatment accorded them by the large trading nations. But what LDCs have been seeking is preferential discriminatory treatment that would enhance their access to the vast markets of developed nations; they have also demanded nonreciprocity in the reduction of trade barriers, which would allow them continued protection for their own markets but easier entry to foreign markets.

Not long after the conclusion of the Kennedy Round, many industrial countries (but not including the United States) did establish generalized tariff preference schemes that were designed to promote export trade of LDCs by granting lower, or in some cases zero, tariff duties to their manufactured and semimanufactured exports, but not to the like products exported by other countries. While preferential tariff arrangements appear to be a clear opening wedge to the principles that have anchored international trade policy for the past forty years, the substantial number of qualifications, exceptions, and the conservative safeguard clauses that are a part of every tariff preference scheme in operation means that such arrangements to date are more symbolic than substantive. This could change somewhat now that the new US Trade Act provides for enactment of the US GSP scheme and if existing GSP schemes operated by other countries were significantly broadened in scope during the course of the multilateral trade negotiations.

Another transition in international trade policy has been the increasing attention given to the issue of safeguards. Safeguards refers to a formula or a means by which countries could contain actually or potentially disruptive imports, and yet they would be constrained in the extent to which they could assert their national freedom by imposing protective barriers against imports on the pretext of an emergency. The safeguard issue has emerged because of the very rapid growth of world trade in manufactures during the 1960s and because of a number of cases of market disruption and various adjustment problems that were alleged to have resulted. Not only developed countries but also several of the more advanced developing countries, such as Taiwan, Korea, Hong Kong, Mexico and Brazil, enjoyed high rates of increases in various manufactured goods exports. But chiefly the industrial countries and their declining domestic industries bore the brunt of others' success. An improved international safeguard mechanism setting out limits within which protection would be justified and also requiring periodic review of such protection is believed to be essential for the negotiation of new trade agreements that would further liberalize international trade and thus make access to markets that much easier for foreign producers.

Safeguards also may be taken to mean policy measures that facilitate (rather than retard) the adjustment of manufacturing and commercial interests to evolving competitive conditions and new trade patterns. Several countries have adopted legislation calling for such safeguards as import relief for industry and adjustment assistance for firms and workers. But with only slim authorizations of funds to back them up, most of these sorts of safeguards have until recently proved wholly inadequate.

A third kind of safeguard has to do with measures designed to assure that domestic producers are able to compete equitably with their foreign counterparts and that standards of fair trade apply to all parties. Specifically, these are procedures that cope with dumping and with subsidies or grants that may excessively stimulate imports or may disadvantage exports. Here again, experience of the past few years has indicated a need for more specific agreement and closer adherence to international standards of fair trade.

International trade policy appeared more and more to be in a state of flux during the latter 1960s and early 1970s, inasmuch as the incidence of violations to free trade, nondiscrimination, and other fundamental principles of the GATT increased and the existing machinery to cope with those violations proved to be ever more ineffective. In a sense, these problems were a reflection of fundamental changes in world trade and economic structure that had arisen in the quarter century since the conclusion of World War II, when GATT was born. The European Common Market had replaced the United States as the largest world trading bloc, and a major redistribution of economic strength from the

United States toward Western Europe and Japan had occurred during that time. It was hardly surprising, therefore, that the rules and regulations of GATT, conceived in a period of paramount US economic strength in the world and at a time of severe dollar shortage, should not be adequate or responsive to trade problems arising years later in a vastly altered world trade environment. Thus, from the US point of view, and from the viewpoint of a number of other countries, a major review of the Articles of the General Agreement for the purpose of reform and amendment emerged as an increasingly important objective of international trade policy. Indeed, it was this requirement, along with similar requirements in the area of international monetary policy and reform of the IMF, that provided much of the impetus for and helped to shape US initiatives in August 1971.

Areas of GATT that to the United States, at least, appeared particularly deficient and in need of reform included exceptions to MFN treatment that gave special quarter to common markets and free-trade areas. According to many observers during the late 1960s and early 1970s, this movement toward regionalism threatened to break the multilateral trading community into a world of competitive factions, each with a distinctive inward focus.

Another kind of violation to the GATT Articles, where existing machinery proved especially permissive if not inadequate, concerned the proliferating number of bilateral commercial arrangements involving the European Common Market and certain other countries, both developing and developed. Although many of those preferential agreements were seen as having little impact on the immediate trade situation, the long-term threat of growing isolation for the United States and for other nations such as Japan with global rather than regional trading interests was viewed more seriously.

There were still other areas of GATT operations that required reform. GATT treatment of subsidies and import charges were found to discriminate in favor of countries whose tax revenues derived importantly from value-added taxes rather than from direct or indirect taxes, and the GATT safeguard clause to protect against balance of payments deterioration had become anachronistic. In late years such countries as England, France, and even the United States in 1971 and Italy in 1974 imposed import restrictions for balance of payments reasons in open defiance of GATT Articles. Finally, in the area of agricultural trade, which had long been heavily controlled and subsidized not only in Europe but in other industrial countries, GATT was able to offer little or no guidance along a path toward freer, more efficient world production, trade, and consumption. (The waiver to Article XI, obtained by the United States in 1951 to permit quantitative restrictions on certain agricultural imports, was the first and perhaps most critical blow to GATT's relevance in this area.) In these various areas redress of existing Articles of Agreement was seen as critically important, not only to the future viability of GATT, but also in terms of ensuring that the international trade system would not deviate further or irreparably from the principles of free and fair trade or from the multilateralist philosophy that had served world interests so well in the past.

In all of these respects, international trade policy had come to be concerned with the pressing issues that had emerged since the end of the Kennedy Round. Some were issues that had received consideration in the past, but only secondarily to the issue of tariffs. All the while, however, the focus of trade policy has continued to concentrate on opening up and assuring access to foreign markets.

Active concentration on the trade policy issues enumerated above, although consistent with the focus on improving access to markets that characterized trade policy in previous decades, signaled an important transition that had already occurred in the realm of domestic economic policy and that has occurred most recently in the area of international monetary policy. That transition has to do with a movement away from the laissez-faire approach of the past, according to which government intervention in the market place for the sake of helping to achieve various economic objectives was minimized, toward a neo-Keynesian approach, whereby active intervention by government to influence and hopefully to improve the workings of the market and to bring closer to reality a whole complex of economic objectives, has become the norm rather than the exception.

The hypothesis is, therefore, that part of the reason for new concern of international trade policy with issues once considered of secondary importance (and certainly not deserving of detailed understandings between governments, or codes of conduct for government intervention, or of highly formalized rules) represents an increasing penchant by governments to effect closer, more active management of prevailing problems and issues of international trade policy. (The other part of the explanation, as indicated already, is that reduced importance of tariffs relative to other trade barriers has inevitably caused greater attention to be given to those other barriers.) With increased proclivity of governments to interfere in the market for the management of both domestic and external economic policy objectives, the need for international ground rules pertaining to such intervention is also increased. And given the growing economic interdependence that has taken place among all nations of the world, the implications of one government's policy objectives loom large for other nations in the international trading community. Accordingly, the need for better cooperation and improved understanding between governments is enhanced; and it is this need which is currently manifesting itself in the realm of international trade policy. There is concentration on a wide variety and growing number of issues, and efforts are now afoot in the multilateral trade negotiations to develop workable understandings and a basis for better management of the problems at hand. While the governmental approach to the management of trade policy issues has altered from an essentially passive to a much more active position, basic allegiance to the fundamental principles of nondiscrimination, reciprocity, and freer trade has continued.

During 1972-1973 almost all industrial countries experienced simultaneously strong expansions in their domestic economies. It was a phenomenon of timing that had no parallel in the recent past, and it was the main instigating factor accounting for shortages in basic materials and products that gripped the world in 1973. Rapidly rising domestic activity created a surge in demand for industrial raw materials and that in turn led to large increases in foreign-exchange earnings of raw-materials-producing LDCs. With increased purchasing power, LDCs demand for imports from industrial countries and from other nations also increased. Thus, the growth of interdependence among national economies, which was necessary to achieve the high level of income and well-being through increased specialization and international trade, was itself a mechanism for spreading inflationary fires among the countries of the world.

Coincidental with rising aggregate demand in the world, poor climatic conditions in Russia, in Australia, and in Europe caused harvests of grains and foodstuffs to drop below forecast levels. Shortfalls in domestic supplies had to be made up through increased imports of feeds and grains from abroad, which in this case turned out to be primarily from the United States and Canada. Poor crops abroad and the rise in import demand were further aggravated by increased real incomes resulting from boom conditions, for that only added to people's willingness to spend more income for meat and other food items earlier regarded as semiluxuries. The world food shortage affected not only developed countries but many less developed countries as well. These developments in world agricultural production and demand added new and very substantial inflationary pressures to those already being unleashed by rapid industrial expansion and excess aggregate demand throughout the world.

The third set of developments exacerbating serious economic circumstances that were rapidly unfolding throughout 1973 concerned the rather brief oil embargo, imposed by the Arab oil-producing nations, and the fourfold increase in crude-oil prices, instigated and carried out by the Organization of Petroleum Exporting Countries between the first quarter of 1973 and the start of 1974. Not only did these developments contribute greatly to inflationary trends in industrialized oil-importing nations, the likes of which had never before been experienced in a time of peace, but they also caused grave new uncertainties about both the short-term economic performance of leading countries and their balance of payments prospects, and also about the prospects for a serious world depression for the first time since 1929. The oil embargo and the sharp increase in prices set in motion policy measures in most oil-importing nations to curtail nonessential oil demand. Those actions caused sharper-than-expected economic downturns in most industrial economies during 1974, a turn of events that has prompted some governments to embark on new programs of economic expansion despite continuation of very strong inflationary trends.

Balance of trade and payments uncertainties for all oil-importing countries, and the especially great concerns regarding the viability of a number of less developed countries that rely to a relatively greater degree than developed countries on oil as a basic energy source, have led to the establishment of a special oil facility within the International Monetary Fund. The oil facility has been set up to help channel funds from oil-producing countries to those oil-importing countries that have severe balance of payments problems as a result of higher-cost oil imports and which therefore need time and financial assistance to implement adjustments in domestic policies that will allow them to cope with the new energy situation. The concern over prospects for a serious world depression remains high, especially in Britain, and skillful handling of financial and economic problems now pending, together with some measurable success in combating inflationary pressures to help restore the confidence of consumers and businessmen throughout the world, are necessary if economic disaster is to be averted.

These recent economic developments laid bare new problems for international trade policy. Over the past several decades, issues of trade policy have principally been of the genre having to do with access to foreign markets. Only occasionally, and then on a limited basis, was access to foreign supply an issue of importance. But the unique success of OPEC in raising export prices of oil, the shortages of certain foodstuffs, fibers, minerals, and other raw materials and industrial supplies, and the still rampant inflationary pressures throughout the world have raised a new set of issues concerned with short supply—problems of equitably sharing limited supplies in an interdependent world and the appropriate application of export controls.

Much uncertainty prevails in respect of the durability of these new issues. Some regard present problems of short supply as essentially short term and likely to disappear almost as fast as they rose initially. According to this view, OPEC constitutes a unique instance of cartel-type pressures to be applied successfully on an international scale, and even it may yet prove to have been a flash in the pan. Alternative sources of oil are bound to become available given the high international prices now prevailing; conservation efforts of oil-importing countries and policies to promote the use of alternative energy forms will, so it is argued, lead to a significant reduction of oil prices within a few short years. According to this school, the likelihood of all major industrial economies again hitting their expansionary phase simultaneously is remote; and the confluence of independent economic events that struck the world during 1972-74 being repeated again at some point in the future is still more slight. Thus, problems of scarcity and the issues of access to foreign supply are seen as temporary and soon to be replaced by the more traditional issues and problems of access to foreign markets.

The other interpretation of recent developments is that we have entered a new era in which population and economic growth trends will outstrip material resources, that technological advances in the area of synthetics or substitute materials are diminishing, and that the increased costs of raw materials and foodstuffs in the year ahead will be so great that profound changes in economic, political, and social structures will result, along with major shifts in competitive relations between industries and between nations. It can be anticipated that nations producing and exporting copper, bauxite, tin, iron, silver, coffee, bananas, and other items will make an effort to form cartels similar to OPEC. This possibility should be taken seriously by consuming countries. According to this view, problems of scarcity and short supply present major new challenges for the long run, not just for international trade policy but for the related areas of monetary and investment policy, economic assistance to less developed countries (especially the so-called least developed, which have limited endowments of natural resources and basic commodities in short supply), and national defense policy.

The difficult question at hand is how should the present problems of scarcity and access to foreign supply be treated in the context of international trade policy and the multilateral trade negotiations now commencing? In view of the greater than usual uncertainties now prevailing in respect of future levels of demand for commodities in question, and their future availability from present sources and from others yet to be discovered, developed and made commercially viable, it may be the best policy to resist the temptation to embark on grand strategies involving long-term commitments that appear to offer the comforts of stable but very high prices and assurances of access to future supply.

But it is too much, and perhaps undesirable, to expect negotiators and the government bureaucracies behind them to do nothing in the face of these extraordinary circumstances. At the least, therefore, efforts might well go toward developing a body of rules, as part of the existing GATT Articles, perhaps pertaining to imposition and use of export controls. It is true that the present GATT Articles are vague and inadequate in this area, and while export controls have not seen anything like the widespread application of import controls in the past, it would be constructive to provide the GATT with a more balanced set of rules and regulations that would be responsive to problems that may arise in either area in the future. To go beyond that stage now and, for example, negotiate long-term commodity agreements with primary-producing nations could well prove to have been premature in just a few years time. In any case, should these problems of access to foreign supply prove as enduring and as disruptive to the international economic structure as some predict, then complex and far-reaching cooperative arrangements between all countries will have to be worked out and amended over a considerable period of trial and error. Ultimately, the mutual interdependence of supplies and markets will have to be accepted as the foundation for any stable economic system, regardless of whether the current intensity of the scarcity problem endures or not.

The current round of multilateral trade negotiations provides a timely and appropriate forum for airing different views of the issues of short supply and, quite possibly beyond that, toward devising a set of rules to govern the use of export controls. Whether agreements are entered into concerning these issues or whether negotiating parties decide to await further information and to allow for valuable perspective afforded by the passage of time, the MTN, which includes many other pressing and important issues on the agenda, must go forward. It is to be hoped that significant and lasting achievements will result from the efforts now being put forth.

For the United States, there has been a real interest in simply getting multilateral trade negotiations underway. By achieving only that much, domestic protectionist forces that posed a significant and possibly lasting danger to the United States economic position in the world in 1970-72 are turned aside. The United States is truly a world trader, and for that reason imposition of any significant trade barriers to protect US markets from foreign competition would be deleterious not only to US exporters, as foreign nations would quite likely take retaliatory measures, but also to US political influence abroad and to our ability to meet military commitments.

In the trade negotiations themselves, a breakthrough in rationalizing international agricultural trade and in laying the groundwork for systematically removing trade barriers in this area that exist in practically all countries may be the single most important outcome. An equally significant breakthrough in negotiations to reduce or remove NTBs would have perhaps an even greater immediate impact on US trade, but considering the long-term comparative advantage of the United States in food production, an agricultural trade agreement may be more significant.

Comprehensive, binding agreements providing security to foreign supplies do not appear in the US interest at this juncture. The United States is both an exporter and an importer of basic materials. On balance, the United States is a net importer of raw materials from LDCs and a net exporter of raw materials to developed countries. With the possible exception of oil, self-sufficiency in the face of serious and lasting world shortages is economically and commercially feasible; and for this reason alone, entering into long-term commodity agreements now, given the high degree of uncertainty that future shortages and prices of raw materials and fuels will match those experienced in recent months, would be premature at best.

For Europeans, and for Japanese too, the short-supply issue looms much larger, and indeed for some of them it may be a preoccupation in relation to other issues of access to markets. But recent months have provided enough opportunities to teach a lesson that hasty bilateral deals to win assurances on future availability of energy or other primary products are not only expensive but also pose potential dangers to national sovereignty and future economic independence, if carried very far. A distinct possibility is that the dramatic economic events of recent months will reinforce European enthusiasm at the bargaining table for issues concerned with access to markets, possibly to an extent unimagined as recently as say late 1973. With commodity and energy prices likely to remain well above pre-1973 levels, but not necessarily higher, or as high as, early 1974 levels, all nations, including Europe, will have to seek ways to earn their way in the world—which in essence means exporting more abroad. And that necessity will be greatly facilitated by agreements at the MTN to enhance access to foreign markets.

This conclusion holds even more strongly for Japan, which simply has no natural resource base of its own to enable it to maintain or expand upon present levels of economic activity and economic well-being. For Japan, the opening of the MTN is only a first step. Major agreements that liberalize access to foreign markets and maintain or improve access to foreign supplies are vital to the long-term interests and to the very survival of the Japanese economy. Of all major trading nations, none has a greater stake in a successful round of multilateral trade negotiations than Japan. This means that when negotiations begin in earnest, Japan will have to give in order to receive.

For less developed countries the great emphasis on generalized tariff preferences over the past decade has provided a theme around which all could rally. But preferences were oversold, for developed countries were never in a position nor willing to deliver benefits to LDCs through this mechanism to the extent demanded. Indeed, it was impossible, given the relatively modest tariff rates in developed countries (and now likely to be even more true if further MFN tariff reductions are achieved in the current round), that tariff preferences could have ever provided more than a very few developing countries with sufficient competitive advantage to break into industrial countries markets in a way that would reap significant increases in foreign exchange earnings, and thereby facilitate realization of economic development ambitions.

While trade is important, more aid and a lot of patience will be necessary to draw increasing numbers of LDCs within shooting range of competitive, large-scale production required just to enter large industrial markets. But as LDCs do approach within that range, their major interest will be in assurances of access to those markets. Rather than tariff preferences, therefore, the future trade policy interests of LDCs lie in international safeguards and in formulation of safeguard standards that give sympathetic consideration to their station in world trade.

For primary-producing countries, present windfall foreign exchange earnings should be used to diversify their economies, to train and educate their labor force for increasingly productive pursuits. There is no guarantee how long the sun will continue to shine for them, and they should make as speedy preparations as possible so that their countries will be able to participate responsibly and compete independently in world trade in the near future. All of this strongly suggests that long-run interests of primary-producing countries lie in the MTN issues of access to markets and liberalization of world trade—not in protectionist policies that may maximize their short-run earnings, nor in the long-term commodity agreements that may serve to inhibit and retard their future growth and economic diversification.

Communist countries have much to gain if progressive reforms result from the MTN; but only a few of them will be active participants in the negotiations themselves. Their increased sharing in the benefits of world trade and their more direct involvement in decision taking in international trade policy will be realized in the future world economic order, which itself will be materially and substantially influenced by results of the current round. Thus, the Communist countries have very considerable interests in the conduct and outcome of the MTN.

All the major international trade negotiations of the past have represented turning points, opportunities for nations to move forward toward a more liberal, more open trading order or to move back to a period of diminished commercial intercourse in which inward-looking nationalistic policies prevailed. In this respect, the current round is no exception. But in addition, there is a closely related question concerning whether nations will be able to work together to achieve better management of international trade issues in our increasingly interdependent world. Better management of trade issues, both old and new, through general understandings and improved rules and regulations, through closer cooperation and frequent consultation, is essential to the future growth and well-being of the international economy.

# Notes

# Notes

## Chapter 1
### Introduction

1. *Report of Board of Governors by Committee of Twenty and Outline of Reform with Annexes*, International Monetary Fund, 14 June 1974.

## Chapter 2
### The Reciprocal Trade Approach:
### 1934-67

1. The philosophy underlying the approach to domestic economic policy making, which endorsed active intervention in the market place, was alien to the philosophy of laissez faire, which was one of the main pillars of classical economics and the Trade Agreements Program, then still in its infancy.

2. For a good review of the Reciprocal Trade Agreements Program, see Walter Krause, *International Economics* (Boston: Houghton Mifflin Co., 1965), chapter 19.

3. See Harley Notter, *Postwar Foreign Policy Preparation, 1935-45* (Washington, D.C.: Department of State, 1949); and William Adams Brown, Jr., *The United States and the Restoration of World Trade*, An Analysis and Appraisal of the ITO Charter with the General Agreement on Tariffs and Trade (Washington, D.C.: The Brookings Institution, 1950).

4. One of the important works that deals with this period is Richard N. Gardner, *Sterling-Dollar Diplomacy: Anglo-American Collaboration in the Reconstruction of Multilateral Trade* (Oxford: Clarendon Press, 1956).

5. Interested readers should again refer to the comprehensive and important book by William Adams Brown, Jr., *The United States and Restoration of World Trade* (Washington, D.C.: The Brookings Institution, 1950), which carries through the establishment and first two years' activities of GATT. Another work spanning the first fifteen years of GATT's operations is by Gerard Curzon, *Multilateral Commercial Diplomacy: The General Agreement on Tariffs and Trade and Its Impact on National Commercial Policies and Techniques* (London: Michael Joseph, Ltd., 1965).

6. United States participation in the GATT has been on the basis of executive agreement and has never been sanctioned by the Congress.

7. The first was at Geneva in 1947, the next at Annecy in 1949, the third at Torquay in 1951, the fourth at Geneva in 1956, the fifth (the Dillon Round) at Geneva in 1960-62, and the sixth (the Kennedy Round) at Geneva from May 1964, until June 1967.

8. For more information on the ITO and on GATT, see John H. Jackson, *World Trade and the Law of GATT* (New York: The Bobbs-Merrill Co. Inc., 1969); Karin Kock, *International Trade Policy and the GATT 1947-1967* (Stockholm: Almquist and Wiksell, 1969); and Kenneth W. Dam, *The GATT Law and International Economic Organization* (Chicago: University of Chicago Press, 1970), esp. chapter 2.

9. Approximately one-half of this duty reduction was attributable to rising prices that lowered the ad valorem incidence of specific duty rates. According to Walter Krause (*International Economics* [Boston: Houghton-Mifflin Co., 1965], p. 418), the reduction was about 50 percent if measured by applying each set of rates to the volume of trade in 1949—from 25.8 to 13.3 percent.

10. U.S. Tariff Commission, *Average Ad Valorem Rates of Duty on Imports into the United States*, Washington, D.C., July 1963.

11. Joint Economic Committee (U.S. Congress), *Trade Restraints in the Western Community*, Washington, D.C., 1961, p. 6.

12. Reference is made to Walter Krause, *International Economics* (Boston: Houghton Mifflin Co., 1965), pp. 421.

13. Ibid., chapter 2.

14. Harry G. Johnson, *The World Economy at the Crossroads* (Oxford: Clarendon Press, 1965), chapter 4.

15. Ibid., p. 58.

16. Ernest Preeg, *Traders and Diplomats* (Washington, D.C.: Brookings Institution, 1970), p. 257. This book is one of the standard references to what took place at the Kennedy Round and what it all meant.

17. For further information on results of the "Kennedy Round," see Karin Kock, *International Trade Policy and the GATT 1947-1967* (Stockholm: Almqvist and Wiksell, 1969), chapter 4; Ernest Preeg, *Traders and Diplomats*, chapter 16; and Thomas B. Curtis and John Robert Vastine, Jr., *The Kennedy Round and the Future of American Trade*, (New York: Praeger Publishers, 1971).

18. See the very good appraisal of US adjustment assistance by Thomas P. Enger, "U.S. Tariff Adjustment and Adjustment Assistance," *Journal of World Trade Law*, September-October 1972, pp. 518-32.

19. For example, see Walter Krause, *International Economics* pp. 425-29.


Chapter 3
**The International Trade Structure:**
**Growing Discontent**

1. If chemicals are included, the shares are 54 percent and 65 percent in 1960 and 1970, respectively. Figures are derived from League of Nations and GATT sources.

2. For a concise review of the evolution in economic thought that took place in this area of economic development, see Walter Krause, "The New Revolt," in *The Economy of Latin America*, Walter Krause, editor (Iowa City: University of Iowa Press, 1966).

3. United Nations, *The Economic Development of Latin America* (New York: United Nations, 1950).

4. *Towards a Dynamic Development Policy for Latin America*, (New York: United Nations, 1963).

5. The objective of UNCTAD has been to contribute to more rapid growth and development of LDCs through improved trade and aid relationships with developed countries. For a review of UNCTAD's impact in these matters, see Robert S. Walters, "UNCTAD: Intervener Between Poor and Rich States," *Journal of World Trade Law* 7, no. 5 (September-October 1973): 527-54.

6. A multivolume *Proceedings*, published by the United Nations.

7. Benjamin J. Cohen, "American Foreign Economic Policy: Some General Principles of Analysis" in Cohen (ed.), *American Foreign Economic Policy* (New York: Harper and Row, 1968), pp. 31-32.

8. The Export Control Act also declared that export controls be used in order "(a) to protect the domestic economy from the excessive drain of scarce materials and to reduce the inflationary impact of abnormal foreign demand; (b) to further the foreign policy of the United States and to aid in fulfilling its international responsibilities."

9. In particular, see Gunnar Adler-Karlson, *Western Economic Warfare, 1947-1967* (Stockholm: Almqvist & Wiksell, 1968), Chapters 8 and 9.

10. Nathaniel M. McKitterick, *East-West Trade: The Background of U.S. Policy* (Twentieth Century Fund, 1966), p. 17.

11. MFN treatment was restored to Poland in 1960, and from the late 1950s onward she availed herself of the PL 480 and Commodity Credit Corporation Programs, purchasing hundreds of millions of dollars worth of subsidized US agricultural goods. See Thomas A. Wolf, *U.S. East-West Trade Policy* (Lexington, Mass.: Lexington Books, D.C. Heath and Co., 1973), pp. 70-72.

12. This finding was in compliance with subsection 231(b) of the Trade Expansion Act of 1962, designed especially for the two countries in question. For more on this point, see Thomas Wolf, *U.S. East-West Trade Policy*, pp. 79-80.

13. For more on the Miller Report, see ibid., pp. 83-85.

14. Ibid., pp. 102-105.

15. Ibid., pp. 105-107.

16. Poland was the first Communist country granted MFN treatment and the only one at the time. See Thomas Wolf, "Effects of U.S. Granting of Most Favored Nation Treatment to Imports from Eastern Europe: The Polish Experience," *The ACES Bulletin* 15 (Spring 1973): 23-42.

17. See Wilbur F. Monroe, *International Monetary Reconstruction: Problems*

*and Issues* (Lexington, Mass.: Lexington Books, D.C. Heath and Co., 1974), chapter 5.

18. For more on NTBs, see Robert E. Baldwin, *Nontariff Distortions of International Trade*, (Washington, D.C.: The Brookings Institution, 1970); and Harold B. Malmgren, *Trade Wars or Trade Negotiations?—Nontariff Barriers and Economic Peace-keeping* (Washington, D.C.: The Atlantic Council of the United States, 1970).

19. For more on the EC preferential trade arrangements and for problems posed for other nations including the US, see Declan O'Sullivan, "New Problems for Countries Outside the Trading Blocs," *Columbia Journal of World Business* 8, no. 1 (Spring 1973).

20. Harold Malmgren, "The U.S., the EEC and the International System," *Money Management* (Year end, 1971).

21. Ibid.

22. Another independent hypothesis of the surge in US direct investment was offered by Raymond Vernon, "International Investment and International Trade in the Product Cycle," *Quarterly Journal of Economics*, May 1966; see also, G.C. Hufbauer, "The Impact of National Characteristics and Technology on the Commodity Composition of Trade in Manufactured Goods," and William H. Gruber and Raymond Vernon, "The Technology Factor in a World Trade Matrix," both in Raymond Vernon, editor, *The Technology Factor in International Trade* (New York: National Bureau of Economic Research, Columbia University Press, 1970).

23. *The United States in the Changing World Economy*, vol. 2: Background Material, chart 55 (Washington, D.C.: U.S. Government Printing Office, 1971).

24. Indeed, the growth of these earnings in the invisibles account of the US balance of payments led some economists to forecast major shifts in the future US trade structure. For example, Lawrence Krause, "Trade Policy for the Seventies," *Columbia Journal of World Business* 6, no. 1 (January-February 1971).

25. See John Makin, "Capital Flows and Exchange-Rate Flexibility in the Post-Bretton Woods Era," *Princeton Essays in International Finance*, no. 103 (February 1974), and John Hewson and Eisuke Sakakibara, "The Impact of U.S. Controls on Capital Outflows on the U.S. Balance of Payments—An Exploratory Study," I.M.F. *Staff Papers*, March 1975.

26. See, for example, Jean Jacques Servan-Schreiber, *The American Challenge*, French translation by Arthur Steel (New York: Atheneum, 1968).

27. See Robert M. Dunn, Jr., "Canada and Its Economic Discontents," *Foreign Affairs*, October 1973, pp. 119-40.

28. The LTA first entered into force October 1, 1962.

29. See Gerald Curtis, "The Textile Negotiations: A Failure to Communicate," and Saburo Okita, "The Textile Negotiations: Japan's Point of View," both in *Columbia Journal of World Business* 8, no. 1 (Spring 1973); and Gary

Saxonhouse, "The Textile Confrontation," in Jerome B. Cohen, ed., *Pacific Partnership: United States-Japan Trade* (Lexington, Mass.: Lexington Books, D.C. Heath and Co., 1972).

30. See the now famous "Three Options" speech of Minister for External Affairs, Mitchell Sharp, in *International Perspectives* (Autumn 1972).

31. See Robert M. Dunn, Jr., "Canada and its Economic Discontents," *Foreign Affairs*, October 1973.

32. See Economic Report of the President, Transmitted to the Congress January 1972 (Washington, D.C.: U.S. Government Printing Office, 1972), chapter 5.

33. Bilateral trade talks between the United States and Japan, the United States and Canada, and the United States and the EC were launched in mid-1971 and continued into 1972. The purpose in each case was to obtain concessions that would permit an improvement of the US trade balance. A mere realignment of exchange rates was not believed sufficient by itself to reverse the trade imbalance, an assessment that was to be proven correct later on.

## Chapter 4
## Less Developed Countries and the
## Current Issue

1. *Proceedings of the United Nations Conference on Trade and Development*, Third Session (Santiago, Chile, 13 April-21 May 1972) vol. 1, annex VIII, I, "Statement Made by the Representative of France on Behalf of the Countries of Group B Concerning Multilateral Trade Negotiations."

2. Ibid., M, "Statement Concerning Multilateral Trade Negotiations Made by the Representative of Ethiopia on Behalf of the Group of 77 at the 119th Plenary Meeting."

3. See the *International Economic Report of the President*, Together with the Annual Report of the Council on International Economic Policy, Transmitted to the Congress February 1974. Appendix C contains the text of the Tokyo Declaration.

4. In the OECD negotiations, eighteen potential donor countries participated, including Canada, the United Kingdom, the six countries then forming the EC, Austria, New Zealand, Ireland, Finland, Norway, Denmark, Sweden, Switzerland, Japan, and the United States. The other donor country, Australia, was not then a member of the OECD.

5. Disagreement prevailed on a number of key issues. First, the United States advocated broad product coverage, including selected primary and semiprocessed products, in order to give maximum benefit to LDC trade. Other countries strongly preferred narrower product coverage, in part to preserve their already existing discriminatory agreements, which they were unwilling either to

give up entirely or to phase out gradually. Second, in respect of a safeguard mechanism to be used in cases where imports into developed country markets became disruptive in some sense, the United States preferred its own traditional "escape-clause" approach along with a list of products (textiles, shoes, petroleum, etc.) to be excepted from the preference list. Europeans and Japanese preferred instead a tariff quota system with practically no exceptions for especially sensitive products. Zero or preferential import duties would be applied up to a certain stipulated limit for each product, and beyond that point tariffs at the usual MFN rate would be imposed. Other issues debated and unresolved had to do with a determination within industrial countries to defend their own "declining" industries, which stood potentially to be seriously displaced by generalized preferences, as opposed to a determination to seek equitable and meaningful adjustment, relocation, and compensation of workers and capital affected. Still other concerns had to do with the fact that an open-ended GSP would benefit primarily a few of the more advanced LDCs, which were already able to compete internationally with light manufacturing industries in Italy, Japan, and elsewhere. The idea was that GSP should not allow a few to reap the lion's share of the benefits at the expense of other more numerous and also less developed LDCs. For more on these various issues, see Harold B. Malmgren, *Trade for Development* (Washington, D.C.: Overseas Development Council, 1971), pp. 44-45.

6. For details of the US proposal, see "The Fifteenth Annual Report of the Trade Agreements Program, 1970," Message from the President of the United States, Washington, D.C., 1971, p. 11.

7. In addition to these countries, certain Socialist countries have entered into arrangements referred to as generalized preference systems in favor of some LDCs. Bulgaria, Czechoslovakia, Hungary, Poland, and Russia have declared their readiness to grant import preferences to LDCs through the operation of their state trading systems; only Hungary has submitted a full description of its system to UNCTAD.

8. See Walter Krause and Ernest V. Zuber, "A New U.S. Foreign-Trade Policy?" *Arizona Business Bulletin*, February 1971; and "The Fifteenth Annual Report of the Trade Agreements Program, 1970" Message from the President of the United States, Washington, D.C., 1971, p. 11. Matters having to do with US trade legislation and the trade bill itself are the subject of chapter 6.

9. See articles by Tracy Murray, "UNCTAD's Generalized Preferences An Appraisal," *Journal of World Trade Law*, July-August 1973, pp. 461-72; "Preferential Tariffs for the LDC's," *Southern Economic Journal*, July 1973, pp. 35-46; "How Helpful is the Generalized System of Preferences to Developing Countries?" *Economic Journal*, June 1973, pp. 449-55.

10. C. Clague, "The Trade Effects of Tariff Preferences," *Southern Economic Journal*, January 1972, pp. 379-89.

11. B. Hindley, "The UNCTAD Agreement on Preferences," *Journal of World Trade Law*, November-December 1971, pp. 694-702.

12. Tracy Murray, "Preferential Tariffs for the LDCs," *Southern Economic Journal*, p. 43.

13. For further thoughts along these lines, see Walter Krause and F. John Mathis, *Latin America and Economic Integration* (Iowa City: University of Iowa Press, 1970), chapter 4.

14. See two UNCTAD studies that conclude that the tariff quota safeguard system is limiting and in fact serves to reduce the value of beneficiary exports which receive GSP treatment. UNCTAD, "Operation and Effects of Generalized Preferences Granted by the European Economic Community," TC/B/C.5/3, 11 January 1973; and UNCTAD, "Operation and Effects of Generalized Preferences Granted by Japan," TD/B/C.5/6, 23 January 1973.

15. This important criticism, that GSP is more "aid" than "trade" because of the existing safeguard mechanisms, is developed in Tracy Murray, "Preferential Tariffs for the LDC's," *Southern Economic Journal*, July 1973.

16. Tracy Murray, "UNCTAD's Generalized Preferences: An Appraisal," *Journal of World Trade Law*, July-August 1973, p. 465.

17. They number twenty-five and include: Botswana, Burundi, Chad, Dahomey, Ethiopia, Guinea, Lesoths, Mali, Malawi, Niger, Rwanda, Somalia, Sudan, Uganda, United Republic of Tanzania, Upper Volta, Afghanistan, Bhutan, Laos, Maldives, Nepal, Sikkim, Western Samoa Yemen, and Haiti. These "hardcore" countries were so designated by the Committee for Development Planning of the United Nations Economic and Social Development Council. For more on problems of these countries, see J. Ahmad, "The Least Developed Among the Developing Countries," *Journal of World Trade Law* (March-April, 1974), pp. 201-208.

18. See UNCTAD, "General Report on the Implementation of the GSP," TD/B/C.5/9, January 25, 1973.

19. Tracy Murray, "UNCTAD's Generalized Preferences: An Appraisal," p. 470. Preferential tariff margins on such products have been limited in many cases to a very few percentage points.

20. LDCs have focused their attentions on NTBs ever since UNCTAD I in 1964. Besides the UNCTAD forum, the International Development Strategy for the Second United Nations Development Decade (adopted by the General Assembly in resolution 2626 (XXV) on 24 October, 1970) addressed itself to tariff and nontariff barriers and to adjustment assistance as a policy measure to expedite removal of such barriers. It was provided specifically that developed countries "will not ordinarily, raise existing tariff or nontariff barriers to exports from developing countries, nor establish new tariff or nontariff barriers nor any discriminatory measures, where such action has the effect of rendering less favorable the conditions of access to the markets of manufactured and semimanufactured products of export interest to developing countries" (Offical Records of the Trade and Development Board, Eleventh Session, Supplement 2 [TD/B/352], annex III, A, paragraph 33; see also paragraphs 34-35).

More recently in 1972, during UNCTAD III in Santiago, a resolution on the liberalization of nontariff barriers was adopted without dissent (Resolution 76 (III), 118th Plenary Meeting, 19 May 1972). NTBs were considered to be an important obstacle to the expansion of international trade generally, and an important obstacle in particular to LDCs' exports of manufactures and semi-manufactures, including processed and semiprocessed products, to developed countries. The need for a continuing examination of NTBs by UNCTAD was recognized; moreover, benefits to be derived from generalized tariff preference schemes were acknowledged as being adversely affected by NTBs relating to exports of less developed countries. Therefore, close coordination between UNCTAD efforts on NTBs and tariff preferences was deemed desirable.

In addition to the identification and analysis of NTBs affecting exports of interest to LDCs prepared by the UNCTAD secretariat, and related work carried out by other international organizations (including the GATT and the OECD), several action steps were adopted in anticipation of the forthcoming multilateral trade negotiations and in recognition of the need to assist less developed countries in preparing for their full and effective participation therein. Specifically, a Sessional Committee of the Committee of Manufactures was established in order to study NTBs in further detail and to maintain up-to-date information on the products, groups of products, and countries affected by existing NTBs so that LDCs would be as well prepared as possible when the time came for multilateral trade negotiations.

21. For general background on NTBs, see Robert E. Baldwin, *Nontariff Distortions of International Trade* (Washington, D.C.: The Brookings Institution, 1970), and Ingo Walter, "Nontariff Barriers and the Free Trade Area Option," *Banca Nazionale del Lavoro Quarterly Review*, March 1969.

22. See Ingo Walter, "Nontariff Barriers and the Export Performance of Developing Economies," Papers and Proceedings of the 83rd Annual Meeting of the American Economic Association, reprinted in *American Economic Review*, May 1971, p. 196.

23. For example, "The Declaration and Principles of the Action Programme of Lima," which was adopted by the Group of 77 at the Second Ministerial Meeting on November 7, 1971, preparatory to UNCTAD III held April-May 1972, spoke specifically to the issues involved. First, in accordance with the International Development Strategy, it was stated "developed countries should strictly observe the principle of standstill. No new tariff or nontariff barriers should be introduced by developed countries nor existing barriers increased, and where tariff and nontariff barriers have been introduced or increased since the Second Conference, these should be eliminated." In regard to liberalization of nontariff barriers, it was declared:

Developed countries should reduce and ultimately eliminate internal taxes, fiscal charges and levies on all primary products, including semi-processed and processed primary products imported from developing countries. Pending such action, developed countries should institute a programme for the full refund of such taxes, fiscal charges and levies to developing countries.

Third, the action program asserted that developed countries should agree "that negotiations for the phasing out and eventual elimination of existing quantitative restrictions and other nontariff barriers should take place within UNCTAD." See "Declaration and Principles of the Action Programme adopted at the Second Ministerial Meeting of the Group of 77," at Lima, on November 7, 1971, reprinted in *United Nations Conference on Trade and Development*, Third Session, Santiago, Vol. 1, report and annexes (New York: United Nations, 1973), Annex VIII, F.

24. For a brief summary of the more important developments during the late 1960s and early 1970s, see *Proceedings of the United Nations Committee on Trade and Development*, third session, Santiago, Chile, April-May 1972, Vol. II merchandise trade (New York: United Nations, 1973), "Programme for the Liberalization of Quantitative Restrictions and Other Nontariff Barriers in Developed Countries on Products of Export Interest to Developing Countries," Report by the UNCTAD Secretariat, pp. 154-56.

25. See debates in the fourth session of the UNCTAD Committee on Manufactures (1970) as noted in the proceedings (UNCTAD documents TD/295-TD/B/C.2/97).

26. Ingo Walter, "Nontariff Barriers and the Export Performance of Developing Economies," AEA Papers and Proceedings, reprinted in *American Economic Review*, May 1971, pp. 195-205.

27. Ibid., p. 198.

28. R.L. Allen and I. Walter, "An Analysis of the Impact of Nontariff Measures Imposed by Developed Market Economy Countries on Representative Products of Export Interest to Developing Countries," UNCTAD Secretariat Working Paper (Mimeo, 1970). Referred to and summarized in Ingo Walter, "Nontariff Barriers and the Export Performance of Developing Economies," pp. 198-200. The six product categories were: prepared and preserved meats, prepared and preserved vegetables, household and ceramic articles, preserved and prepared fruits and juices, starch derivatives and products, and sugar confectionery and chocolate.

29. Ingo Walter, "Nontariff Barriers and the Export Performance of Developing Economies," p. 200.

30. Ibid., p. 201.

31. Walter's findings of preliminary evidence, suggesting that LDCs are especially susceptible to NTBs applied to their exports by developed countries and that the structure of protection indicated by such NTBs may be systematically biased against them, are supported by similar conclusions of other writers. See Bela Belassa, *The Structure of Protection in the Industrial Countries and its Effects on the Exports of Processed Goods from Developing Countries*, UNCTAD Document TD/B/C.2/36, 25 May 1967; and Hal B. Lary, *Imports of Manufacturers from Developing Countries* (New York: National Bureau of Economic Research, 1968).

32. "Programme for the Liberalization of Quantitative Restrictions and Other

Nontariff Barriers in Developed Countries on Products of Export Interest to Developing Countries," circulated at UNCTAD III as TD/120/Supp. 1, 3 January 1972, and reproduced in *Proceedings of the United Nations Conference on Trade and Development*, Third Session, Santiago, Chile, April-May 1972, Vol. II, merchandise trade (New York: United Nations, 1973).

33. In 1968, cotton textiles covered by the Long-Term Arrangement accounted for about one-quarter of the value of all 1968 imports into developed market-economy countries subject to nontariff barriers. At the end of 1973, the LTA was renegotiated and broadened to include all textiles.

34. Petroleum products comprised over 75 percent of the value of manufactured or semimanufactured goods imported into developed countries from LDCs subject to NTBs and over 50 percent of the value of all such affected imports, including those in semiprocessed and processed agricultural product groups.

35. Report by the UNCTAD Secretariat, "Programme for Liberalization of Quantitative Restrictions and Other Nontariff Barriers in Developed Countries on Products of Export Interest to Developing Countries."

36. Respectively, Decision 1 (IV) of the Committee, and paragraphs 33-34 of UN General Assembly Resolution 2626 (XXV), 24 October 1970.

37. For a summary of such proposals, see the Report by the UNCTAD Secretariat, "Programme for the Liberalization of Quantitative Restrictions . . . ," pp. 156-163.

38. *Trade for Development*, p. 53 and "Discussion," Papers and Proceedings of the 83rd Annual Meeting of the American Economic Association, reprinted in *American Economic Review*, May 1971, pp. 206-207.

39. Resolution, 16 (II). See "Problems and International Action Concerning Commodities Covered by Conference Resolution 16 II," Report by the UNCTAD Secretariat in *Proceedings of the United Nations Conference on Trade and Development*, Third Session, Vol. II, merchandise trade, pp. 61-66.

40. See the two articles in *Challenge* (September-October and November-December 1974): The first, by C. Fred Bergsten, "The New Era in World Commodity Markets," interprets the current move toward cartels as the beginning of a new age of "commodity power." The second article, by Raymond Mikesell, "More Third World Cartels Ahead?" argues that oil is a special case and that producer cartels in other raw materials are unlikely to succeed. For further discussion of this issue, see chapter 5.

41. For instance, excessive economic dependence on production of a very few commodities for which world demand rises at a slow pace over time.

42. For a more detailed discussion of some of the possibilities along these lines, see C. Fred Bergsten, *Completing the GATT: Toward New International Rules to Cover Export Controls*, British North American Committee, National Planning Association, October 1974. These matters are considered again in chapters 5 and 7.

43. See, for example, the recommendation to this effect in annex A.III.6 to

the Final Act of UNCTAD I in 1964, *Proceedings of the United Nations Conference on Trade and Development*, Vol. I, Final Act and Report, pp. 39-40; Paragraph 35 of the "International Development Strategy for the Second United Nations Development Decade"; and Annex I, 72.III, "Adjustment Assistance Measures," Resolutions and other decisions adopted by UNCTAD III, 118th plenary meeting, May 19, 1972, in *Proceedings of the United Nations Conference on Trade and Development*, Third Session, Vol. I, Report and Annexes (United Nations, New York: 1973), pp. 81-82.

44. For more on adjustment assistance as it concerns LDCs, see "Adjustment Assistance Measures," Report by the UNCTAD Secretariat, in *Proceedings of the United Nations Conference on Trade and Development*, Third Session, Vol. II, merchandise trade (New York: United Nations, 1973), pp. 171-204.


## Chapter 5
## Developed Countries and the Current Issues

1. John Jackson (*World Trade and the Law of GATT* [Indianapolis: Bobbs-Merrill Co., Inc., 1969], p. 502) has concluded that the existing rules against the use of export controls are riddled by so many exceptions as to be of very little effective use. In his Statement before the Subcommittee on Economic Growth of the Joint Economic Committee of the Congress, July 23, 1974, Ambassador William Eberle concluded that the prohibition on export quotas as set forth in Article XI of the General Agreement "is virtually worthless because the exceptions are so broadly defined."

2. Guido Colonna di Paliano, Philip H. Trezise and Nobuhiko Ushiba, *Directions for World Trade in the Nineteen-Seventies*, A Report of the Trilateral Task Force on Trade (The Trilateral Commission: New York, 1974). Also, C. Fred Bergsten, *Completing the GATT: Toward New International Rules to Govern Export Controls* (British North American Committee, October 1974).

3. Among those who regard the threat as great, see articles by: C. Fred Bergsten, "The Threat From The Third World," *Foreign Policy*, (Summer 1973), pp. 102-124; "The Threat is Real," *Foreign Policy* 14 (Spring 1974): 84-90; and "Response to the Third World," *Foreign Policy*, forthcoming, 17 (Winter 1974-75); and Zuhayn Mikelashi, "Collusion Could Work," *Foreign Policy* 14 (Spring 1974): 57-68. Others believe that cartels are likely to be difficult to organize and to sustain. See Stephen D. Krasner, "Oil is the Exception," *Foreign Policy* 14 (Spring 1974): 68-84; and *Directions for World Trade in the Nineteen-Seventies*, A Report of the Trilateral Task Force; and Bension Varon and Kenji Takeuchi, "Developing Countries and Non-Mineral Fuels," *Foreign Affairs*, April 1974, pp. 497-510.

4. See *The New York Times*, 26 August 1974. p. 28.

5. One set of proposals is by C. Fred Bergsten, *Completing the GATT:*

*Toward New International Rules to Govern Export Controls* (British North American Committee, October 1974).

6. For more discussion of these matters, see Chamber of Commerce of the U.S., "The Scarcity Problem and U.S. Trade Policy," Washington, D.C., 11 June 1974.

7. See the discussion on agricultural issues in this chapter.

8. For some suggestions along these lines, see C. Fred Bergsten, *Completing the GATT: Toward New International Rules to Govern Export Controls* (British North American Committee, October 1974).

9. See the "Declaration on the Establishment of a New International Economic Order" (1 May 1974) which emanated from the Special Session of the UN General Assembly in New York, April 1974, on Raw Materials and Development.

10. Bernard Norwood, "The Next World Trade Negotiations," in C. Fred Bergsten and Wm. G. Tyler, *Leading Issues in International Economic Policy* (Lexington, Mass.: Lexington Books, D.C. Heath and Co., 1973), p. 131.

11. During and after the Kennedy Round of trade negotiations considerable attention was devoted to the differential between effective and nominal tariffs. See Bela Belassa, "Tariff Protection in Industrial Countries: An Evaluation," *Journal of Political Economy*, December 1965, pp. 573-94; Harry G. Johnson, "The Theory of Tariff Structure with Special Reference to World Trade and Development," in *Trade and Development* (Geneva: Institut Universitaire de Hautes Etudes Internationales, 1965); and also by Johnson, "The Theory of Effective Protection and Preferences," *Economica*, May 1969, pp. 119-38. More recently a conference was sponsored by the GATT and the Graduate Institute of International Studies with the proceedings published in a book edited by Herbert G. Grubel and Harry G. Johnson, *Effective Tariff Protection* (Geneva: GATT and Graduate Institute of International Studies, 1971).

12. See the Thames Essays by Gerard and Victoria Curzon, *Hidden Barriers to International Trade* (London: Trade Policy Research Centre, 1970) and *Global Assault on Non-Tariff Barriers* (London: Trade Policy Research Centre, 1972).

13. The Text of the Tokyo Declaration appears in *International Economic Report of the President*, together with the Annual Report of the Council on International Economic Policy, Transmitted to the Congress February 1974, appendix C.

14. See, for example, William D. Eberle, "Negotiating a New World Market-place—An Overview"; and Geza Feketekuty, "Toward an Effective International Trading System," both in *Columbia Journal of World Business*, Fall 1973.

15. See Gerard and Victoria Curzon, *Global Assault on Non-Tariff Barriers*, for more on Gatt's work in respect of NTBs.

16. *Directions for World Trade in the Nineteen Seventies* (The Trilateral Commission, New York, 1974).

17. For further thoughts on ways to approach NTB's problems, see Harold B.

159

Malmgren, *Trade Wars or Trade Negotiations?*– Non-Tariff Barriers and Economic Peacekeeping (Washington, D.C.: Atlantic Council of the United States, 1970), and John C. Renner, "Trade Barriers, Negotiations and Rules," *Columbia Journal of World Business*, Fall 1973, pp. 53-54.

18. G.K. Helleiner, "Manufactured Exports from Less Developed Countries and Multinational Firms," *Economic Journal* 83 (March 1973): 21-47.

19. For a good discussion of the issues, of the existing safeguard mechanisms, and of possible reformulations, see Jan Tunlir, "A Revised Safeguard Clause for GATT?" *Journal of World Trade Law* 7, no. 4, (July-August 1973): 404-20.

20. *Directions for World Trade in the Nineteen Seventies*, New York: The Trilateral Commission, 1974.

21. John C. Renner, "Trade Barriers, Negotiations and Rules," *Columbia Journal of World Business*, Fall 1973, pp. 54-56.

22. *Directions for World Trade in the Nineteen Seventies* (New York: The Trilateral Commission, 1974).

23. Howard L. Worthington and Mary E. Chaves, "Agricultural Trade Negotiations," *Columbia Journal of World Business*, Fall 1973, p. 45.

24. Raul Prebisch, Hans Singer, and others made numerous contributions to economic literature in regard to the long-term deterioration in LDCs' terms of trade. As producers and exporters of raw materials and foodstuffs, they had to sell increasing volumes over time just to earn sufficient foreign exchange to pay for the same volume of imported manufactured goods.

25. One promising approach to a balanced agricultural settlement, which would cover both the concerns of security of supply and of improved market access, has been recently suggested by Paliano, Trezise and Ushiba, *Directions for World Trade in the Nineteen Seventies*. This approach would make use of the EC concept *"montant de soutien,"* or level of support, which was first introduced during the Kennedy Round. Another idea, suggested before the food shortages in 1973 had been fully realized, has to do with the so-called sectoral approach. A sectoral agreement, as opposed to the more typical single commodity agreement, implies a coordinated, comprehensive program spanning both external and domestic restrictions pertaining to production, consumption, and prices of commodities involved for all participating countries. See Howard C. Worthington and Mary E. Chaves, "Agricultural Trade Negotiations," *Columbia Journal of World Business* (Fall 1973), pp. 47-48.

26. On the need to reform CAP, see Gian Paolo Casadio, "External Relations of the EEC," *Journal of World Trade Law* 7, no. 4 (July-August 1973).

27. This is reprinted as Appendix C in the *International Economic Report of the President*, together with the Annual Report of the Council on International Economic Policy (February 1974).

28. See Karin Kock, *International Trade Policy and the GATT, 1947-1967* (Stockholm: Almquist and Wiksell, 1969), chapter 11, for an account of how LDCs' problems gradually came to be recognized in the GATT and what steps were taken.

29. After the chairman of the panel, Gottfried Haberler. The official title is, *Trends in International Trade. A Report by a Panel of Experts*, (Geneva: October, 1958).

30. For more discussion on the issues involved in GATT's recognition of special problems faced by LDCs, see Kenneth W. Dam, *The GATT Law and International Economic Organization*, (Chicago: University of Chicago Press, 1970), chapter 14; and John H. Jackson, *World Trade and the Law of GATT* (New York: Bobbs-Merrill Co., Inc., 1969), chapter 25.

31. *Directions for World Trade in the Nineteen Seventies*, New York: The Trilateral Commission, 1974; and C. Fred Bergsten, *Completing the GATT: Toward New International Rules to Govern Export Controls*, (British North American Committee, October 1974).

32. See Walter Krause and F. John Mathis, "The U.S. Policy Shift on East-West Trade," *Journal of International Affairs* 28, no. 1 (1974). See also the section "Trends, Prospects and Policies for East-West Trade" in Papers and Proceedings of the 86th Annual Meeting of the American Economic Association, three papers reprinted in *American Economic Review*, May 1974: Gregory Grossman, "Prospects and Policy for U.S. Soviet Trade"; Alexander Eckstein and Bruce Reynolds, "Sino-American Trade Prospects and Policy"; Alan A. Brown, Paul Marer, and Egon Neuberger, "Prospects for U.S.-East European Trade." Also, *International Economic Report of the President*, Together with the Annual Report of the Council on International Economic Policy, (Transmitted to Congress, February 1974), part II, chapter 6, entitled, "New Approaches to Foreign Trade in Communist Countries." Further discussion of potential U.S. East-West trade is found in Thomas A. Wolf, *U.S. East-West Trade Policy* (Lexington, Mass.: Lexington Books, D.C. Heath and Co., 1973), chapter 8.

33. Much in the spirit of the approach taken by the International Monetary Fund, Olivier Long, director general of GATT, is reported to have proposed recently that a high-level group of not more than twenty representatives be established inside the GATT in order to deal more effectively with crisis situations involving trade issues in the world economy. Presumably, the large trading nations would dominate such a committee. "International Trade Panel Proposed by GATT Head," *The Washington Post*, 5 July 1974.

34. For a good survey of the aspects of GATT needing reform, see Peter Bratschi, "GATT: Targets for Reform," *Journal of World Trade Law* 7, no. 4 (July-August 1973): 393-403. For more in this vein on the need for GATT reform, but in a broader context, see Richard N. Gardner, "The Hard Road to World Order," *Foreign Affairs*, April 1974, pp. 556-76.

35. For more on this approach to GATT reform, see *Directions for World Trade in the Nineteen Seventies*, The Trilateral Commission, New York, 1974; and Special Advisory Panel to the Trade Committee of the Atlantic Council of the U.S., "Interim Report on Reform of the International Trade System" (11 February 1974).

36. See Bernard Norwood, "The Next World Trade Negotiations" in *Leading Issues in International Economic Policy*, C. Fred Bergsten and William G. Tyler, editors (Lexington, Mass.: Lexington Books, D.C. Heath and Co., 1973), pp. 140-42.

37. For more detailed suggestions along these lines, see Special Advisory Panel to the Trade Committee of the Atlantic Council, "Second Interim Report on Reform of the International Trade System. Trade Measures and the International Monetary System: Proposals for Institutional Reforms" (26 March 1974).

## Chapter 6
## Formulation of US Trade Policy:
## The Trade Reform Act

1. For a good discussion of this ongoing process, see C. Fred Bergsten, "Crisis in U.S. Trade Policy," *Foreign Affairs* 49, no. 4 (July 1971).

2. Ibid., p. 622.

3. Lawrence Krause, "Trade Policy for the Seventies," *Columbia Journal of World Business* 6, no. 1 (January-February 1971).

4. A similar thesis to explain American labor's increasingly protectionist position is offered by Thomas P. Enger ("Foreign Trade Policy of American Labor," *Journal of World Trade Law*, July-August 1973, pp. 449-60). Enger argues that both structural change in the US economy toward the service sector and the various operations of multinational corporations threaten worker job security and the continued well-being of unions in the production sector.

5. Philip H. Trezise, "Making America's Foreign Economic Policy" in *Perspectives on U.S.-Japan Economic Relations*, Alan Taylor, editor (Cambridge, Mass.: Ballinger, 1973), p. 220.

6. See I.M. Destler, "Comments on the Framework for Foreign Economic Policy Decision-Making In Japan and the United States," in *Perspectives on U.S.-Japan Relations*, Alan Taylor, editor (Cambridge, Mass.: Ballinger, 1973), pp. 227-30.

7. See Walter Adams, "The New Protectionism," *Challenge*, May-June 1973, pp. 6-10; and Nat Goldfinger, "The Case for Hartke-Burke," *Columbia Journal of World Business* 8, no. 1 (Spring 1973): 22-26.

8. In 1971, the first US trade deficit since 1893 was recorded in the amount of $2.7 billion. The purposeful actions of the US administration were designed to counteract that trend. The Smithsonian Agreement of December 19, 1971 provided for a realignment of the world's leading currencies, including devaluation of the dollar. But the desired effects of those changes were slow to emerge—much slower, in fact, than widely anticipated. Indeed, an even larger US trade deficit of almost $7 billion occurred in 1972. With improvement so slow to materialize, and with a growing body of evidence in support of the claim that

the first realignment had not gone far enough, yet another devaluation of the dollar was agreed to by the major industrial countries in February 1973.

9. Stephen P. Magee, "The Welfare Effects of Restrictions on U.S. Trade" in *Brookings Papers on Economic Activity*, 3: 1972, pp. 645-708.

10. *United States International Economic Policy in an Interdependent World*, Report to the President submitted by the Commission on International Trade and Investment Policy, July 1971, Washington, D.C.

11. For a brief summary of the Williams Commission Report and its recommendations affecting US trade policy, see: *Sixteenth Annual Report of the Trade Agreements Program*, Message from the President of the United States (Washington, D.C.: U.S. Government Printing Office, 1973), pp. 8-9.

12. Congress authorized the council on August 29, 1972, in Public Law 92-412.

13. The complete text of the Tokyo Declaration appears as Appendix C in the International Economic Report of the President, Together with the Annual Report of the Council on International Economic Policy. Transmitted to the Congress February 1974.

14. Copies of the Trade Act of 1974, or a short summary of its provisions, are obtainable from the U.S. Government Printing Office, Washington, D.C., 20402.

15. See Guy F. Erb and Charles R. Frank, Jr., "U.S. Trade Reform and the Third World," *Challenge* (May-June 1974), pp. 60-67.

16. Ibid.

17. See the statement by Charles Frank in "Hearings Before the Committee on Finance," U.S. Senate, 93rd Congress, 2nd Session, *The Trade Reform Act of 1973—Part 3*, March 1974, p. 879.

18. See the reform recommendations offered by Guy Erb and Charles Frank, "U.S. Trade Reform and the Third World," pp. 63-64.

19. Ibid.

20. Rachel McCulloch ("United States Preferences: The Proposed System," *Journal of World Trade Law*, March-April 1974, pp. 216-26) reaches similar but slightly more optimistic conclusions. Prior to competitive need exclusions, she estimates 1971 US imports eligible for GSP to be $3.2 billion, and after the exclusions, $1.5 billion. This latter amount is equal to about 3 percent of total US imports from all sources.

21. U.S. Tariff Commission, *Probable Effects of Tariff Preferences for Developing Countries* (U.S. Tariff Commission, Washington, D.C., 1972).

22. David Dunford, "Trade Effects of Alternative U.S. Systems of Generalized Preferences," U.S. Department of State, February 1973 (unpublished). These estimates are reviewed briefly in Rachel McCulloch, "United States Preferences: The Proposed System," *Journal of World Trade Law*, March-April 1974, pp. 216-26.

23. See the Chamber of Commerce of the US, "The Scarcity Problem and U.S. Trade Policy," Washington, D.C., 11 June 1974, for a brief summary of

Senator Chiles's proposals and proposals put forth by others in the Congress and by the administration.


## Chapter 7
## Some Remaining Issues of
## International Trade Policy

1. See Alan A. Brown, Paul Marer and Egon Neuberger, "Prospects for U.S.–East European Trade," Papers and Proceedings of the 86th Annual Meeting of the American Economic Association, reprinted in *American Economic Review*, May 1974, p. 303. Also, see A. Malish, Jr., "An Analysis of Tariff Discrimination on Soviet and East European Trade," *The ACES Bulletin* 15 (Spring 1974): 43-56.

2. And specifically, the long and difficult debates over the granting of MFN status to so-called nonmarket economy countries.

3. A. Malish, Jr., "An Analysis of Tariff Discrimination on Soviet and East European Trade."

4. For a good but brief discussion on the pros and cons of US-Soviet trade and the intertwining of economic, political, and military considerations, see Gregory Grossman, "Prospects and Policy for U.S.-Soviet Trade," Papers and Proceedings of the 86th Annual Meeting of the American Economic Association, reprinted in *American Economic Review*, May 1974, pp. 289-93.

5. Steven C. Haas, *Impact of MFN on U.S. Imports from the PRC*, Office of East-West Trade, US Dept. of State, Washington, D.C., 17 August 1973. Referred to in Alexander Eckstein and Bruce Reynolds, "Sino-American Trade Prospects and Policy," Papers and Proceedings of the American Economic Association, 86th Annual Meeting, reprinted in *American Economic Review*, May 1974, p. 298. Haas estimated that granting MFN to the PRC would raise US imports by 16 percent, or to about $60-70 million in 1973 imports.

6. Alexander Eckstein and Bruce Reynolds, "Sino-American Trade Prospects and Policy." Projections based on information from UN, OECD, and US Department of Commerce sources.

7. Walter Krause and F. John Mathis ("The U.S. Policy Shift on East-West Trade," *Journal of International Affairs* 28, no. 1 [1974]: 34) also express the view that low-technology manufactured goods produced in and exported by Communist countries are likely to provide direct competition with the same goods exported by LDCs.

8. The case for this is forcefully argued in C. Fred Bergsten, *Completing the GATT: Toward New International Rules to Govern Export Controls*, British North American Committee, October 1974. The same idea or connection between export control regulations and commodity agreements is also to be found in *Directions for World Trade in the Nineteen Seventies*, The Trilateral

Commission, New York, 1974, and Chamber of Commerce of the United States, "The Scarcity Problem and U.S. Trade Policy," 11 June 1974.

9. This argument with respect to bauxite was made recently by Ambassador William D. Eberle. See, *Journal of Commerce*, 15 August 1974.

10. In the spirit of W.W. Rostow's classic work, *The Stages of Economic Growth* (London: Cambridge University Press, 1960).

11. J.H. Dunning, editor, *The Multinational Enterprise* (New York: Praeger, 1971) and F.M. Scherer, *Industrial Market Structure and Economic Performance* (Chicago: Rand McNally & Co., 1970).

12. Raymond Vernon, "Competition Policy Toward Multinational Corporations," Papers and Proceedings of the 86th Annual Meeting of the American Economic Association, reprinted in *American Economic Review*, May 1971, pp. 276-82.

13. Ibid., p. 277.

14. If such a body were to be created, it would have as its precedent for action chapter 5 of the defunct ITO charter, which was intended to cover facets of private investment and business practices. In the days when ITO was being considered, however, all of these matters bore quite a different meaning than they do today, for the multinational corporation did not exist. See Walter Krause, "The Implications of UNCTAD III for Multinational Enterprise," *Journal of Interamerican Studies and World Affairs*, February 1973, pp. 46-59.

15. Sigmund Timberg, "An International Antitrust Convention: A Proposal to Harmonize Conflicting National Policies Towards the Multinational Corporation," Tokyo Conference on International Economy and Competition Policy, 1973 mimeo, referred to in Vernon, "Competition Policy Toward Multinational Corporations," p. 280.

16. Karin Kock, *International Trade Policy and the GATT, 1947-1967* (Stockholm: Almquist and Wiksell, 1969), p. 288.

17. One proposal offered by Walter J. Levy, an internationally known oil consultant, is that the strongest importing nations limit the inflow of surplus Arab oil money to amounts no higher than the deficits in their own oil trade. Levy believes that if oil-exporting countries were faced with a refusal by the large industrial countries to finance the continued high price of oil, they might soften their stance. Walter J. Levy, "What Can Oil Importers Pay?" *The Washington Post*, 1 September 1974.

18. Preamble to the General Agreement on Tariffs and Trade.

19. See chapter 5 for discussion and reference to these alternative approaches.

# Indexes

# Index of Names

# Index of Subjects

Italy, 16, 65, 136

Japan, 4, 16, 23, 25, 36, 42, 46-68,
54, 57, 62, 65, 76-77, 80, 85-86,
98, 115, 123, 131
Johnson administration, 41, 98

Kennedy administration, 17-19, 41
Kennedy Round, 2, 15n, 43, 73, 79,
84, 119, 127, 133-134
impact on world trade composition,
28-29
results of, 22ff

Kuwait, 125

Latin American Free Trade Association, 31
League of Nations, 27n
Least developed countries, 58-59, 121
Less developed countries
discontent, 30ff, 51, 134
economic assistance, 8, 59
future trade policy interests,
119-122
interest in trade negotiations, 8,
51-53, 69ff, 86-88
international trade shares, 2-3, 29
safeguards, 70-71
and the Trade Expansion Act, 19
and U.S. trade policy, 19, 33
worsening terms of trade, 30-31

Marshall Plan, 14, 26, 37-39
Miller Report, 41
Mills Bill, 96, 98
Most-favored-nation treatment, 2,
10-11, 19, 29, 38, 80, 104, 114,
120
Multilateral safeguards. See Safeguards
Multilateral Trade Negotiations, 93,
101-102, 140-143. See also Tokyo
Round
Multinational corporations, 99,
122-124

National Association of Manufactur-
ers, 94, 96
National security safeguard, 12, 17, 20
New Zealand, 54, 62, 84
Nixon administration, 55, 94, 97-100,
103

Non-tariff barriers
emergence of, 43-44, 133
future problems concerning, 127
and LDC trade, 51, 61ff
proposals to alleviate, 65-67, 80, 98
studies on, 62, 79
North Atlantic Treaty Organization,
38
North Korea, 39
Norway, 23, 54

Organization for Economic Cooperation and Development, 62, 76, 79,
91
Organization of Petroleum Exporting
Countries, 67-68, 125, 138

People's Republic of China, 4, 40, 43,
84, 88-89, 115, 126
Peril-point provisions, 12, 17, 20
Philippines, 11
Poland, 38, 40, 43n, 124
Prebisch proposals, 30ff

Randall Commission, 12
Reciprocal Trade Agreements Program
comparison with Trade Expansion
Act, 23ff
extension record, 11ff
foundations of, 1-2, 9ff
impact on world trade composition,
27
principal features, 10
results of, 15
Reverse trade preferences, 35-36, 44,
59
Roosevelt administration, 9-10
international trade policies, 9-10.
See also Reciprocal Trade Agreements Program
Russia, 4, 37, 40, 84, 88-89, 105-106,
115, 126

Safeguards, 70-71, 80-81, 135
future problems concerning, 128
and LDC interest, 52
Security of foreign supply, 67-68,
73-77, 125
as a long-run problem, 117-119,
139-40
and U.S. trade bill, 109-111
Senate Finance Committee, 97-98

# About the Author

**Wilbur F. Monroe**, an international economist with the U.S. Department of Treasury, is presently serving as Technical Assistant to the U.S. Executive Director to the International Monetary Fund. From 1970-72, he was Assistant Financial Attache in the American Embassy in Tokyo and more recently he was Guest Scholar at the Brookings Institution. He received the Ph.D. in economics from the University of Iowa in 1969, having done some study at the London School of Economics and Political Science. Dr. Monroe is the author of *Japan: Financial Markets and the World Economy, International Monetary Reconstruction: Problems and Issues*, and a number of articles on international economic and financial topics which have appeared in professional journals.